Wage Theft in America

ALSO BY KIM BOBO

Organizing for Social Change: Midwest Academy Manual for Activists

Kim writes a regular column for the IWJ print newsletter "Faith Works" and online e-newsletter (www.iwj.org)

Wage Theft In America

WHY MILLIONS OF WORKING AMERICANS ARE NOT GETTING PAID—AND WHAT WE CAN DO ABOUT IT

Kim Bobo

THE NEW PRESS

NEW YORK
LONDON

Requests for permission to reproduce selections from this book should
be mailed to: Permissions Department, The New Press, 38 Greene Street,
New York, NY 10013.

Originally published in the United States by The New Press, New York, 2009
This revised and updated edition published in the United States by The New
Press, New York, 2011

Distributed by Perseus Distribution

ISBN 978-1-59558-717-6 (pb.)
CIP data available

The New Press was established in 1990 as a not-for-profit alternative to the large,
commercial publishing houses currently dominating the book publishing industry.
The New Press operates in the public interest rather than for private gain, and is
committed to publishing, in innovative ways, works of educational, cultural, and
community value that are often deemed insufficiently profitable.

The movement against wage theft that was spurred by the first edition of this
book illustrates the impact books can have on social change.

www.thenewpress.com

Composition by Westchester Book Group
This book was set in Janson

Printed in the United States of America

1 2 3 4 5 6 7 8 9 10

Contents

Acknowledgments

This book is the product of many people, but especially the staff and leaders of the Interfaith Worker Justice (IWJ) affiliated workers' centers. These centers are in the front lines of the fight against wage theft. The staff and leaders of these centers were generous with their stories, experience, and wisdom in both the first and this second edition. Thank you especially to Laura Boston, Martin Chartrand, Tiffany Crain, Fernando Garcia, Annica Gorham, Hamilton Gramajo, Patrick Hickey, Adam Kader, Anna Karawicz, Veronica Mendez, Pete Meyers, Dan Moore, Brian Payne, Alfredo Pena, Don Sherman, Rael Silva, Jeanette Smith, Garrett Stark, Marie Thompson, Abigail Thornton, and Cristina Tzintzun.

I am grateful to current and former Department of Labor leaders who shared their ideas for improvement of the agency and reviewed mine in order to weed out the really dumb ideas and correct many of my misunderstandings (any totally wild ideas and misunderstandings that remain are all mine and not theirs!). They were patient with my inquiries and open to new ways of doing things. Thank you especially to John Fraser, Rae Glass, Libby Hendrix, Michael Kerr, and Timothy Reardon.

Labor friends, advocates, policy experts, and attorneys offered key insights and directions. Jules Bernstein read every page of both editions with a careful editor's eye. I am grateful for all the comments from Bruce Boyens, Jody Calemine, Matthew Capece, Johanna Chao-Kreilick, Janice Fine, Ariel Jacobson, Tom Kochan, William Lurye, Edith Rasell, Catherine Ruckelshaus, Gerry Shea, Michael Wilson, and David Weil.

Lots of friends and colleagues commented on drafts and improved the document's readability and focus. Thank you to Eric Boria, John Howard, Dean Lawrence, Kathryn Mitchem, Kelly Quakenbush, and Laurie White.

Thank you to the Twink Frey Visiting Social Activists Program at the Center for the Education of Women at the University of Michigan, which offered me a space away from work to think and write. Everyone at the Center was so kind and welcoming to me. Thanks especially to Beth Sullivan, who coordinates the Twink Frey Visiting Social Activists Program and Gloria Thomas, the Center's director.

I owe special thanks to all the IWJ staff members who took on extra work enabling me to take time in 2008 and then again in 2011. I am particularly grateful to Aina Gutierrez and Charese Jordan who served as joint acting directors in 2008 and Aina Gutierrez and Ted Smukler who juggled extra responsibilities in 2011. Ted also gave extensive comments on both drafts. My two beloved assistants, Cathy Junia in 2008 and Honna Eichler in 2011, protected me from e-mails and calls, arranged trips and calls for me, and helped me track down information, including Appendices A, B, and E. Anne Janks, coordinator of Can My Boss Do That (www.canmybossdothat.com), compiled an updated list of workers centers and legal clinics for the second edition. Other current and former colleagues, including Cynthia Brooke, Dianne Enriquez, Jose Oliva, and Danny Postel, gave meaningful content suggestions. Joan Flanagan helped proof the galleys. Thank you to the IWJ Board of Directors, led by Bishop Gabino Zavala, who supported my carving out time for the original writing and then the revision. In addition to Jules Bernstein and Edith Rasell, mentioned above, several board members were very helpful, including Charles Whitaker, who copyedited the first edition before I even sent it out to readers, Karen McLean Hessel (and her husband Dieter), who helped integrate the Scriptures, and Hussam Ayloush, Bob DeRose, Jeff Korgen, Linda Lotz, Mary Priniski, and Bennie Whiten who offered content suggestions.

The book was significantly improved by the stories, examples, and corrections offered by all these colleagues. Nevertheless, as someone coming to this work primarily out of concern for workers, as opposed to great legal skill, and trying to make the confusing array of workplace issues comprehensible, I suspect that despite my best efforts I have not explained something clearly, or perhaps have even gotten something wrong. Any errors or lack of clarity are my fault. If you find something confusing or you think something is incorrect, please let me know via the book's website (www.wagetheft.org). I'd also love to hear your stories of wage theft. Did you have wages stolen? If so, what did you do? Were you a manager or an employer, and did you find ways to stop wage theft in your company or in a subcontractor? If so, what did you do?

Thank you to Jennifer Phillips and Phil Tom for encouraging the Joyce Foundation and the Presbyterian Church USA to provide financial support for my writing time in 2008 and the Twink Fey Visiting Activists Program for the time in 2011.

Thank you to Marc Favreau at The New Press for pushing me to consolidate chapters and document the extent of the crisis and to Debbie Masi and Melody Negron at the Westchester Book Group for their careful production editing. Ellen Adler, Publisher of the New Press, has been a tireless supporter of the project.

And finally, thank you to my beloved husband Stephen Coats (who commented on the manuscript) and our twin sons Eric Coats and Benjamin Bobo for their overall support and encouragement.

Introduction

Thou shalt not steal.

—Exodus 20:15 (KJV)

Americans understand that the nation faces a jobs crisis. We simply don't have enough jobs for all those who are willing to work. Most Americans also understand that we have an income and benefits crisis. There aren't enough jobs that pay living wages with family-supporting benefits. Too many are without jobs. Too many with jobs don't get paid enough to make ends meet. Wages are stagnating. Health and pension benefits are disappearing. Workers' rights to organize unions are under attack. There are many excellent books on these subjects—my two favorites being *Nickel and Dimed: On (Not) Getting By in America* (2001) by Barbara Ehrenreich and *The Big Squeeze: Tough Times for the American Worker* (2008) by Steven Greenhouse.

Unfortunately, most Americans are shocked to learn that we *also* have crises of wage theft and payroll fraud. Unscrupulous employers are stealing money from workers by cheating them of wages owed or not paying them at all and lying to public agencies about having employees.

Since 1996, I've had the honor and pleasure of leading Interfaith Worker Justice (IWJ; www.iwj.org), a national network that engages people of faith in issues and campaigns to improve wages, benefits, and working conditions for low-wage workers. We work with an awesome network of more than fifty religion–labor groups and twenty-five workers' centers. Originally, IWJ had planned to work primarily with labor unions, because they are the best antipoverty and antiwage theft vehicles around. Unfortunately, we quickly realized that unions didn't exist in many communities and that their capacity to organize and represent workers in many low-wage sectors is not as strong as we would like.

As a result, we began developing and supporting workers' centers, which are essentially drop-in centers for workers in low-wage jobs who are having trouble with wages or health and safety. Like the Catholic Labor Schools of the 1930s and 1940s or the farm worker service centers in rural communities, the workers' centers train workers to understand their rights in the workplace and organize to improve their situations.

The number one problem the workers' centers face is wage theft—people not getting paid for their work. When I tell people about the wage theft and payroll fraud crises, they are surprised to learn how wide-spread the problems are. Although sometimes people have actually experienced wage theft or payroll fraud themselves, they thought it was an isolated incident—one bad employer, one bad apple. Unfortunately, the problems are at epidemic proportions.

Although I know there are many fine ethical businessmen and women in the United States who employ workers and do their best to treat workers both legally and ethically (a few of whom are profiled in Chapter 8), my experience from IWJ and particularly the workers' centers provides a disheartening view of the mean underbelly of the economy. Millions of workers are having billions of dollars of wages stolen each and every year. The protections that exist are inadequate or not enforced. As consumers and sometimes as employers, all of us participate either knowingly or unwittingly in supporting businesses that steal wages from workers and revenues from the public.

This book outlines the crises of wage theft and payroll fraud in the nation, proposes ways that we as a nation can combat them, and suggests how each of us can help. Wage theft and payroll fraud hurt both middle-class and poor workers. Wage theft and payroll fraud by unscrupulous employers place ethical employers at a competitive disadvantage against those who don't pay workers and cheat on taxes. Payroll fraud withholds needed revenues from public entities that serve the broader public's needs. And wage theft denies needed economic stimulus to struggling communities. Wage theft and payroll fraud are bad for all of us.

The first edition of the book, which came out before the 2008 elections, had a particular focus on the Wage and Hour Division of the U.S. Department of Labor, because it is the primary federal agency responsible for enforcing wage payment laws. Although this new edition continues to support an enhanced role for the Wage and Hour Division of the Department of Labor in stopping and deterring wage theft, it adds chapters on strengthening state and local enforcement agencies, reflecting the amazing progress made to strengthen state and local enforcement in the past few years.

I've added a chapter on payroll fraud, which details the thievery of employers who lie about having employees and paying people "under the table."

The new chapter that I've had the most fun with is a chapter on ethical business leaders who are modeling alternative ways to pay and treat people. The conversations with these ethical business leaders have given me renewed hope for the future of our nation.

Throughout the book I draw from the Hebrew, Christian, and Muslim scriptures to ground the concern about wage theft in the religious justice-seeking traditions. These references are not intended to be used as "proof texts" but as a way to illumine how the religious texts speak to the matter of wage theft that transcends time and culture. I use various translations of the scriptures, including the King James Version (KJV), the New Revised Standard Version (NRSV), and Today's New International Version (TNIV).

Some of the selected texts, when read out of context, will sound harsh or judgmental. But what they represent is a stream of multiple messages in our religious traditions that demonstrate God's commitment to justice in the context of hope. God gives commandments along with promises for peace and reconciliation. There is a part of that tradition that does offer judgment but always with the message of hope and love for those who listen and act.

My dream for the first edition of the book was that it would build awareness of the crisis of wage theft and stimulate the needed public determination to stop it. The issue of wage theft has gotten significant media attention, the phrase "wage theft" has become standard usage, politicians are reevaluating their enforcement practices, unions are recognizing wage theft within their industries, and some (not enough) business leaders are beginning to challenge wage theft within their sectors. A lot of progress has been made since the first edition was published. In this second edition, I continue to seek to build awareness and public will for stopping wage theft, but also to draw lessons from the incredible organizing work that has stepped up enforcement and created new tools for educating workers and employers.

As a nation, we are capable of stopping most wage theft, but only if people begin to understand wage theft as a serious problem we must face. Stopping wage theft requires political will. It requires us to support workers and ethical businesses and punish those who steal wages from workers. Some of the necessary changes are simple; others are more complicated. Nationally, the leadership for these changes must come from the president, the secretary of labor, and Congress, but it is our job to create the political space for them to want to make the changes. Locally, the leadership must come from ethical businesses, religious leaders, unions, workers' centers, immigrant rights groups, attorneys, local elected leaders, and workers themselves.

Wage theft and payroll fraud are all around us. If you talk with your friends, family, and neighbors, you'll find workers who haven't been fully paid what they are owed. If you talk with workers in your community's businesses, you will find more workers who haven't been paid. If you talk with government officials, you'll learn about businesses lying about having employees in order to defraud the government. As consumers, we all purchase goods and services from businesses that steal wages. Wage theft and payroll fraud are not somewhere else. They are here—in my community and yours. We are all surrounded by wage theft and payroll fraud.

There is some good news about wage theft and payroll fraud: they can be stopped. Compared with many problems our nation faces, these problems are relatively simple to address. The history of our nation is one of constant change and constant striving for the common good. We don't have to accept wage theft and payroll fraud as inevitable. We can end both, but only if we recognize the problems and build the political will to address these abuses. Together, we can create the will and the programs needed to stop wage theft and payroll fraud and build a nation that truly offers justice for all its workers.

Kim Bobo, April 2011

Part I

Wage Theft

1

The Crisis of Wage Theft

Do not take advantage of a hired worker who is poor and needy, whether that worker is an Israelite or is a foreigner residing in one of your towns. Pay them their wages each day before sunset, because they are poor and are counting on it. Otherwise they may cry to the Lord against you, and you will be guilty of sin.

—Deuteronomy 24:14–15 (TNIV)

And O my people! Give just measure and weight, nor withhold from the people the things that are their due.

—Qur'an 11:85

A few years ago, I heard about a garment factory near my house where workers weren't making the minimum wage, or so I was told. I couldn't believe that such a place operated four blocks from where I live. I didn't even know it existed.

I'd heard about this place because some workers had visited Arise Chicago's workers' center and told their stories. In addition, I'd heard that this place was a sole subcontractor for a leading national company. I wanted to know what was going on.

With the help of Interfaith Worker Justice (IWJ) colleagues, we organized a fact-finding delegation of religious leaders to investigate what was happening. One cold Chicago morning, twenty-five of us dropped in at the factory. The place was located in a largely residential neighborhood in a small turn-of-the-century industrial building that faces the Metra train stop. There was no sign outside identifying the facility. The front door was unlocked, so we marched on up to the second floor.

Sure enough, when we opened the second door at the top of the stairs, we stepped into a small entryway, which then had a door opening to a large high-ceiling room full of Latina immigrant women huddled over sewing machines. Despite twenty-five folks, including some in clerical collars, dropping in unexpectedly, no one looked up from their machines. (I can't believe it was because they were accustomed to regular visitors.)

Despite the cold outside, the workroom was quite warm. We all imagined how hot the room would be in August. Such Chicago buildings have impressive boilers but no air conditioning.

We scoured the place looking for the manager. Once the manager got over the shock of seeing us in her place, she quickly tried to shoo us back into the lobby area. I must confess, we were not the most cooperative crowd. It took us a while to get back to the lobby.

Once back and contained, we began peppering her with questions.

"What do you pay these workers?"

"I pay them the minimum wage, $5.15 per hour."

"But this is Illinois; the minimum wage is $6.15, not $5.15."

Slapping her forehead, "Why didn't they tell me!"

"Do you provide any health insurance for the workers?"

"Well, I asked them if they wanted health insurance, but none of them did. They all get it through their husbands. Oh, and these workers are like my family. We celebrate birthdays and babies."

Meanwhile, one of our colleagues went to use the bathroom. A worker jumped up to give her a few sections of toilet paper.

So we asked the manager, "What's the deal on the toilet paper?"

"Oh, I used to provide it, but the workers would steal it, so now they prefer to bring their own." Right.

But this manager was not the only culprit here. The workers claimed this garment sweatshop was sewing exclusively for Cintas, the nation's largest industrial laundry. Cintas is not a mom-and-pop shop that doesn't know any better. It is a leading national company. The Cintas website describes itself as follows:

Cintas is a publicly held company traded over the Nasdaq Global Select Market under the symbol CTAS, and is a Nasdaq-100 company and component of the Standard & Poor's 500 Index. Cintas designs, manufactures and implements corporate identity uniform programs, and provides entrance mats, restroom cleaning and supplies, promotional products, first aid and safety products, fire protection services and document management services for approximately eight hundred thousand businesses.

Cintas operates more than 420 facilities in the U.S. and Canada, including four manufacturing plants and eight distribution centers that employ more than 30,000 people.

Cintas revenues were $3.5 billion in fiscal year 2010, with a net income for the year of $216 million. Cintas was founded by Richard T. Farmer, Chairman of the Board. Scott Farmer was appointed Chief Executive Officer in 2003, and Bob Kohlhepp serves as the Chairman of the Board.

Several months after our call at the factory, IWJ published a report called "Airing Dirty Laundry" based on the delegations and other interviews; as a result, Cintas threatened to sue IWJ and all its affiliates. When I called to talk with the attorney representing the company, he told me Farmer and Kohlhepp were willing to meet with some religious leaders. At the meeting, we came with stories we had gathered from workers around the country. Farmer and Kohlhepp were prepared with their PowerPoints, their directors of contracting and diversity and health and safety, and so on. Our spokespeople included a man who had taught Kohlhepp's children in confirmation classes, a Methodist bishop, a Baptist pastor, a nun, and a few others. We brought no real expertise, just a concern for workers.

The Cintas officials assured us they had excellent subcontracting guidelines in place. We assured them that the subcontracting guidelines weren't working.

On a personal level, Farmer and Kohlhepp and their staff were all very nice and pleasant. They give generously to their churches and the community. I'm sure they are great with their own families. I'm sure they are very nice people. Oh... and did I mention that Farmer is one of the richest men in the state of Ohio?

Still, Cintas is a part of the crisis of wage theft in the nation.

Arise Chicago's workers' center helped Cintas's subcontractor's workers file complaints for the lost wages, for the subminimum wages they received, with the Illinois Department of Labor. Eventually, the workers recovered $209,867.82 in back wages and penalties.

Cintas, as the ultimate employer of these workers, had essentially stolen over $100,000 from poverty wage workers with no benefits by allowing them to receive less than the minimum wage, the lowest amount that workers can legally be paid. This is what I mean by wage theft.

And Cintas and its subcontractor are not alone. Not by a long shot!

Billions of dollars in wages are being illegally stolen from millions of workers each and every year. The employers range from small neighborhood businesses to some of the nation's largest employers—Wal-Mart, Tyson, FedEx, McDonald's, Target, Pulte Homes, federal, state, and local governments, and many more.

Wage theft occurs when workers are not paid all their wages, workers are denied overtime when they should be paid for it, or workers aren't paid at all for work they've performed. Wage theft is when an employer violates the law and deprives a worker of legally mandated wages.

Wage theft is widespread and pervasive across all types of companies. Various surveys have found that:

- 60 percent of nursing homes stole workers' wages.[1]
- 89 percent of nonmonitored garment factories in Los Angeles and 67 percent of nonmonitored garment factories in New York City stole workers' wages.[2]
- 25 percent of tomato producers, 35 percent of lettuce producers, 51 percent of cucumber producers, 58 percent of onion producers, and 62 percent of garlic producers hiring farm workers stole workers' wages.[3]
- 78 percent of restaurants in New Orleans stole workers' wages.[4]
- Almost half of day laborers, who tend to focus on construction work, have had their wages stolen.[5]
- 100 percent of poultry plants steal workers' wages.[6]

Although wage theft is most pernicious when employers steal money from workers earning low wages, wage theft affects many middle-income workers too, including construction workers, nurses, dieticians, writers, bookkeepers, and many more. Wage theft affects young workers, mid-career workers, and older workers. Although some of the worst wage theft occurs when immigrant workers aren't paid minimum wage or aren't paid at all, the largest dollar amounts are stolen from native-born white and black workers in unpaid overtime.

In 2009, *Broken Laws, Unprotected Workers: Violations of Employment and Labor Laws in America's Cities* documented results from a landmark survey of 4387 workers in low-wage industries in New York, Chicago, and Los Angeles. The results were startling. One out of four workers wasn't paid the minimum wage. Of those who worked overtime (more than 40 hours per week), 76 percent weren't paid for it. The survey found routine employer disregard for the nation's labor laws and pervasive retaliation when workers sought to complain or organize.[7]

Millions of workers are having their wages stolen. More than three million workers aren't being paid the minimum wage. More than three million additional workers are victims of payroll theft in which their employers lie about their workers' status, calling them independent contractors when they are really employees; this means their employers aren't paying their share of payroll taxes and many workers are being illegally denied overtime pay. Untold millions more aren't being paid overtime because their employers wrongfully claim they are exempt from the overtime laws. Several million more aren't being paid for their breaks or have illegal deductions made from paychecks. The scope of these abuses is staggering.

The Economic Policy Foundation, a business-funded think tank, estimated that companies annually steal $19 billion in unpaid overtime.[8] Labor lawyer colleagues suggest the number is much higher.

Cases of unscrupulous employers stealing wages have reached epidemic proportions. As a nation we are facing a crisis of wage theft.

Studies Demonstrate Widespread Wage Theft

The scope and pervasiveness of wage theft are confirmed by state and federal government surveys as well as academic studies. Here are some findings for particular groups of workers:

CONSTRUCTION WORKERS: More than $500 billion is spent each year on residential construction, and more than one million workers are employed in the industry. The number of workers is expected to grow significantly in the next ten years.[9] In many cities, construction work was historically done primarily by construction firms that hired union members. These firms paid people well, and the unions made sure wage laws, as well as health and safety standards, were rigorously enforced. With a decline in unionization, construction work is now divided dramatically between union and a few other ethical high-road employers, which are concentrated in commercial building, and those construction companies that exploit workers, primarily by squeezing subcontractors, which are concentrated in residential construction.

A recent study prepared by the Fiscal Policy Institute of the construction industry in New York City found that approximately fifty thousand workers (one in four of the estimated two hundred thousand workers) are either misclassified as independent contractors instead of employees or employed by construction contractors completely off the books.[10] Misclassifying and paying off the books are schemes for stealing wages from workers and avoiding tax obligations.

Although there are no national studies of wage violations in the construction industry, if you google "wage violations in construction," you will find hundreds of stories about it. Workers' centers regularly assist underpaid workers from the construction industry. Cristina Tzintzun, coordinator of the Workers Defense Project in Austin, Texas, confirms the problems faced by construction workers. She says, "Most construction workers we see have experienced the most egregious wage theft—they haven't been paid at all."[11]

GARMENT FACTORY WORKERS: Wage theft is a significant problem among the nation's seven hundred thousand garment workers. Garment industry surveys in 1999 and 2000 in Los Angeles, San Francisco, and New York City showed overall compliance rates of 33 percent, 74 percent, and 35 percent, respectively. Fewer than half of garment factories surveyed in Los Angeles were paying minimum wage. The average back wages (the amount of wages that were owed because what was paid was not enough according to the law) owed per shop were more than $4000 in Los Angeles and $12,000 in New York City. Although subsequent surveys in the garment industry in 2001 did show improvements in compliance and reduction in the seriousness of violations, garment workers continue to have their wages stolen. It is an industry sorely in need of regular oversight and enforcement.

For example, Laundry Room Clothing in Westminster, California, run by Milton and Sharon Kaneda, produced goods for national retailers including Forever 21 and Ross Stores, Inc. The 115 low-wage workers were cheated of $380,000 in minimum wage and overtime compensation from 2009 to 2010.[12]

NURSING HOME WORKERS: Almost six hundred thousand nursing assistants work in nursing homes.[13] These are difficult jobs with high turnover rates because they are physically demanding, pay little, and provide few benefits. The national hourly rate for a nursing home certified nurse assistant (CNA) is $10.33.[14] The annual salary for a CNA averages only $23,716 per year.[15]

The U.S. Department of Labor's Wage and Hour Division's 2000 Nursing Home Compliance Survey found only 40 percent overall compliance, meaning that 60 percent of nursing homes surveyed had cheated workers of wages. The FY 2004 Annual Report of the Department of Labor showed compliance rates in nursing homes had risen to 55 percent, which is still low.[16] The biggest problems were with workers not getting paid for the overtime they had worked. According to the Nursing Home 2000 Compliance Survey Fact Sheet, most overtime violations occurred because the nursing homes misclassified workers as exempt workers, when they should have been nonexempt. (For a detailed explanation of the misclassification problem, see Chapter 2.) Other problems included not compensating workers for hours worked during their meal breaks, failing to include bonuses or shift differential payments into the employees' regular rate of pay (base rate for "time-and-a-half" computation), being paid straight time for overtime hours worked (the regular wages instead of the wages times 1.5), and failing to pay for pre- and postshift work.

The bottom line here is that more than half of nursing homes surveyed are violating wage and hour laws. The workers most affected are CNAs. These are the hardworking people who push patients in wheelchairs, lift them in and out of beds, help them to the bathroom, wash them, and serve them. These workers care for our family members. These same workers are not receiving all their pay. So if you have a loved one in a nursing home, the odds are good that the nursing home is cheating some of its workers of their pay.

FARM WORKERS: The roughly two million farm workers are among the poorest and most hardworking workers in the nation. They plant, tend, and harvest the food we eat. Unfortunately, things are not much different from when the famous 1960 CBS television documentary *Harvest of Shame* shocked the nation by showing slavelike working and living conditions for farm workers. The median hourly wage for farm workers is $7.95, but farm workers usually don't work year-round. As a result, most farm worker families, despite working hard and doing work essential for the society, live well below the poverty line.

One visit to most farm labor camps will convince you that something is dreadfully wrong in our society. In 2007 I visited a farm labor camp with a Farm Labor Organizing Committee (FLOC) organizer in North Carolina. The "camp," a long squat building, looked like a converted chicken coop. There was no heat and certainly there was no air conditioning. The floors were concrete. The walls were just unpainted boards. The building was divided into five or six large rooms. One was the kitchen with a couple of stoves, a couple of fridges, and a long wooden picnic table for eating. Food was piled in open shelves. This room and all others had dreary lightbulbs hanging from the ceiling, but somehow no light seemed to enter the few windows. The kitchen was dirty and unpleasant.

The bathroom was the worst—a long row of toilets and a few showers. There were no stalls, no shower curtains—no privacy of any sort.

There were a few dormitory-type rooms with eight to ten beds lined up in each. Workers didn't even have a dresser or a table for personal belongings.

Because the inside conditions were so horrible, most of the farm workers hung out outside. The workers were all immigrants from Chiapas, Mexico, and with one or two exceptions, all were very young. They had come to the United States to harvest our crops because their own families were starving and needed income. They were in North Carolina picking tobacco. They were not being paid minimum wage.

By federal law, farm workers are covered by minimum wage, but are exempt from overtime coverage, which means that the employer doesn't legally have to pay the workers overtime pay (1.5 times the regular pay for the hours worked over 40 hours). The employer *is* required to pay minimum wage. Yet in many cases, workers are not getting paid for all the hours they work, illegal deductions are being taken from their paychecks, or workers are paid by the piece at such low rates that their hourly wages don't meet minimum wage. (It is legal to pay workers by the piece as long as their hourly wage reaches the minimum wage.) These forms of wage theft often go undetected and unabated for years. Crop workers are employed by the same employer for an average of four and a half years.[17] Such longevity indicates that workers have both loyalty and experience, but those traits don't translate into better wages, working conditions, or benefits.

Wage theft is rampant in agriculture. Department of Labor Wage and Hour surveys in 1999 and 2000 in various agricultural crop categories found compliance rates ranging from 38 percent to, at most, 75 percent.[18] A 2000 Human Rights Watch report investigating child labor abuses in agriculture found that approximately one-third of those interviewed reported earning significantly less than minimum wage.

POULTRY WORKERS: When I first helped organize IWJ in 1996, I repeatedly heard about the wage theft and safety problems poultry workers faced. I heard stories from union friends, board members (especially Reverend Jim Lewis, who had just begun a ministry with poultry workers on the eastern shore of Maryland), and workers themselves. One of IWJ's first actions was a fact-finding delegation investigating working conditions for Case Farms's poultry workers in Morganton, North Carolina.

Workers at a variety of plants told stories of being clocked out (that is, officially "leaving" work), but still having to continue working on the line until the last chicken passed by, not being paid for time spent putting on and taking off safety and protective gear (referred to as "donning and doffing"), and not being paid for overtime. IWJ called upon the Department of Labor to investigate. We were thrilled when then Secretary of Labor Robert Reich responded to our press conference by announcing a poultry investigation.

The division's first survey in 1997 found only 40 percent compliance, meaning 60 percent of plants were violating wage and hour laws.

Poultry companies were stealing wages from both poultry workers and from catchers, the guys (almost all guys) who go around to various chicken farms and catch the birds with their hands (unbelievably horrible work, by the way). Conditions were so dreadful that the division decided to reinvestigate the industry in 2000. What do you think was found? Every single one of the fifty-one plants investigated was found to be violating wage and hour laws. One hundred percent noncompliance. One hundred percent of chicken plants were stealing wages from workers, even though they'd been informed of the violations a few years previously.

In 2002, the Department of Labor helped workers recover more than $10 million in back wages owed to Perdue's twenty-five thousand workers for donning and doffing violations, $450,000 owed to Sanderson Farms's five hundred workers, and $148,000 owed to Continental Grain workers. In 2006, the Department of Labor recovered $1.24 million for five thousand poultry workers employed by George's Processing Inc. in Missouri for underpayment of overtime wages. These settlements were long-standing cases begun from the prior administration.

But the issue of donning and doffing continues. In June 2010, the Department of Labor announced that Tyson Foods Inc. had agreed to a nationwide injunction that required the company to pay its poultry processing workers for all the hours they worked. A similar consent judgment was made with Pilgrim's Pride in January 2010.[19] Even though it may take only a few minutes in the morning to "don" clothes and protective gear and a few minutes in the evening to "dof" them, that time is compensable and adds up over weeks and years. For low-paid poultry workers, getting paid for all their time worked is important.

RESTAURANT WORKERS: Restaurants are notorious for stealing wages from workers. Eleven different Department of Labor-directed enforcement initiatives at restaurants in 1999 uncovered compliance rates ranging from 22 percent in New Orleans to 70 percent in northern New Jersey.[20] Every single IWJ-affiliated workers' center regularly sees restaurant workers who haven't been paid, with the worst abuse happening with dishwashers, table clearers, and cooks who work in the back of the restaurants.

The Chinese Progressive Association in San Francisco released a survey of 433 restaurant workers in Chinatown in 2010. Half of the workers weren't paid minimum wage. Three-fourths weren't paid overtime.[21]

In 2011, the Restaurant Opportunities Centers United (ROC United) released surveys of restaurant workers in Los Angeles, Miami, and Washington, D.C. Those reporting minimum wage violations ranged from 5 percent to 22 percent of those surveyed. More than a third of all workers weren't paid the legally required overtime rates. In 2010, ROC United released similar surveys of restaurant workers in Chicago, Detroit, New Orleans, and Maine. All four reports showed widespread violation of laws.[22] The National Restaurant Association's 2011 fact sheet says there are 12.8 million workers employed by restaurants.[23] Given the wage theft indicated in the government and private surveys, there are likely millions of restaurant workers who have been and are today being cheated of wages.

DAY LABORERS: There are two major kinds of day laborers in the nation. One group works for day labor agencies that usually operate out of storefronts. The other stands on street corners and sells their labor to whoever comes by and bids for it.

The formal agencies have mixed records. Some, especially the smaller agencies that avoid registration, routinely steal wages. Ian Armstrong visited the Cincinnati Interfaith Workers' Center complaining about not getting paid. He had signed up with Quickstaff Employment Agency in Covington, Kentucky, and went to work at a convention center. He didn't get paid the $350 he was owed. Even worse, he got a W-2 from a payroll service claiming he'd been paid $780, so he would have to pay taxes on money he never received. The Covington Police said other workers had been victimized too and issued a warrant for the owner's arrest.[24]

Other larger agencies, such as Labor Ready, which signed a 2003 voluntary compliance agreement with the Department of Labor, are seeking to comply with labor laws.[25]

The worst abuses occur among corner day laborers. The largest survey of day laborers, *On the Corner: Day Labor in the United States* by Abel Valenzuela Jr., Nik Theodore, Edwin Meléndez, and Ana Luz Gonzalez was published in 2006 after interviews with 2660 day laborers from 264 randomly selected day labor sites.[26] The survey showed that nearly half of all day laborers (49 percent) had wages completely stolen by at least one employer during the two months prior to being surveyed, meaning they were not paid at all for their work, and 48 percent had been paid less than their employer promised or the law required. Stealing of wages was a particular problem in the Midwest, where 66 percent of workers reported having wages stolen and 53 percent were underpaid (less than promised or less than the law required). The report then goes on to say, "Wage theft is just one type of employer abuse endured by day laborers. During the two months prior to being surveyed, 44 percent of day laborers were denied promised food, water and legally mandated breaks; 32 percent worked more hours than agreed to with the employer; 28 percent were insulted or threatened by the employer; and 27 percent were abandoned at the work site by an employer (instead of being transported back to the location where they were hired, as is customary)."[27] According to the survey, almost half (49 percent) of the abused workers were hired by homeowners or renters who sought assistance with projects, and most of the rest (43 percent) were hired by contractors for jobs in construction and landscaping.[28]

A smaller survey of day laborers conducted by the Fairfax County Department of Systems Management for Human Resources in Virginia found similar problems with wage theft. "The majority of the respondents (84 percent) listed having one or more problems with their employers. The problems reported most frequently included not receiving any time for breaks (59.3 percent), payment less than that which was agreed upon (54.6 percent), and non-payment for work performed (53.1 percent)."[29] Once again, half the workers had been cheated out of wages.

Still another survey of day laborers in Newark, New Jersey, conducted by the Immigrant Workers' Rights Clinic at the Center for Social Justice of Seton Hall University School of Law confirmed the crisis. Almost all those surveyed (96 percent) had experienced wage theft. The biggest problems were not getting paid what they were promised (77 percent), not being paid at all (62 percent), and not getting paid the overtime premium for hours worked over 40 (88 percent).[30]

The General Accountability Office in its recommendations to the Secretary of Labor about how to better protect day laborers states that "available information indicates that day laborers face numerous potential violations. Many of these potential violations involve nonpayment of wages, including overtime."[31] Day laborers, among the poorest of the poor, are routinely being cheated of wages.

LANDSCAPE WORKERS: Although there have been few studies of landscape workers, the industry is known throughout the advocacy world for its violations. In 2009, the Philadelphia district office of the U.S. Department of Labor's Wage and Hour Division announced it was investigating landscapers. According to an article about the investigation, "Of the companies investigated by the local office in the last five years, only 25 percent were in compliance with wage laws."[32]

FREELANCERS: Increasing numbers of workers are freelancers, meaning they don't work for one employer. Some freelancers really want to be freelancers—they enjoy the freedom of setting and working their own schedules. Others are freelancers primarily because they can't find a full-time job. Most freelancers have had the problem of getting paid.

Jason Wisdom, a Rutgers-educated freelance computer consultant contracted for $70 per hour with a client who had a contract with Sirius Satellite Radio. At first, he was paid on time. Then payments were late. Then payments stopped. By February 2010 he was owed $20,000. He ended up racking up money on his credit card and withdrawing money from his retirement account to make ends meet. Wisdom spent months complaining to the client, Sirius, the Better Business Bureau, and finally the district attorney's office.[33]

Stiffing freelancers is such a common problem that the Freelancers Union has organized a new campaign called Getting Paid Not Played. Check it out at www.freelancersunion.org.

Department of Labor Suits and Settlements

The Department of Labor only catches a small percentage of employers who steal wages (for reasons that will be explained later), and there is no readily available list of all its suits and settlements. Nonetheless, the following table shows a few of the settlements; the table of many more wage theft cases presented in Appendix A demonstrates the pervasiveness of

Alleged ways wages are stolen	Date on Department of Labor press release	Company	Suit or settlement	Back wages owed (or estimated)	Number of workers owed $
not paying overtime	1/25/2007	Wal-Mart	settlement	$33 million	86,680
misclassifying workers	8/30/2007	Southern California Maid Services and Carpet Cleaning	suit	$3.47 million	385
not paying overtime	8/8/2007	Pilgrim's Pride Corp.	settlement	$3 million	500
not paying required wages (to non-immigrant workers)	6/7/2007	Patni Computer Systems Inc.	settlement	$2.4 million	607
not paying overtime	2/15/2007	ABC Professional Tree Services Inc.	settlement	$1.8 million	2501
not paying minimum wage	1/14/2010	MT Transportation & Logistics Services	settlement	$1.8 million	500
not paying prevailing wage	8/17/2010	Smartsoft International Inc.	settlement	$1 million	135
not paying all hours worked and not paying overtime	6/14/2010	Umatilla Chemical Depot	settlement	$4.2 million	603

A sampling of wage and hour settlements. See Appendix A for the larger list.

the wage theft crisis in our nation and offers an overview of the ways employers steal wages.[34] The table clearly shows that wage theft is not a minor problem involving just a few employers who don't understand the laws. It is a major crisis cutting across industries, regions, and many sizes of firms.

Private Lawsuits Explode

There is perhaps no better evidence of the breadth of the crisis than the explosion of private lawsuits seeking to recover unpaid wages. The Fair Labor Standards Act (FLSA), which covers minimum wage and overtime issues, provides workers the "private right to sue," which means they can take their cases to private attorneys. They are doing so in record numbers.

Current business magazine headlines, including a front-page *Business Week* cover story and management-side law firms' articles tell the story:

> *Wage Wars: Workers—From Truck Drivers to Stockbrokers—Are Winning Huge Overtime Lawsuits*[35]
>
> *Wage and Hour Violations: An Employer's Single Greatest Uninsured Risk*[36]
>
> *Time Bomb Waiting to Explode: Wage and Hour Claims over Exempt Employees*[37]
>
> *Wage and Hour Audits: Wage and Hour Laws Are Violated More Often Than Any Other Employment Law*[38]
>
> *Wage and Hour Laws Are Violated More Often Than Any Other Employment Law*[39]
>
> *Overtime Pay: A Ticking Time Bomb*[40]

According to the Administrative Office of the U.S. Courts, there were 6073 FLSA lawsuits filed in 2009,[41] compared to only 1257 in 1990, 1580 in 1995, and 1935 in 2000.[42] Between 1990 and 2000, the cases increased by a little more than 50 percent. Between 2000 and 2010, the suits filed more than quadrupled.[43] These figures account for only the federal lawsuits and do not include wage cases filed in state courts under state wage laws. Most of the wage and hour lawsuits were filed for large groups of workers, which means that these cases are recovering wages for several hundred thousand workers. The number of workers recovering wages would be much higher if workers didn't have to "opt-in" to the suits.[44]

Company	Alleged violation	Employees affected	Settlement amount	Year settled
Farmers Insurance Exchange	unpaid overtime	2402 claims adjusters	$200 million	2004
State Farm Group	unpaid overtime	2600 California claims adjusters	$135 million	2005
Allstate Corp.	unpaid overtime	3000 California-based adjusters	$120 million	2005
Citigroup Global Markets (Smith Barney)	unpaid overtime	20,000 brokers	$98 million	2006
UBS Financial Services	unpaid overtime	13,000 brokers	$89 million	2006
UPS	unpaid overtime, meal and rest period pay, and pay stub penalties	20,000 drivers	$87 million	2007
IBM	unpaid overtime, misclassified workers	32,000 tech workers	$65 million	2006
City of Houston, TX	unpaid overtime	600 paramedics	$72 million	2004
Albertsons LLC	unpaid overtime	7000 employees	$53.3 million	2007
Farmers Insurance Exchange	unpaid overtime	2800 claims adjusters	$52 million	2006
Dick's Sporting Goods	unpaid overtime	not disclosed	$15 million	2011
Staples	misclassification	5500 assistant store managers	$42 million	2010
Spherion Pacific Workgroup	didn't pay for all worked time unpaid overtime and unpaid holiday pay	not disclosed	$13 million	2010
Wal-Mart		232,000 workers	$86 million	2010

A sampling of private wage and hour lawsuits. See Appendix B for the larger list.

(In many class-action suits, one is automatically covered in the class unless one chooses to "opt out." Unfortunately in federal FLSA suits, workers are required to "opt in," which makes it harder to build the class.) "Lawyers on both sides estimate that over the last few years companies have collectively paid out more than $1 billion annually to resolve these claims."[45]

Most of the big wage and hour lawsuits deal with overtime pay. The FLSA has been clear since 1938 that all workers, except those exempt from the law, are eligible for overtime pay (1.5 times the FLSA "regular rate") for hours worked over 40 each week. The real issue is who is exempt and who isn't. Thousands of workers and their attorneys claim they are "nonexempt" workers and thus due overtime pay. But many of the employers claim the workers are exempt and thus not due overtime. The crux of the matter is the classification of workers—whether they are really exempt or nonexempt. In an effort to clarify and streamline the overtime provisions, the Department of Labor issued new overtime regulations in 2004. Unfortunately, the regulations remain complicated, and employers continue to break the laws. Whether out of ignorance or willfulness, employers who illegally deny workers overtime are stealing wages. Following is a table (and Appendix B provides a fuller list) showing some recent lawsuits for unpaid overtime wages, again demonstrating the breadth of wage theft across industries, regions, and size of employers.

Workers' Centers and Wage Theft

Wage theft is acutely felt at the nation's workers' centers and legal clinics where workers whose wages have been stolen seek help. Jeffrey Steele is one such worker who sought help in New Orleans.

Steele, an African American from Atlanta, wanted to be part of history in rebuilding New Orleans after Hurricane Katrina. Responding to a flyer advertising "Free Room and Board, Free Food, Pay $10/Hour," he signed up with Workforce Development Corp. Inc., run by Carroll Harrison Braddy, and boarded a van to New Orleans in mid-October 2005. As it turned out, Braddy reneged on his flyers' promises. Steele's first few days were particularly miserable: he received no food, he had to sleep in the van, and he was made to work long hours. A few weeks after arriving in New Orleans, he was finally fitted for an aspirator, a critical piece of health and safety equipment for all those involved in the cleanup and exposed to dangerous contaminants.

When Steele's first paycheck was due, he calculated he was owed $1400, not even assuming any overtime pay (1.5 times the regular rate over 40 hours per week). But Braddy only paid him $230. By mid-November, Steele left Braddy's employment and went to work for another cleanup firm called JNE where he was promised $18 per hour. After four weeks of very long hours (almost 100 hours per week), Steele estimated he was owed about $7000. He was initially paid $300 and then got another $1000. In January 2006, he started working for a third employer, with whom he stayed for nine months. This third employer paid him as an "exempt" salaried employee, even though he was probably legally eligible for overtime coverage (more on this issue later), which means he probably had wages stolen with this employee too. At the last New Orleans job he worked, Steele injured his hand, which then required surgery. He received no workers' compensation for his injury, nor did his employer provide any medical insurance. In all, Steele had four employers in New Orleans—and all of them stole wages or workers' compensation from him. In testimony before the Domestic Policy Subcommittee of the Oversight and Government Reform Committee on June 26, 2007, Steele said,

> I went to New Orleans to help and to be part of history. I did the dirty, hard work that was needed. Yet, I was exploited by contractor after contractor who crammed us into filthy living spaces, provided next to nothing to eat, offered practically no safety precautions or equipment and paid workers late and so much less than even promised. If this is how this country allows employers to get away with treating hard working citizens while companies make a profit—then shame on us. I've worked hard all my life and I pay taxes. I'm a United States citizen. I've been working since I was 9 years old. I've never been to jail and I've never asked the government for nothing. If another catastrophe happens in this country, I hope you never let any one else treat workers and the people they are trying to help like they did in New Orleans.[46]

Although wage theft was particularly bad in New Orleans immediately after Katrina, workers' centers throughout the nation help thousands of workers annually who have had their wages stolen. (More background on workers' centers is provided in Chapter 6.)

Throughout the book, many of the examples of wage theft involve immigrants. This makes sense because the examples come from many of the IWJ workers' centers that work with immigrants. Although the centers work with all workers in low-wage jobs, it is undocumented immigrants—who are most fearful of approaching government agencies—who flood the workers' centers seeking help. Nonetheless, if you review the lists of the more than five hundred Department of Labor settlements (Appendix A) or the private wage and hour lawsuits (Appendix B), you will find that most of the workers whose wages are stolen are U.S. citizens. Perhaps the worst exploitation occurs among immigrants, but the crisis of wage theft would exist even if there were no immigrant workers in the society.

Wage theft affects all American workers by lowering the nation's workplace standards, but especially those in middle- and low-income jobs. Stealing wages hurts workers and their families. Workers who aren't paid their wages still have to pay their rent or their child care. Workers who are required to work long hours without overtime compensation are deprived of the opportunity to get another job or spend time with their families. Workers who are cheated of wages can't save for their kids' college or save for a home. For some earning the lowest wages, not getting paid means their families go hungry or become homeless. As a society, when we allow employers to steal wages from some workers, it drives down wages and standards for all workers.

Wage theft places ethical employers at a competitive disadvantage. Those businesses that pay workers legally and fairly and pay all their taxes as required are undercut by businesses that steal from workers and don't pay taxes and insurances as required. In addition, wage theft steals from public coffers and deprives communities of the economic stimulus generated when workers spend their wages.

Throughout the book, we will examine how and why employers steal wages. We will look at how unions, workers' centers, and ethical employers are combating wage theft. We will look at how we can strengthen enforcement agencies—federal, state, and local. And finally, we will look at how you and I can stop and deter wage theft.

Stopping wage theft is good for America and something that we can do. Unlike many of the problems we face as a nation, stopping wage theft can be accomplished. Wage theft is a national crisis, but we can stop it.

2

How Employers Steal Wages

They plot injustice and say, "We have devised a perfect plan!" Surely the mind and heart of man are cunning.

—Psalm 64:6[1] (TNIV)

Employers steal their employees' wages in a variety of ways. Although some employers may be confused about the law and their legal responsibilities to their workers, most of them know precisely what they are doing or *should* know what they are doing.

I do believe that there are some small employers, especially those who have just started employing staff, who may not understand the labor laws and may not realize that many of these laws cover their businesses. When you read Chapter 5 on how U.S. labor laws fail workers, you will appreciate how confusing these laws are. As someone who runs a nonprofit organization, I too often have struggled to stay abreast of all the laws and regulations.

Most employers, however, who steal wages from workers do so intentionally, either by directly putting in place systems and approaches for stealing wages or by indirectly failing to install systems to prevent wage theft, especially in supply chains and contracting. Think of these as sins of both commission and omission.

Sins of commission are committed when an employer pays a worker less than the minimum wage or pays workers for fewer hours than were worked or pays workers in cash in order to avoid paying payroll taxes. This theft is done overtly, intentionally, and maliciously.

Sins of omission are committed when senior managers, often of very large firms, put great financial pressure on their local store managers, branch managers, contractors, or suppliers to keep costs low without putting in place equally strong measures to prevent wage theft. The senior managers "omit" putting in place strong legal and ethical standards and disincentives to discourage wage theft.

Wal-Mart is the classic example of this problem. Wal-Mart's pressure on its managers to cut costs, without equally strong standards preventing wage theft, resulted in wage theft at the local store level. The Wal-Mart senior leadership may not have had a policy that told managers to steal wages, but it did not institute systems designed to prevent wage theft. As a result, the company has faced lawsuits all over the country.

On December 23, 2008, Wal-Mart announced that it had agreed to settle sixty-three of the wage and hour lawsuits against it for at least $352 million, but no more than $640 million.[2] The amount the company will end up paying depends on how many workers claim the money. A year later, it settled an additional $40 million in a suit in Boston,[3] and in 2010 Wal-Mart agreed to pay up to $86 million to settle a suit in California.[4] By the end of 2010, there were still at least six additional wage and hour class cases not yet settled. The problems workers faced were common across stores and states. Managers "shaved hours" to keep workers' records under forty hours so Wal-Mart wouldn't have to pay overtime, required people to work through meal and rest breaks but did not pay them for the time, and required workers to come early or stay late, working off the clock. In addition, there were consistent problems with assistant managers being exempted from overtime provisions even though they did similar work to hourly workers (and thus should not have been exempt from overtime pay) and contracted janitorial firms that were hired by Wal-Mart underpaying workers.

Whether through commission or omission, wage theft has become a ubiquitous feature of the American workplace. Any effective solution has to take into account the complexities of the problem and the myriad challenges workers face when payday comes. The following are primary ways that employers steal wages from workers:

Paying less than the minimum wage. Most people are legally covered by minimum wage laws, either the federal or the state minimum wage,[5] but more than two million, possibly as many as three million, workers are not paid the minimum.[6] The large survey of more than 4300 workers in

Chicago, Los Angeles, and New York (referred to in Chapter 1) found that one in four low-wage workers was not paid minimum wage.[7]

Shurbrite-Hi-Speed Car Wash is the largest of six area car washes owned by members of the Smith family in Nashville, Tennessee. Shurbrite employs between thirty and sixty primarily homeless workers and people with felony records who have trouble finding other work. At Shurbrite, approximately 95 percent of the workers are African American and the other 5 percent are white.

In June 2008, several workers filed an FLSA suit alleging that workers were paid below minimum wage. More than forty-five workers joined the suit within two weeks of it being filed. This car wash had an elaborate scheme to steal wages from workers. Workers were required to be present at the car wash for fairly long periods of time, but the managers would clock workers in when customers were present and clock them out when there were not. So, a worker might be at the work site from 7:00 A.M. until 7:00 P.M. but only be paid for 6 hours of work. Using the June 2008 minimum wage rate of $5.85, Homeless Power, a Nashville homeless rights organization supporting the workers, estimates that the forty-five workers alone who have joined the suit to date are owed $85,000. As workers are added, so will the back wages owed.[8]

Workers' centers across the nation are seeing similar problems. For example, a worker named Claudia visited the Houston Interfaith Workers' Center expressing concerns about her pay. She worked at Refresqueria Tampico, a place that sold snow cones but ironically made its employees work in an overheated shack with no air conditioning. Her 2007 hourly wage, because she got no overtime, averaged about $2 per hour, well below the state minimum wage. She wanted her money but was afraid to formally complain for fear of losing her job.[9] Miguel's story is no different. He worked 11½ hours a day, seven days a week, at a grocery store in Madison, Wisconsin. His weekly pay was $200, from which $50 was deducted for housing. Essentially, he earned less than $3 per hour—once again, way below the minimum wage. In the spring of 2008, Miguel sought help from the Madison Workers Rights Center, which helped him file a claim with the Wisconsin Department of Workforce Development Equal Rights Division. The agency determined that he was owed $12,365 for his 5½ months of unpaid wages.[10]

The minimum wage laws are very clear: workers must be paid the current minimum wage for *all* hours worked. Although some deductions are legal, they cannot bring a worker's pay below minimum wage. *Not paying workers for all the hours they work.* Under the law, employers are required to keep records of hours that employees work and then pay them for all those hours. Yet in many cases, employers simply issue paychecks that do not reflect the total compensation owed to their workers.

When Raymundo started working at the high-end Tres Agaves Restaurant in San Francisco, he was told that the first week of work was a "deposit" and would not be paid until he left employment. Raymundo accepted this since other workers had agreed to that policy and he needed the job to help support his four daughters. Nevertheless, when Raymundo was dismissed less than six months later, he was not paid for that week of work. Raymundo and seven other workers who were fired the same day went to Young Workers United (YWU). When YWU obtained employee records and compared them to the daily receipts that some workers had saved, YWU discovered that they were not being paid for all hours worked. After public protests in front of the restaurant, Tres Agaves agreed to pay a $5000 settlement to Raymundo.[11]

Abel came to the Houston Interfaith Workers' Center with both his pay stubs and a copy of his punch clock record of hours. They did not match. He had worked at two different locations of the chain of restaurants called Las Rosas Mexican Grill. There was clearly a pattern of underpaying workers. Because this was a fairly large business, which was systematically underpaying workers, it was a perfect case to refer to the Department of Labor. Although Abel's case has not yet been resolved, the Labor Department is conducting a full investigation of this chain of restaurants.[12]

Some employers arbitrarily decide that some work tasks aren't worth paying for. In March 2011, after I gave a talk on wage theft in Ann Arbor, Michigan, the woman who'd served food told me how her employer, a successful caterer in town, didn't want to pay servers for the driving time to and from a catering job out of town (5 hours total). He told her, "Most of the servers will be texting the whole way anyway." She insisted that the employer pay them for all the hours worked, including the time getting to and from an out-of-town job.

Giving checks that bounce. Some employers pretend to pay workers but actually give them checks that bounce. Tin Oo was 57 years old and the main income earner for his family of six. Aung Bee was 63 years old and the main income earner for his family of seven. Dah La Klee was 20 years old, and his wife was pregnant with their first child. All three families are ethnic Karens (a hill tribe group located primarily in Myanmar and northwest Thailand) who had lived in a refugee camp before being admitted (legally) into the United States and settling in Indianapolis, Indiana. Because refugee families are only given six months of support before they must work and pay their own way, these men quickly sought work. They took a job in May 2007 building new homes. The employer owed them approximately $2500 for their work, but only gave them one check for $500 and told them he would pay them more soon. When that check bounced, the workers refused to work for the employer anymore. Low-wage workers, especially those in construction, often find that they are paid with checks that bounce.

Not paying overtime/misclassifying "exempt" and "nonexempt." Many middle-class workers and most workers in low-wage jobs are eligible for overtime pay, which is 1.5 times the FLSA regular rate over 40 hours. When the overtime premium pay was initiated in 1938, it was enacted both to ensure that workers got paid extra when they worked long hours and to discourage employers for working people excessively long hours. Yet, millions of workers who should be paid overtime are not. Almost 90 percent of back wages collected by the Department of Labor are for overtime violations.[13]

In 2011, the Department of Labor ordered Levi Strauss and Co. to pay more than $1 million to 596 assistant store managers who were misclassified as exempt from overtime even though they should have been paid for their overtime hours. These assistant managers worked off the clock during late night closings, early morning openings, and staff shortages.[14] Assistant store managers in retail firms and restaurants are often misclassified.

Many employers just don't pay workers any overtime, or they tell workers they are not covered by overtime for some made-up (and not legal) reason. Others misclassify workers by claiming they are "exempt" employees (exempt from the overtime regulations), when they really are "nonexempt" employees (covered by overtime). This misclassification has resulted in the multimillion dollar settlements described in Chapter 1.

This is particularly a problem for workers in low-wage jobs. The 4300-person survey of low-wage workers referred to previously found that three-fourths of low-wage workers who worked overtime were not paid for it.[15] Three-fourths!

Employers who tell secretaries, cooks, retail workers, and others that they are professional or administrative staff and exempt from overtime regulations are simply lying. The exempt categories have very specific management guidelines (control of staff and money decisions). Moreover, anyone earning less than $455 per week, regardless of their responsibilities and title, is automatically covered by overtime (again unless the person is one of the exempted categories of jobs such as a farm worker).

Five janitors who worked for the DB Parking Lot and Janitorial Maintenance Company—a janitorial firm serving small parking lots, as well as national chains, including Walgreens—recently showed up at the Chicago Interfaith Worker Rights Center. These workers had documents showing they had worked approximately 70 hours per week. They were provided vans to drive from location to location but had to pay for the gas. They worked seven days a week and received no overtime. Because they were paid a salary, they were told that they weren't eligible for overtime. These five workers are owed many thousands of dollars for overtime work over the last two years.[16]

Jose worked as a cook. He originally went to the Madison Workers Rights Center because he was concerned that none of the Latino cooks at the restaurants where he worked were getting health insurance. He worked for the same boss and the same supervisor, but in two different restaurant locations. Most weeks, he worked 40 hours in each restaurant for a combined 80 hours, but the employer counted each set of 40 hours separately in order to deny him overtime. The Madison Workers Rights Center helped him recover $6701 in unpaid overtime pay.[17]

Paul Strauss, a Chicago labor lawyer, tells the story of an asparagus packing house owner in California. During the growing season, workers often worked seven days a week. In order to avoid overtime (steal wages from workers), the employer required workers to bring him another person's name and social security number. Then the employer would pay the one worker under two names, thus ensuring, or so he hoped, that workers would not get overtime pay. On payday, workers would each collect two different paychecks. When Strauss helped the workers file suit, the employer quickly settled for $60,000 in back wages.[18]

Paying by the day or the job. A common way that employers steal wages from workers is by paying workers "by the day" or "by the job" in a way that results in the workers not receiving minimum wage or overtime. Usually, such employers pay in cash so that none of the required payroll taxes, unemployment insurance, or workers' compensation are paid either. This robs workers and robs public agencies of taxes due. Day laborers who are picked up on the corner are usually cheated this way, but so are many others.

IWJ released a report in May 2008 on working conditions for construction workers building homes for Pulte Homes, the nation's largest home builder. During fact-finding investigations, workers described a variety of payment arrangements with six Pulte Homes contractors. Most of the workers whom the delegations interviewed reported that they were paid "piece rates." Under "piece-rate" arrangements, workers are paid per unit of work that they complete. For example, workers earn 50 cents per square foot of drywall they hang or $800 per house they paint. If workers end up not getting minimum wage or not getting what they would be owed if overtime wages were calculated, then paying by the piece rate is illegal and steals wages.

Making workers pay for a job. Workers' center leaders describe employers who make workers pay for their jobs another form of treachery.

There's a large car wash not too far from the IWJ office in Chicago. I stopped going there after I heard that workers had to pay for the "right" to dry cars with rags. The dryers worked solely for tips—no wages were paid. Ironically, this car wash's owner played up the plight of these poor workers when fighting a neighborhood zoning change that threatened his business.

Not paying the "prevailing wage." Projects that use government monies are usually required to pay the "prevailing wage" for various construction trades and service jobs. The prevailing wage is the standard and customary wage rate in a particular area for a particular job category. For example, skilled electricians might have a prevailing wage rate of $40 per hour, janitors a prevailing wage rate of $10 per hour, while laborers receive $12 per hour. These rates vary by community.

Unethical employers will steal wages from workers by not paying the prevailing wage rate, even though their contracts were bid and *the employers were paid* based on the prevailing wage rates stipulated in the bid documents. In fiscal year 2004, the Department of Labor conducted 654 investigations under the Service Contract Act. More than 80 percent of those investigations found that employers operating under the Service Contract Act did not pay the wages or benefits owed to workers. In this relatively small number of investigations, 14,000 service contract employees were owed $16.4 million in unpaid back wages and fringe benefits.

In 2007, six workers—one Polish, one Mongolian, three Mexican, and one Honduran—visited the Arise Chicago Workers' Center because they were upset with their wages and working conditions. They were working for an electrical contractor, LOPAR Limited (not a joke), that was providing service on a large government-funded housing project. All other workers on the job were union members getting paid the prevailing wage. These six workers had been coached to tell anyone who asked that they were union members, which they were not. If they had been union members, the union would have ensured that they were paid the prevailing wage. The prevailing wage for electricians during the months they worked was $37.95 per hour. The workers were paid between $10 and $15 per hour. The employer, who was paid a good rate that *assumed* workers were paid the prevailing wage rates, was stealing roughly $23 to $28 per hour from each worker.[19] Eventually, the contractor agreed to pay the workers $21,000 in back wages, although had they actually been paid the prevailing wage they would have received closer to $80,000 in back wages. The workers chose to accept the lower amount because they could get it quickly instead of seeking the larger amount, which would have taken more time.

Taking illegal deductions from workers' paychecks. Another way employers steal wages is by taking illegal deductions from workers' paychecks. Workers don't know that the deductions are illegal and often are told by employers that various deductions are legal. For most workers, the federal rules on deductions are minimal. Essentially, the employer cannot make deductions that bring the worker's paycheck below minimum wage, no matter what the reason. State rules on deductions vary.

Alberto Jimenez is a retail cleaning worker and member of Centro de Trabajadores Unidos en la Lucha (CTUL). Alberto worked for National Floor Maintenance cleaning, a Lunds & Byerly's store in the Twin Cities,

Minnesota, metro area. In the summer of 2010, National Floor Maintenance deducted more than $200 from Alberto's paycheck, claiming that
he had damaged merchandise in the store. As CTUL began investigating
this issue, it became apparent that it was common practice at this company to deduct wages from workers' paychecks for alleged accidents that
damaged merchandise. According to reports from workers, one worker
had over $1300 deducted from his wages for allegedly damaging mer-
chandise at the store that he cleaned!

It is against Minnesota state labor law to deduct wages from workers'
wages without their written permission. An employer who violates this law
can be held liable for double the wages illegally deducted from workers'
wages. Despite the fact that Alberto and other workers had complained to
their supervisors about the deduction of wages from their paychecks, the
company did nothing. Alberto together with CTUL wrote a letter to
National Floor Maintenance and sent a copy of the letter to Lunds &
Byerly's. Several days later, Alberto and several other workers received a
check for double the amount of wages that had illegally been deducted
from their paychecks, for a total of an estimated $10,000 in back wages.[20]

Four women employed by Paragon Packaging went to the Houston
Interfaith Workers' Center seeking help in recovering stolen wages.
The employer had deducted $1900 from each of their paychecks, claim-
ing he had to use the money to pay a notary to petition for the women's
citizenship. As these workers did not know, notaries don't practice immigration law, nor do they charge this much money. When the women
complained, the employer told them that the notary had run off with the
money without producing anything and that he was as mad as they were.
When Laura Boston, the workers' center advocate, called and talked with
the employer, he agreed to repay the workers at the rate of $130 per
month.

Most deductions made are smaller than $1900, but many are still il-
legal and still constitute theft of wages. Even though the laws for what
deductions are legal vary tremendously between states, the basic federal standard is that deductions for broken or lost equipment or missing
cash in a register may be taken only if it doesn't bring the worker's paycheck below minimum wage.

Anka Karewicz, the Polish-speaking workers' rights advocate at the
Chicago Arise Workers' Center, says, "Every time I think I've heard the

most ridiculous paycheck deduction, I hear another." Workers have told her of deductions for:

- The "convenience" of cleaning women being picked up and taken to various houses for cleaning (charges of up to $30 per day for the "convenience").
- Washing uniforms.
- A security deposit in case they might break something while cleaning a home.
- Food and rent.
- Water.

Farm workers and farm worker advocates talk a lot about illegal deductions, such as:

- Claiming to withhold social security tax payments, but then pocketing the money instead of sending it to the federal government.
- Deducting from workers' pay the cost of work-related equipment provided by the employer, including safety equipment that the government requires employers to provide.
- Deducting from workers' pay the supposed costs of providing worker housing (which fewer and fewer employers do). One Arizona employer, for example, reportedly deducted from his workers' pay the entire cost of his ranch's use of electricity, despite the fact that the workers each lived in shacks lighted with a single bulb.
- Deducting from workers' pay a fee for transporting them to and from the work site. For some workers, transportation time and expenses represent a huge burden. Workers transported from the Yuma area of Arizona to the agricultural area west of Phoenix, for example, travel 2½ hours each way, for which they reportedly pay $12 of their $40 daily wage.
- Failing to provide drinking water as required by law, and then selling workers soda or beer for $1 or $1.50 each.

Restaurant workers are particularly vulnerable to illegal deductions because their wages are so low and restaurant employers deduct for many things, including meals, uniforms, broken dishes, and missing cash.

Automatically deducting for breaks that workers don't get. Some employers automatically deduct a half hour or an hour from workers' hours, assuming the workers take breaks, whether or not they actually take the breaks. Under federal law, employers do not have to pay for breaks, but workers must be allowed to take them. If employees work through their breaks, they must be paid for that time. The Department of Labor settled a suit against Raceway Petroleum Inc., a gas station company throughout central New Jersey. Not only did the employer deny the overtime premium (and some of the workers claimed to have worked as many as 100 hours per week), but the employer automatically deducted for 2 hours of breaks, even though workers said they seldom got more than 30 minutes.[21]

Stealing workers' tips. Many wait staff and other service workers earn a significant percentage of their pay from customer tips. Employers are allowed to pay tipped staff a lower minimum wage assuming they receive additional wages through tips.[22] Yet despite this reduced wage, the increase in lawsuits against employers stealing tips demonstrates how common it is for employers to take workers' tips.

Maria worked at Azteca Taqueria in San Francisco for ten years as a waitress. She was supporting her daughter and trying to go to school part-time at night, but it was hard to get enough money to pay rent and food for her daughter and at the same time save for community college tuition. During her time at Azteca Taqueria, Maria repeatedly saw the manager, who is also the owner's brother, take cash from the tips jar. Days after she complained about it to the owner, she was terminated. With the help of YWU, she filed a claim against the employer for stealing tips, retaliation, and other violations of the labor code. Three other workers agreed to testify in support of her claim.[23]

The Shurbrite-Hi-Speed Car Wash workers described earlier who weren't getting paid the minimum wage believe their tips were stolen too. They claim that they were told that they will be fired if they take tips directly. Customers all put their tips in a jar. At the end of the week, the managers take the tip jar into a back room and divide it up. No worker has ever made more than $20 per week, which seems slim to the workers. The workers suspect theft of the tips, given the theft of minimum wage.[24]

Cash tips aren't the only ones stolen. There are extensive reports of employers keeping the amount added to a credit card bill that should have been given to the wait staff. This problem is so prevalent that Department of Labor colleagues have urged me to give all tips in cash.

Tip stealing isn't done just by small employers. The luxury Canyon Ranch Spa in Lenox, Massachusetts, used to charge its wealthy clients an 18 percent service charge on all bills at the resort. Clients were told that tipping wasn't necessary because of the service charge. Unfortunately, the workers didn't get any of the tips. In 2008, the spa agreed to pay $14.75 million to hundreds of spa staff for the collected, but unpaid, tips.

Supervisor kickbacks. In construction, landscaping, and farm work, industries that often have crew leaders or site supervisors, workers are sometimes compelled to provide kickbacks in order to keep their jobs. Juan Manuel Avalos worked for Charles Evleth Construction for five months. His verbal hiring agreement was that he would work five days a week for $750. Once on the job, he actually worked six days a week, usually 12-hour shifts. He was paid in cash weekly, but discovered two months into the job that the site supervisor was cashing his check and stealing up to $500 per week from him.[25]

Nine former workers at the Super Great Wall Buffet restaurant in South Portland, Maine, filed a suit against the owner for unpaid wages and squalid housing conditions, but among the complaints was that the manager collected kickbacks in cash from the wait staff, ranging from $210 to $250 every two weeks.[26]

Not paying people at all. Some workers don't get paid at all. Every study of day laborers finds that most day laborers have experienced working all day or all week and not getting paid at all.

Four men were recruited in Detroit by a Chicago-based employer hired to deliver phone books in Madison, Wisconsin. He gave the workers his van to drive from Detroit to Madison and use for delivering the phone books. The employer promised to pay for the workers' hotel and wages. On Sunday morning at 6 A.M., after having worked Monday through Friday of the previous week, the workers heard the van start up outside their motel room and caught the owner trying to take off. He told them they were fired for refusing to work in the rain on Saturday and that he wasn't going to pay them the money he owed them. The workers showed up at the workers' rights center with their luggage in their hands and no place to go. The Madison Workers' Rights Center pressured the phone company, which in turn pressured the contractor and finally got $400 paid back to each worker.[27]

Reverend Mark Wendorf, a former IWJ board member, saw wage theft firsthand when his 22-year-old son came home from college. His son, a qualified USA Cycling Mechanic (a high-grade bicycle mechanic), was hired at a local bicycle shop. The employer didn't pay him for three months, although he continued to promise to pay. Finally, Mark's son quit and sought help from the Maine Department of Labor to recover his unpaid wages.

Residential construction workers often get paid for a first job but not the second. A worker visited the Arise Chicago Workers' Center in the spring of 2008 and explained how this happens. He had a written agreement between himself and the owner for a first project. The owner was pleased with the work and paid him promptly according to the agreed-upon terms. Then, as if an afterthought, the owner asked him to undertake another smaller job on the house, this time without a contract. A verbal agreement was made, but nothing was put in writing. Upon completing this project, without any contract to enforce payment, the worker was denied compensation.[28]

Michael Baker had been homeless for several years, but he was excited about getting his life together and getting a job. He was hired by a mechanic to do clean-up work at his shop and occasionally to do some work at his home. He was promised $50 a day. Most days he worked between 8 and 10 hours a day. Michael was staying at a homeless shelter, ate breakfast and dinner at free-food places, but struggled to have food for lunch. Every so often the employer would give him a little cash for lunch. The employer kept promising to pay him but didn't. Michael was trying to do the right thing, going to work faithfully, but he didn't get paid. After three months with no pay, he asked the Northwest Arkansas Workers' Center to help him get his money. The center calculated that he was owed approximately $5000. He eventually recovered $3000, but he was more discouraged than ever about the possibility of escaping homelessness.[29]

Not paying last paychecks. Many workers are not paid their last paychecks. Sometimes a worker quits in the midpay period, and the employer refuses to pay for the days or hours the employee worked. Others are fired, and the employer refuses to pay for the work done before the firing. Still others finish a short-term job only to discover that the employer refuses to provide the final paycheck. The law is clear that workers must be paid for the time worked, but this issue of last paycheck is such a problem that forty-seven states have passed special laws attempting to ensure that workers who are fired or quit get paid their final paychecks.

Factory worker Enemis Figueroa was fired from her job when her employer, Scholl Truss and Component Company, received a social security no-match letter with her name on it. Although no-match letters clearly state that employers should not take any adverse action against an employee whose social security number appears on the list, some employers have used the letters as an excuse to fire workers. When Enemis was fired, she was told that she would not receive any compensation until she provided a copy of her social security card. Scholl Truss and Component Company withheld Enemis's last check for over 60 hours of work. Advocates at the Houston Interfaith Workers' Center contacted Scholl Truss and Component Company, which paid Enemis's last check of $478.[30]

Failing to give sixty days' layoff notice or pay. Large employers, those with 100 full-time workers, are required by the Worker Adjustment and Retraining Notification Act (called the WARN Act) to provide sixty days' advance notice to workers and communities of a plant closing or mass layoff. If the employer does not provide the notice, the employer must at least provide the workers with sixty days of pay. According to a Government Accountability Office study in 2003, only 36 percent of employers covered by the WARN Act complied with the law.[31] If workers in plants are represented by a union, the union leadership will know the laws and insist on workers getting paid for sixty days. When workers aren't represented, they often don't know the law and thus don't get either sixty days' notice or sixty days' pay.

Paycheck kickbacks. Another way unethical employers steal from workers and attempt to hide it from government inspectors is by requiring workers to return (kickback) part of their paycheck to the employer or crew chief. In 2010, employees of the Hamilton Avenue Animal Hospital and Clinic and the Sycamore Animal Hospital complained to the Cincinnati Interfaith Workers' Center that their employer required them to return their overtime pay premium to their employer via a check or in cash. The workers were paid at a rate of $8 per hour; therefore, hours over forty were supposed to be paid at $12 per hour. The employer would pay the $12 per hour, but then turn around and require that the workers pay her back the $4 per hour overtime premium. The workers filmed their employer taking cash kickbacks. They also had canceled checks that had been deposited into the animal hospital's account. Although the hospital did not admit guilt, it did agree to pay $9225 in overtime and interest to nineteen employees.[32]

Kickback schemes are particularly a problem on prevailing wage construction jobs. These are jobs that involve federal or state dollars and thus require employers to pay workers a wage that is standard in that area for a particular kind of work. Unethical employers will give workers checks at the prevailing wage rate, so they can show it in audits and then turn around and require the workers to kick back part of the wage.

San Andreas HVAC, an installer of heating and air-conditioning units, stole lots of money from its workers. The company bid and won a contract in Santa Clara County, California, to work on the Jasmine Square Apartments in Morgan Hill. The prevailing wage for this skilled trade was $54 per hour. The workers received checks at the prevailing wage, but were instructed (via sticky note) to return about 75 percent of the money to the bosses in cash. The employees ended up being paid about $13.50 per hour, instead of $54.[33]

Denying workers' compensation. Workers' compensation is a no-fault insurance program created by state statutes that is designed to replace workers' wages and provide injury-related health care coverage when workers are injured on the job. The programs vary by state, but most employers are required to carry workers' compensation insurance. When a worker is injured on the job, the worker is supposed to file a workers' compensation claim. The workers' compensation insurance then covers the worker's wages for the time the injured worker is off work, plus the medical expenses incurred. If the worker is permanently disabled, the worker receives a lump sum of money for the injury. Each state has its own rate sheets for injuries.

Employers steal wages and health coverage from workers when they unjustly deny workers' compensation. This occurs in several ways. Some employers don't provide workers' compensation when they should, and so, when a worker is injured, he or she is just laid off or fired. Others technically provide workers' compensation coverage, but discourage workers from filing a workers' compensation claim in order to keep their claims low or tell the workers that they are not covered by workers' compensation. Employers will say, "You are not eligible because you haven't been on the job long enough," or "Your position is not covered by workers' compensation," or "I'll give you this $500, so don't file a workers' compensation claim." (Workers' compensation insurance is like personal car insurance. If you use it, your rates go up. So if employers can discourage workers from filing for workers's compensation, their rates will not be raised.)

However, when workers don't file workers' compensation claims, they lose both the opportunity to get wages for the time they are off work and health coverage that could be due them while they are injured or recovering. Some unethical companies take the position that all claims, even obviously compensable ones, are to be denied. The thought process behind this "method of claims management" creates a chilling effect in the workplace. The employer hopes to discourage employees from filing future claims if they watch their coworkers having a difficult time with their claims. Unjustly denying workers' compensation is indeed another form of stealing wages.

In March 2011, the Washtenaw Workers' Center staff and I met with a worker who had been employed at an International House of Pancakes as a janitor. What he told us was that at one point while he was mopping, he slipped and fell, injuring his back. He couldn't even get up from the floor. His manager did not call the ambulance, but his coworkers did. When he went to the hospital, he clearly reported that his injury occurred at work. The doctor told him to stay off work for at least four days, which he did, but he had a large medical bill and an ambulance bill. When he returned to work, his employer fired him on the spot. Several weeks later, when we met with him, he was still having back problems. Workers' compensation should have paid for this worker's ambulance, medical care, and wages for lost time—easily several thousands of dollars, especially if he continued to need back care. The worker should have been cared for by his employer—that's the law. Instead, the worker was saddled with bills he can't afford to pay. If the worker ends up not paying the medical bills, the costs for that get shifted to all those paying for health insurance.

Payroll fraud is the last significant way that employers steal wages from workers. This problem has become so widespread that an additional chapter was added in this revised edition just on this topic. Read on.

3

Payroll Fraud

Do not steal. Do not lie. Do not deceive one another.

—Leviticus 19:11

Payroll fraud is one of the most common forms of wage theft. Payroll fraud occurs when an employer intentionally lies to public agencies about how many employees it has and denies workers the wages, contributions to taxes, and insurances and protections due employees. Payroll fraud is perpetrated in two primary ways. Some employers fraudulently call workers independent contractors instead of employees in order to shirk their responsibilities as employers. This involves lying to the Internal Revenue Service (IRS), state workers' compensation boards, state unemployment boards, and other agencies that regulate and collect monies from employers. This also requires lying to workers by telling them they are not employees and thus denying them the legally mandated protections and wages due employees.

The other primary way unscrupulous employers perpetrate payroll fraud is by paying workers completely in cash and "off the books." Again, this requires an employer to defraud government agencies and workers and steal from both public coffers and workers.

Neither workers themselves nor employers can arbitrarily call workers independent contractors when they are really employees. Doing so is illegal and has enormous consequences for workers and public revenues.

Payroll fraud is widespread and involves billions of dollars in lost revenue to the states, federal government, and workers. FedEx is an example of a company that has built its business on the practice of calling its drivers independent contractors. FedEx has approximately 15,000 drivers who are called independent contractors, even though they should be employees. The drivers drive the areas FedEx assigns, deliver its packages in FedEx-approved trucks, and can only take time off if FedEx approves their replacement plans. FedEx clearly controls this working environment. "In recent years, courts and government agencies have debunked FedEx Ground's misleading independent contractor model."[1] Despite FedEx losses over this issue, it continues to fight court cases and rulings because of the sheer amount of money involved. It saves millions, perhaps billions, by its payment practices. As Ray Marshall, former Secretary of Labor from 1977 to 1981 said, "The damage FedEx Ground does to workers' rights by misclassifying employees as independent contractors goes far beyond employers' fairly common anti-union tactics. These misclassifications would nullify the protections that the U.S. and other advanced democracies have extended to all workers. Wage and hour, anti-discrimination, occupational safety and health, pension protection, and unemployment compensation policies are all designed to protect employees from discriminatory actions by employers, as well as from damage that could be done to workers, their families, and the public by unemployment or substandard wages and working conditions."[2] FedEx, a nationally touted company, has a practice that is illegal and harmful to workers, but it saves the company money.

Payroll fraud involves more than money. When workers who are victims of payroll fraud get injured, they not only are denied their owed wages, they often are denied the medical care they should have received.

Quelino Ojedo Jimenez moved to Chicago in August 2010 to build roofs, working for a subcontractor hired by Imperial Roofing Group. One day, as Quelino pulled a sheet of metal he thought was secured by nails, he fell backward more than 20 feet to the ground. When he woke three days later, he was a quadriplegic and connected to a ventilator. The nonprofit hospital cared for him without receiving any reimbursement from workers' compensation insurance, which should have covered his care, for four months. The hospital tried to find a long-term care facility to take him, but without the workers' compensation insurance he should have had, no institution wanted him. On December 22, 2010, the hospital management whisked him away, without his or his appointed guardian's consent, and dumped him in a hospital in Oaxaca,

Mexico, his hometown, that did not have rehabilitation services or even new filters for his ventilator.[3]

Chicagoans were upset by the behavior of the hospital, and rightly so, but the bigger problem is that this worker was a victim of payroll fraud. His employer did not have workers' compensation insurance as is required of all employers. The roofing contractor hired contractors who illegally called employees independent contractors and then denied them basic protections, such as workers' compensation. Workers' compensation insurance would have made sure that this worker was paid for his time off work and for all the health care he needed—even if his care required years of rehabilitation, which it probably will.

Employers who lie about not having employees don't pay workers' compensation. Companies that lie about not having employees do not ensure that health and safety guidelines, such as the one that says workers should not be more than 6 feet off the ground without proper fall protections, are followed. Payroll fraud can have devastating human consequences.

Stealing from Public Coffers

Employers who commit payroll fraud steal needed revenues from public coffers, thus forcing other businesses and citizens to pay more than their fair shares. Employers who commit payroll fraud do not pay the following:

FEDERAL INCOME TAX: Employers are required to withhold monies from employee's pay for workers' personal share of federal income taxes. Workers who are illegally called independent contractors are given 1099 forms, so the government gets a record of their income, and then they are required to pay the taxes. Without having income taxes deducted on a regular basis workers must save money for taxes and pay them on their own. This is difficult for many workers and means they are likely to have problems with the IRS for underpayment of income taxes.

For workers who are paid in cash off the books, it is unlikely that most regularly report all their income to the IRS. Thus, payroll fraud encourages underpayment of federal income taxes.

STATE INCOME TAX: In most states, employers are required to withhold monies from employees pay for state income taxes. Thus again, those who are paid as independent contractors must make sure to save and pay their state income taxes on a regular basis, which is difficult for many struggling to make ends meet. Most of those paid in cash probably do not report and pay state income taxes. Consequently, payroll fraud encourages the underpayment of state income taxes.

SOCIAL SECURITY AND MEDICARE TAXES: Social security and Medicare are paid through payroll taxes, half of which are paid for by workers themselves and half by employers. Employers who commit payroll fraud shift their share of these taxes to the workers or don't pay social security and Medicare taxes at all. If workers are paid as independent contractors, they will end up paying their share and their employer's share of social security and Medicare taxes. Those paid in cash probably won't pay either share.

UNEMPLOYMENT INSURANCE TAXES: Unemployment insurance is a joint federal and state program that is financed through employer taxes. Employers are required to pay a percentage on the first $7000 of each employee's annual wages to cover unemployment insurance. (Three states also require employees to pay in as well.) Employers who lie about not having employees don't pay into this fund. This means that when their workers actually need unemployment insurance, they won't be able to get it. It also means that these scofflaw employers don't pay their share of general support for the unemployment system, which shifts the burden to ethical employers. Given the current economic crisis, many state unemployment insurance funds are in deep financial trouble and could benefit by *all* employers paying into the funds.

WORKERS' COMPENSATION INSURANCE: Most employers are required by their states to buy workers' compensation insurance either through a state fund or a private insurance company. This insurance covers wages, medical care, and rehabilitation for workers who are injured or sickened (e.g., black lung) because of their jobs. The workers' compensation system was established as a no-fault system,[4] meaning all workers would get the coverage regardless of who was at fault. The system is supposed to make sure that workers get cared for and that employers don't have huge liabilities for workplace injuries and illnesses. Payroll fraud steals monies from the workers' compensation fund or private insurance companies, steals from workers and their families, and shifts burdens of care to others in the community. Like most insurance-type programs, the system works by everyone paying in and then just those who need it use the funds. Employers who are committing payroll fraud are not paying into these insurance pools that create the resources for any worker who is injured.

When a worker whose employer did not have workers' compensation gets injured, the worker often ends up getting charity care at a private hospital, which shifts the burden to the general public. If the worker is without an income for a while, the worker and his or her family may well end up using public services, which they would not have required if the employer had paid his or her fair share of workers' compensation insurance. Shifting health care responsibilities for injured workers to the public and income replacement responsibilities to the public causes both private health care insurance rates and state taxes to rise. Ethical employers and the general public end up paying for problems caused by unethical employers refusing to pay their workers compensation coverage for their employees. Raising rates for ethical employers makes it even harder for them to compete against the scofflaws.

OTHER PAYROLL TAX BENEFITS: Massachusetts requires employers with eleven or more full-time employees (or eleven FTEs—full-time equivalents) to provide a "fair share" toward workers' health insurance. If an employer lies about the number of employees it has, it might exclude it from eligibility and won't be paying enough toward its "fair share." California has a state disability insurance program that is paid for through payroll taxes. Similarly, employers who lie about not having employees do not pay for this public benefit that serves all workers. Any additional state benefits that are provided through payroll taxes get stolen through payroll fraud.

Under the new health care bill passed by the Obama administration in 2010, small employers can get special subsidies to help with health care costs. Employers who lie about the number of workers they have will not only be withholding their fair share of taxes, but they might get an extra benefit from taxpayers because of the disguised (and wrong) size of their payroll.

As Senator Patty Murray from Washington State said, "Right now too many employers across the country misclassify their employees as independent contractors in order to avoid paying their fair share of taxes and workers compensation. This costs the government and workers billions of dollars, it puts responsible employers who pay these taxes at a competitive disadvantage, and it's stealing—plain and simple."[5]

Stealing from Workers and Denying Labor Protections

Willie Wilcox, who worked as a janitor and handyman for a property management company for seven years, sought help from the Workers' Center of Eastern Maine (WCEM) after he had been fired. He had cleaned and repaired two buildings, faithfully, often working more than 40 hours a week without overtime pay. His pay was often given to him late.

About nine months before he was fired, Willie had talked with the WCEM about his employment status. His employer claimed he was an independent contractor even though his employer controlled his daily activities and schedule and set his pay (characteristics of employees, not contractors). All work was done in the employer's buildings. Willie had no other employment besides this. The IRS was requiring him to pay taxes as if he were an independent contractor. Plus, his employer pressured him to sign a form from the Workers Compensation Board saying he was an independent contractor (and thus not eligible for workers' compensation if he was injured).

For seven years, Willie was not given a single vacation day or sick day. When his daughter died, he took two days off, but management reprimanded him for taking the days.

Even though Willie wanted benefits and was pretty sure his employer was committing payroll fraud, Willie decided not to protest it because at least he had a job.

In 2010, Willie's employer fired him. When he applied for unemployment benefits, he was denied because of his employer's payroll fraud. WCEM connected Willie with two attorneys who agreed to help him appeal his case based on employer payroll fraud. Willie should have been paid as an employee and thus eligible for unemployment.

Waiting for his appeal was brutal. Willie had no income for eighteen weeks. He survived on donations from many kindhearted members of Food AND Medicine (FAM). He sold or pawned everything of value including his guitars and his kitchen rug. FAM's donations kept his truck from being repossessed. At one point, he got so discouraged he attempted suicide. Times could not have been tougher for a man who just wanted to do a good job and be treated fairly.

Finally, Willie won the appeal to get unemployment. Then, WCEM assisted him in recovering his unpaid overtime. Eventually Willie accepted a settlement of $20,000. Payroll fraud has serious human consequences.[6]

Employers who lie about workers' status as employees steal from workers and deny their workers basic rights and protections afforded employees. Employees, not independent contractors, are covered by the following workplace protection laws:

• *Minimum wage laws.* Many workers falsely called independent contractors or paid in cash end up earning less than minimum wage; examples are painters or drywallers who are paid $300 per week but work 60 hours a week. Payroll fraud can result in workers not getting paid the minimum wage.

• *Overtime laws.* Most employees are supposed to get time and a half for hours worked over 40. Independent contractors aren't covered by overtime laws, so when workers are called independent contractors when they should be employers, their employers do not pay them for overtime. Although it is not illegal to pay workers in cash and it is technically possible that workers paid in cash could get paid overtime as required by the law, most workers who are paid in cash are being paid completely off the books and are not paid the overtime they are owed. Payroll fraud almost always results in workers not getting paid the overtime owed them.

• *Discrimination laws.* Key laws prohibiting workers from being discriminated against because of disability or age do not apply to independent contractors.

• *Health and safety laws.* Employers don't have to keep track of health and safety issues for independent contractors as they must for employees.

• *Family Medical Leave Act (FMLA).* This law helps workers employed by larger companies be able to take time off to care for a family member without fear of losing their job. This law only protects employees, not independent contractors.

- *National Labor Relations Act.* This law protects employees' rights to organize and engage in collective bargaining. This too covers only employees, not independent contractors.
- *Unemployment insurance.* Employers are required to provide unemployment insurance coverage for employees. Workers who are treated as independent contractors will not be able to get unemployment if they are laid off from their jobs unless they can prove they were really employees. Even if the workers can prove they were employees, it will be a long and arduous process.
- *Workers' compensation insurance.* Most employers are required to provide workers' compensation insurance for their employees in case they get injured on the job. The cost of the insurance varies based on the kind of work. Construction jobs have fairly high premium rates because the work is dangerous. If a worker who is called an independent contractor or who is paid in cash gets injured, it will not be a smooth process to get help with the injury or illness because the worker will first have to go through a time-consuming hearing process to get coverage. In practice, most of the time workers won't get the health coverage and wages for lost worktime they deserve.

Businesses with large payrolls, especially in fields like construction, have significant workers' compensation costs, which is why unethical employers commit payroll fraud. Mauro and Keren Aguirre owned Escapade Acoustic Drywall Company in Lafayette, Louisiana. For workers' compensation coverage purposes, they allegedly reported having thirty-five employees and a payroll of about $145,000, when in fact they had, according to the state of Louisiana, more than three hundred employees and a payroll of more than $4.2 million. The state's Insurance Fraud Task Force arrested them in September 2009.

Payroll fraud steals from public coffers, shifts the burden of public costs to other employers and taxpayers, steals from workers, and denies workers a range of workplace protection laws. Payroll fraud is a serious crime, but too often it is not prosecuted.

Payroll Fraud Connected to Outlaw Behavior

Employers who commit payroll fraud are often involved in much broader illegal schemes. In 2009, the U.S. Attorney's Office in the Southern District of Florida successfully prosecuted Juan Rene Caro and the company he owned, La Bamba Check Cashing, on one count of conspiracy and fifteen substantive counts of failing to file currency transaction reports. This check-cashing company had been set up to cash checks, primarily for local construction companies and subcontractors that were trying to hide their payroll expenses via shell companies. Over two years, La Bamba "laundered" $132 million for the shell companies.[7]

Estaban Stubbs, who ran a drywall business, was sentenced to prison in 2010 in Anchorage, Alaska, for "currency construction." Stubbs based his business on payroll fraud, paying his workers in cash and not paying any payroll related taxes or insurances. Stubbs knew that withdrawing more than $10,000 from a bank would trigger the bank filing a report to the IRS, so he would regularly deposit payments in multiple banks and branches and then withdraw cash amounts ranging from $1500 to $5000 to pay his workers. Over a four-year period he withdrew more than $500,000 in cash to pay workers.[8]

That same year, the Oregon Attorney General convicted Maurilio Castillo Vega for racketeering that bilked the state out of $8 million in unpaid taxes. The employer paid workers in cash under the table through sham companies. The press statement said, "In addition to the lost taxes, the State Accident Insurance Fund estimates it lost millions in unpaid workers' compensation funds. This type of scam is happening all across the country."[9] Indeed, it is.

Payroll Fraud Undermines Ethical Employers

Imagine if you play by the rules, paying all the employer taxes and insurances that you are supposed to, and your competitors don't. Your competition can bid jobs at a much lower rate than you, and so ethical employers are hurt. Employers who commit payroll fraud save approximately 30 percent on their payroll costs. This is a huge difference in industries that are primarily dependent on labor costs.

Lawbreaking employers undermine ethical ones. Some employers try to compete by lowering their standards—setting in motion a driving down of standards within the industry and the society. Some employers will respond by cutting back their own number of employees. Thus the entire community is hurt by having fewer workers employed by ethical employers. And still other employers shut down because they can't operate in an environment that is so stacked against them.

Luckily, some ethical employers are beginning to fight back against payroll fraud and other forms of wage theft. Chapter 8 lifts up such ethical employers operating in sectors fraught with wage theft.

Extent of Payroll Fraud

Payroll fraud is a common practice in many industries. In the last few years, numerous federal and state agencies have investigated payroll fraud in order to prompt their agencies into cracking down on this illegal behavior.

In August 2009, the Government Accountability Office issued a report on payroll fraud that admitted that the national extent of the problem is unknown.[10] It did, however, refer to a 2000 Department of Labor study that found that "from 10 percent to 30 percent of firms audited in nine selected states had misclassified employees as independent contractors."[11]

The Institute for Public Policy and Social Research at Michigan State University issued a report in 2009 suggesting that 30 percent of employers had some payroll underreporting or inaccurate reporting of employees. Perhaps some of the employers were simply "confused" and made unintentional errors, but most made intentional decisions to commit payroll fraud in order to pocket more profits. The report suggested that the state's unemployment trust fund lost $17 million each year and probably an estimated $20 to $35 million in state income tax.[12] This is serious money stolen from Michigan public coffers.

Another study, *The Economic Costs of Employee Misclassification in the State of Indiana*, published in 2010 but looking at 2007–2008 data, found that 16.8 percent of employees were illegally called independent contractors. The study estimated that the state lost $36.7 million in unemployment insurance taxes and $147.5 million in unpaid state income taxes. Workers' compensation insurance premiums were underpaid by $24.1 million. In addition, local governments lost an estimated $59.9 million in local tax revenues.[13]

Similar studies have been undertaken in at least a dozen states. Each has discovered widespread payroll fraud.

Quite a few states have established task forces and divisions focusing on payroll fraud and the underground economy. These task forces have uncovered widespread fraud and abuse among employers and recovered significant revenue for public treasuries.

The Washington State Department of Labor & Industries' Fraud Prevention and Compliance Program recovered $137.4 million in 2010, collecting $7 for every dollar invested in the program.[14] Clearly, investing in this type of law enforcement is a good financial investment for taxpayers.

In its 2009 Annual Report of the New York State Joint Enforcement Task Force on Employee Misclassification, the task force reported it had identified more than 12,300 instances of payroll fraud and had recovered more than $4.8 million in unemployment taxes, $1 million in unemployment insurance fraud penalties, $12 million in unpaid wages, and over $1.1 million in workers' compensation fines and penalties.[15] The report described the task force's Main Street Sweeps in which the task force conducted door-to-door investigations of 304 businesses along four retail and commercial strips. In 67 percent of the businesses visited, the investigators found evidence of violations that required follow-up enforcement action, including 11 percent of the businesses that were not registered for unemployment insurance and 7 percent that didn't have workers' compensation coverage.[16]

The Massachusetts Joint Enforcement Taskforce on the Underground Economy and Employee Misclassification reported in its 2010 Annual Report that it had recovered $6.5 million for state agencies from companies that had evaded paying part or all of their unemployment insurance, Fair Share contributions (the state health program), income tax, and workers' compensation insurance.[17]

The bottom line is that no one knows precisely how extensive payroll fraud actually is, but it is quite widespread and many worker advocates believe that the problem is growing, not diminishing, despite the new enforcement efforts. Increasingly, companies are contracting out services that previously might have been performed by their own employees to smaller firms that may or may not be paying people legally. Unfortunately, when businesses "contract out," too often they absolve themselves of taking responsibility for ensuring that workers are paid fairly and legally. The rapid expansion of contracting jobs and functions that are central to companies' businesses has certainly exacerbated the prevalence of payroll fraud.

Outlaw Industries

Payroll fraud is widespread throughout the economy, but is particularly prevalent in a few industries.

CONSTRUCTION: The construction industry is notorious for payroll fraud. The industry's use of subcontracting has made it particularly challenging to investigate and prosecute. Large builders employ local contractors to do most of the work. The local contractors hire people and call them independent contractors instead of employees or pay them completely off the books in cash. Even though the prime contractor really controls the job, the relationships are not direct, and the practice of payroll fraud has become widespread.

TRUCKING/DRIVING: FedEx is the most visible trucking company that has treated its truck drivers as independent contractors, even though the company controls the routes, schedules, and working conditions for the workers, which strongly suggests that the workers are employees and not independent contractors. In 2010, Massachusetts Attorney General Martha Coakley won a $3 million settlement with FedEx Ground to settle claims that the company misclassified drivers. As other states strengthen the payroll fraud laws and establish stronger enforcement systems, FedEx will face other state investigations.

Drivers at the nation's ports are suffering from payroll fraud. An estimated 82 percent of the nation's 110,000 port truck drivers are now treated as independent contractors. In a survey conducted by the Partnership for Working Families, the average work week for a port truck driver was 59 hours. The independent contractors were paid only $28,

783 per year, and that was before all the taxes required of independent contractors were subtracted. The survey indicated that minimum wage and overtime violations were widespread.[18]

RESTAURANTS: Restaurants are notorious for hiring workers, especially those in the kitchen, as independent contractors or paying them in cash. This is clearly fraudulent behavior. Cooks and dishwashers are employees and must be paid as such.

JANITORIAL SERVICES: Many small janitorial firms pay all their workers as independent contractors, even though the contractors control the workers' hours, locations, assignments, and quality of work. Janitorial firms that pay workers as independent contractors are hired by nationally recognized retail stores that may pay their own workers legally but turn the other way when hiring contracted workers to clean their stores. Even religious congregations and nonprofits have been known to hire janitorial services that routinely pay workers as independent contractors. If a price for services is ridiculously low, you can bet that the workers aren't paid fairly or legally.

When Charanga Restaurant, in San Francisco, California, lost its janitorial contractor, it hired Carlos, a 22-year-old refugee from El Salvador. He was assigned to clean the kitchen for 2 hours a day, seven days a week. He was promised $550 a month for this work. Soon after he started, Carlos was assigned to clean other areas, which resulted in him working more than 3.5 hours a day in order to finish. Because he was working at least 105 hours per month, he earned less than $5.25 per hour, which was well below the minimum wage in San Francisco at the time. When he approached the owner about paying him the minimum wage, she refused and told him she did not have to follow labor laws because Carlos was a subcontractor and she was doing him a favor because he did not have a janitorial business license. Carlos learned about the San Francisco Workers' Center, YWU, from a presentation at his English class and approached them to help him recover his back pay.[19]

INSTALLATION SERVICES: Many firms that provide installation of products in people's homes are paid as independent contractors. Workers who install satellite TV, cable TV, and Internet services are often victims of payroll fraud. Based on the work they do, these installation workers almost always should be categorized and paid as employees, not independent contractors, regardless of what they are called.

MOVERS: Moving companies regularly commit payroll fraud by misclassifying workers as independent contractors and not paying workers as employees.

CHURCH MUSICIANS: Even though this is not a huge category of workers, it is a group of workers who are often paid as independent contractors when by definitions in laws they are employees. Even congregations commit payroll fraud.

Employee versus Independent Contracting Definitions

Unfortunately, there is no one simple way to define an employee versus an independent contractor. According to a recent Government Accountability Office study report, "No definitive test exists to distinguish whether a worker is an employee or an independent contractor. The tests used to determine whether or not a worker is an independent contractor or an employee are complex and subjective, and differ from law to law. For example, the NLRA, the Civil Rights Act, the FLSA, and the Employee Retirement Income Security Act each use a different definition of an employee and various tests, or criteria, to distinguish independent contractors from employees."[20]

The federal courts have offered the following guidelines for determining who is truly an independent contractor under the FLSA:[21]

1. The extent to which the services rendered are an integral part of the principal's business.
2. The permanency of the relationship.
3. The amount of the alleged contractor's investment in facilities and equipment.
4. The nature and degree of control by the principal.
5. The alleged contractor's opportunities for profit and loss.
6. The amount of initiative, judgment, or foresight in open market competition with others required for the success of the claimed independent contractor.
7. The degree of independent business organization and operation.[22]

And frankly, if one uses common sense, the definitions are not that difficult or complex. All the definitions have a common theme: If someone else controls what you do, when you do it, and how you do it, you are an employee.

Because there are various definitions, states have been developing their own laws on misclassification. A great summary of many of the bills and initiatives around this can be found at the following website: www .payrollfraud.net. Most of these laws have tightened definitions, increased punishments for payroll fraud, and established investigative task forces. See more about these state laws in Chapter 11.

Unscrupulous employers will sometimes use the excuse of the varying definitions to justify their illegal behavior. In almost every situation, it really is not hard to determine who is or should be reported as an employee. Those who commit payroll fraud are not confused: they are out-and-out criminals.

Beware of All Contracting

As consumers, we must be extraordinarily careful about any contractors we hire for our homes or our businesses. Contracted services, such as construction or janitorial services, regularly commit payroll fraud. If you don't bother to check, you could pay thousands of dollars to a firm that steals from workers, the public, and you.

One day a few years ago as I arrived at my office, which is located at the Edgewater Presbyterian Church, I saw scaffolding going up around the building. Soon thereafter, workers appeared outside my window repairing the tuck-pointing. The workers were drilling out the crevices without masks on. As we gagged and coughed inside from all the dust, we debated what we should do.

It wasn't long before I got a call from the union representing tuck-pointers informing me that the church from whom we lease space had signed a large contract with a nonunion firm. Even though I believe that a firm that operates without a union can be ethical (although many of my labor friends disagree with me), most large nonunion construction firms that operate in union markets are "bad apples." Needless to say, I had to investigate the situation.

When I expressed my concerns to the church staff members, including explaining that if a picket line went up, none of my staff would cross it, they were understandably a bit defensive. They explained that they had a good relationship with the contractor; he did quality work, and the price was reasonable. I asked if the church leaders would find out how the workers were paid. They agreed to inquire.

Sure enough, the tuck-pointing workers were paid as independent contractors. The church leaders, like most people, didn't understand that the employer was committing payroll fraud.

Payroll fraud is one of the most common forms of wage theft. Lying about the status of one's workers robs money and protections from workers, diverts needed revenues from public treasuries, and creates an environment of lawlessness throughout the society. As we'll see in Chapter 11, there are major important campaigns to clamp down on payroll fraud. Payroll fraud is wrong and must be policed.

4

Why Employers Steal Wages

Woe to him who builds his house by unrighteousness, and his upper rooms by injustice; who makes his neighbors work for nothing, and does not give them their wages.

—Jeremiah 22:13 (NRSV)

But those who want to be rich fall into temptation and are trapped by many senseless and harmful desires that plunge people into ruin and destruction. For the love of money is a root of all kinds of evil, and in their eagerness to be rich some have wandered away from the faith and pierced themselves with many pains.

—I Timothy 6:9–10 (NRSV)[1]

As I've crisscrossed the United States talking about wage theft, people want to know "Why?" Why are employers stealing wages in such epidemic proportions?

The causes of the wage theft crisis are complicated. Fundamentally, major changes impacting the structure of work are occurring in our society. Both societal values and business practices are pushing companies toward wage theft, and there are inadequate countervailing values and forces pushing back to stop or deter wage theft. Let's review some of the fundamental push factors and the *lack* of pushback factors.

Societal Context Impacting Workers and Employers

The workplace of the early twenty-first century is different from that of the mid-twentieth century, when most of the existing labor laws were put into place. Our job structures, job training, and laws have not kept pace with changes. While the societal contexts do not *cause* wage theft, they form the environment in which workers and employers operate. The environment sets the conditions in which workers and employers operate, and many of those conditions make it easy for employers to steal wages. The following five trends in our society have created the environment encouraging of wage theft.

GLOBALIZATION: U.S. companies and U.S. workers compete in a global market. Some would argue that the trend toward globalization is not new, but rather one that has emerged over hundreds, if not thousands, of years. Although this is certainly true, the rate at which production and trade have been globalized has increased dramatically, owing in large part to rapid changes in technology. Globalization clearly is a major factor in the decline of manufacturing, significant job loss in particular sectors, and the overall lowering of wages in the United States. Globalization plays a major role in the squeeze employers place on contractors in industries such as the garment industry, which is struggling to survive in the United States because it is competing against cheap clothing imports from China and elsewhere. But globalization does not affect only manufacturing firms. Globalization is consolidating some service industries, such as janitorial firms and security firms, into global corporations. Many call centers have been set up overseas, so U.S.-based industries compete in the global marketplace.

Even though wage theft existed before the dramatic expansion of globalization, it has exacerbated wage theft problems as companies are allowed to move more of their work around the world searching for low wages and lax or nonexistent worker protections. This globalization has enabled big firms to escape responsibility for their suppliers and contractors, while at the same time pressuring U.S. workers to accept poor working conditions for fear that their jobs will be shipped elsewhere.[2] Globalization is not the driving force per se for employers stealing wages, but it is a major context in which employers and workers operate that puts new pressures and expectations on both.

CONTINGENT WORK AND WORKERS: In the 1990s, the ties between workers and employees began to loosen. More and more workers became free agents, working on part-time or short-term assignments. Although definitions vary over exactly what is contingent work or a contingent worker, the Bureau of Labor Statistics defines contingent workers as "those who do not have an implicit or explicit contract for ongoing employments."[3] Employers don't have to worry about paying pensions, health care, disability insurance, or other benefits that may be provided to full-time employees. Employers for good reasons often hire contingent workers to fill various job gaps and temporary work needs. When employers (including me) hire contingent workers, we don't feel as responsible for them as we do for our "regular" employees.

Using the broadest measurement of contingency, the Bureau of Labor Statistics suggests there are 5.7 million contingent workers. More than half of these workers would have preferred a permanent job.[4] As companies get used to relying on contingent workers, they become accustomed to not being responsible for workers' benefits for these workers. If they have hired workers through a temp agency, they have not been responsible for all the taxes and normal payroll accounting. This creates a context for employers in which they do not feel obligated to pay for such things. Similarly, when workers get used to being contingent, they too don't find it unusual for employers not to provide such things as taxes and overtime pay. I suspect that the growth and prevalence of contingent work creates the context for widespread payroll fraud, which as the previous chapter described constitutes a major way that employers steal money from workers and the public. Because independent contractors or workers paid off the books are treated like contingent workers, and so many employers are used to hiring contingent workers and employees are used to being contingent, the payroll fraud may appear to be reasonable to both, even though it is illegal.

UNEMPLOYMENT AND DISGUISED UNEMPLOYMENT: While official unemployment figures are high (8.9 percent in February, 2011),[5] the real unemployment figures are much higher, probably almost double because of the way unemployment figures are calculated. Those who have gotten discouraged and given up hunting for a job are not counted as unemployed. Also, those who take a part-time job because they can't find a full-time job are not counted as unemployed.[6] Having one in six workers unemployed or underemployed makes other workers anxious about losing their jobs. If workers are anxious about their jobs, they are reluctant to complain about their jobs for fear of losing them and not finding others. On the flip side, if employers know there are lots of workers willing and able to take jobs, they feel no pressure to improve wages and standards or comply with laws. Regularly, workers who complain are told by their bosses, "If you don't like conditions, go find another job." In a time of high unemployment, few will risk their jobs.

TOO FEW GOOD JOBS: In addition to too few jobs altogether, there are too few good jobs for people with college degrees, and even *fewer* good jobs for people without college degrees. The factory jobs, which were primarily unionized and were good-paying jobs with benefits, are disappearing. The attacks on public sector jobs in 2011 provoked such a vocal outcry from workers because public sector jobs are some of the few remaining jobs available to workers without specialty skills that provide benefits. If more good jobs were available, especially for people without college educations, there would be more competition and employers would be more likely to pay people fairly and well. In addition, workers would be less reluctant to leave bad employers if they thought they could find other good jobs. Many workers talk about how bad their jobs are, but that having a bad job is better than no job. The lack of good jobs available in the society also discourages workers from complaining or organizing to improve conditions for fear of losing their jobs and not being able to find better, or even replacement, jobs. When employers know that there aren't very many good jobs out there, few are inclined to raise wages and benefits if they don't have to do so. Again, this establishes a context for wage theft.

UNRESOLVED IMMIGRATION ISSUES: In the last few decades, millions of new immigrants have come to the United States in search of jobs. Estimates are that there are now ten to twelve million undocumented immigrants in the nation. Because our nation has no rational immigration system providing a path to citizenship and no strong worker protections for immigrants, many immigrants find themselves in vulnerable situations. They are desperate to work to support themselves and their families; at the same time, they face enormous backlash from communities that are scapegoating the nation's economic woes on immigrants (hardly a new approach in U.S. history), and they are terrified of being deported. This creates a context that makes it easy for employers to exploit undocumented immigrants. Immigrants are not the cause of wage theft, but the unresolved immigration issues in the society create an atmosphere in which immigrants are often fearful of and unwilling to complain about wage theft. Our workers' centers have seen employers who didn't want to hire anyone who was a citizen. Why? Obviously because undocumented immigrants are easier for unscrupulous employers to exploit.

Societal Challenges (Sins) *Pushing* toward Wage Theft

In addition to the current context in which workers and employers operate, certain societal challenges push employers and consumers toward wage theft. Let me outline three significant challenges: greed, racism, and sexism.

GREED: Greed is a primary cause of wage theft. Michael Constantine and his wife Devon Lynn Kile ran a roofing business in Santa Ana, California. The couple engaged in payroll fraud, reporting their payroll as $3 million a year, when it was actually $32 million. They stole wages from workers and taxes and insurance payments from the state. At the time of their arrest, investigators said they owned five properties, multiple luxury vehicles including a Bentley, two Ferraris, and a Range Rover, and they spent more than $2.1 million over a two-year period on jewelry, clothes, and personal items.[7] Greed is not a new problem. The prophet Amos railed against those who lay on beds inlaid with ivory and trampled the needy and perverted justice in the courts. Greed is a problem for all of us. It is easy to point fingers at those who amass enormous wealth through paying low wages and stealing wages—and I do. But most of us, and I can certainly speak for myself, are not exempt from the sin of greed. We desire more than we need while others around us struggle for the basics. We push for a "good deal" without thinking of the consequences for workers. We fail to advocate justice at every moment we could. We don't treat our neighbors as we would like to be treated. Greed is one of the moral challenges for all of us. As the Apostle Paul says in Romans 3:23, "We've all sinned and come short of the glory of God."

Now that doesn't mean we should accept greed in ourselves or others. As people of faith, or even just as people of good will, we must constantly strive against and challenge greed, both in ourselves and in others. Greed is wrong. We must publicly denounce it, while recognizing that most of us are not without fault ourselves.

RACISM: As a society, we struggle with racism. As much as any of us would like to pretend we are "beyond" racism, we live in a society that accepted slavery (the ultimate wage theft) for centuries and that continues to accept segregated and inferior schools. Despite the enormous gains that individual people of color have made and that we as a society have made, the vestiges of slavery and our ongoing struggle with racism are evident in the workplace treatment of workers by race and ethnicity. Racism locks people into specific low-paying jobs. Under slavery, black people weren't considered human beings. They were workers who could be bought and sold for the benefit of others. They were segregated into particular jobs that were deemed "appropriate." Slaves were given the messy jobs, the behind-the-scenes jobs, the hidden jobs, the backbreaking jobs. Despite some changes in who occupies various jobs, these segregated job roles still exist. In the Delaware peninsula, which is known for its chicken processing, Central American immigrants dominate the chicken processing lines and African American workers are the chicken catchers. At my mother's retirement community, white workers have most of the office jobs, African American women are the aides, and immigrant youth serve the food. Most restaurants in the nation have white and black workers as wait staff and Mexican or Central American immigrants as cooks and cleaning crews. African Americans and immigrants disproportionately hold the nation's 1.1 million security guard jobs.[8] Black slaves used to serve as farm workers, planting and harvesting food; now immigrants fill that function.

Racism justifies treating some workers as disposable human beings. A few years ago I helped organize a delegation of Christian ethics professors to meet with a building contractor in Phoenix who was known to mistreat his workers. We met first with the immigrant workers who described various problems they had with wage theft and lack of benefits. What most upset them, however, was the disrespect the employer showed toward them. The ethics professors were skeptical about the seriousness of their allegations until the professors met with the employer. He talked about the workers as if they weren't human beings. He called them all "his boys." It seemed clear to us that the employer viewed all the workers as disposable human beings. Over the years, I've met with many employers about workplace problems, and I'm regularly struck by employers not viewing their workers as human beings like themselves, especially when the workers are predominately of another race or ethnicity. Both the racism of particular employers and the racism in the core structure of society enable groups of workers to be viewed as disposable commodities.[9]

Racism is also used to set workers against one another. Throughout our nation's history, workers have been pitted against one another on the basis of race and ethnicity. Employers have often hired the newest immigrant groups, setting them up against the existing workers who may have fought to improve working conditions. The Irish and German workers, for example, were hated by native-born workers when they came in the 1800s, and later eastern European immigrants encountered hostility from the mainly northwestern European immigrants when they came to the United States in the great wave of immigration between 1890 and 1914. When white workers would try to organize to improve working conditions, black workers would be brought in as strikebreakers. Today, racism continues to be used to set black and immigrant workers against one another—and immigrant workers are being scapegoated as the source of our economic troubles. Before the workers were unionized, black and immigrant workers at Smithfield Foods in Tar Heel, North Carolina, shared with me how managers used to teach them to fear one another. Immigrant workers were told that black workers didn't want them in the plants, whereas black workers were told that immigrants were taking their jobs.

Racism is structured into our labor laws. Farm workers, who were historically black and are now largely immigrant, are excluded from overtime protection. Home health aides, primarily black and immigrant women workers, are also excluded from overtime protection. Whenever we look at what groups of workers in low-wage jobs have not had the political power to win passage of basic laws to protect them, we invariably find that they are people of color.

SEXISM: Women have made enormous strides in the last hundred years toward obtaining fair and equitable treatment in the workplace.

Nonetheless, discrimination against women workers still exists. In 1963, women earned 59 percent of the wages men earned. By 2005 the wage gap had narrowed to 81 percent, with older women workers experiencing the largest disparity of wages.[10] Similar to the role racism plays in the society, sexism tends to "typecast" women in particular roles, undervaluing their role in caregiving for children and the elderly, as well as their roles in caring for our homes and buildings. Jobs categories that are dominated by women are also those in which wage theft is prevalent. Workers in the garment industry, an industry known for wage theft, are almost always immigrant women. Hotel maids and in-home cleaners are almost always women, and wage theft is widespread in nonunion places. Certified nursing assistants and home health aides are primarily women—additional sectors with widespread wage theft. Child care workers (98 percent of the 1.4 million child care workers are women) earn median annual salaries of $17,630[11] *and* experience wage theft. And like job categories dominated by people of color and excluded from labor law protection, so too are many women's jobs, such as home health aides, private child care workers, and domestic workers in homes. Although it is hard to quantify the degree to which sexism in the society *causes* wage theft, it is easy to recognize the role of sexism and the continued devaluing of women's contributions.

Business Practices *Pushing* toward Wage Theft

Some employers are just greedy and don't want to share profits with their employees. Some don't view the minority or female workers as human beings, who have the same needs and desires as they. But other employers, including some of our nation's largest companies, have business practices that *push* them toward wage theft. Following are four of the significant business practices that lead employers to engage in wage theft:

Expansion at all costs. In a competitive environment, many companies must grow and expand or die. Companies push to expand rapidly and shave costs in all other places in the company other than expanding. In sectors of the economy where overall profit margins are slim, the main way to cut costs is to reduce wages. In competitive environments in which other employers routinely steal wages from workers, it is hard to compete *without* stealing wages.

Preoccupation with short-term profits versus long-term profitability. Much has been written about CEOs who receive exorbitant bonuses for lifting shareholder earnings by slashing workforces, shedding pension responsibilities, and cutting short-term costs. "Even when companies perform well in an increasingly competitive business environment, it is not uncommon for their stock prices to fall when they do not exceed Wall Street's expectations. The intense pressure to show profits and the relentless push to demonstrate continuous growth, no matter what, has no doubt fueled the spectacular failures of companies such as Enron, Worldcom, Global Crossing, and Adelphi. Pressure of this kind often leads executives to take actions that bring short-term reward at long-term cost."[12] Under this kind of shareholder pressure, employers can be tempted to steal wages or turn a blind eye when contractors or subcontractors steal wages.

Understaffing. One way companies keep costs down is to keep their staffing levels low and pressure managers to work with unrealistically low staffing levels. When staffing levels are below what is required to accomplish the tasks, stressed managers push workers to work through their breaks, work off the clock, or work overtime without getting paid for it. Because the managers' rewards are based on keeping staffing levels low, they even "shave" hours off workers records, meaning that they falsify timesheets. If managers' prime reward structures are based primarily on keeping staffing levels low, it will create a powerful *push* toward wage theft.

Weak internal systems to guard against wage theft. It's one thing to establish a policy against wage theft, but it's another to figure out how wage theft occurs and how to institute systems to stop it. Cintas management showed me its contracting policies against wage theft. It did not figure out how to stop it. Pulte Homes has subcontractors throughout the nation building its homes by stealing wages from workers. I'm sure Pulte Homes has great policies on paper too, but it clearly has an inadequate internal system for monitoring its subcontractors.

Wal-Mart's business practices demonstrate all these push factors. Thomas Kochan, the George Maverick Bunker Professor of Management at MIT's Sloan School of Management and co-director of both the MIT Workplace Center and the Institute for Work and Employment, explained this in his expert testimony in a 2006 case charging Wal-Mart with not paying its hourly associates. He says, "Wal-Mart executives have established corporate policies that are ethical and appear to conform to legal requirements. However, Wal-Mart has also established financial and business objectives that managers find difficult to achieve without circumventing those rules. Importantly, there are strong financial and career advancement incentives for store managers to meet Wal-Mart's financial objectives, but there are essentially no financial or career advancement incentives to adhere to corporate policies that protect and/or benefit hourly employees (i.e., providing rest breaks and full compensation). Store managers can also lose their jobs for failing to meet Wal-Mart's profitability objectives. The result is that managers ignore rules of this type to make their financial objectives."[13]

Lack of Pushback Forces

One reason for the crisis of wage theft in the society is that the *push* forces are far stronger than the *pushback* forces. Following are four important *pushback* factors.

Weak unions and worker associations. Unions and worker associations in the workplace are a countervailing power to shareholders and owners who would seek to maximize profits at all costs. Unions and worker associations push for profits to be shared between owners and shareholders on the one hand and workers on the other. Organized workers push back against efforts to squeeze or steal workers' wages. Chapter 6 explains in some detail why and how unions are critical in challenging and preventing wage theft.

The declining power of unions in the society and the increasingly lower percentages of workers represented by unions are major reasons why wage theft now abounds in the society. Unions create a pushback force for challenging greed and maximization of profit at all costs.

Weak laws. The United States has some of the weakest labor laws in the industrialized world. What labor laws exist are woefully inadequate and incredibly confusing. Chapter 5 reviews the confusing array of laws that are supposed to protect workers. Strong and effective labor laws could be a countervailing force to restrict or minimize wage theft in the workplace.

Even weaker enforcement and meaningless consequences. The labor laws that are on the books are not being adequately enforced, and the consequences of getting caught stealing wages are often meaningless. The primary reason for poor enforcement is the ridiculously low staffing levels of the labor law enforcement agencies. Lack of leadership and creativity in enforcement approaches reduces their effectiveness as well. And then when companies are "caught" stealing wages, many of them are not given consequences that are sufficient for changing behavior. Penalties must be significant enough to be a countervailing balance to the pressures of profit maximization and greed. If every company knew that its wage payment systems would be investigated annually and the penalties would be serious if they were found guilty of stealing wages, companies would put in place systems to reward and encourage managers and subcontractors for paying workers. A strong enforcement approach with meaningful consequences would provide an important countervailing force in society.

Few business community pressures. The business community can influence how businesses act when issues are discussed and leaders are rewarded for their values. Many in the business community have taken up environmental concerns. Conferences are held to discuss environmental problems, awards are given for "green" leadership, and business leaders are ostracized for polluting. The same should become true for the issue of wage theft. The business community should create its own pushback factor to address this crisis in the society.

The causes of wage theft are complicated and multifaceted: current contextual factors that make workers and employers ripe for wage theft; the societal sins of greed, racism, and sexism that affect how all of us treat one another and operate in the society; the business practices that push companies toward wage theft; and weak pushback forces in the society. Needless to say, there is not one simple answer to why wages are stolen. The causes are complex, but not so complex that we can't address them. Together we can challenge the contexts, address our individual and societal sins, establish stronger worker-friendly business practices, and strengthen the pushback factors. We can do this.

In the next chapter we will explore our nation's labor laws and why they are inadequate. Then we will turn in the next section, Vehicles for Stopping Wage Theft, to look at how unions, workers' centers, ethical business leaders, and workers themselves can serve as countervailing forces in society to fight wage theft. The following section, Strengthening Enforcement, focuses on how federal, state, and local enforcement agencies can become strong pushback institutions against wage theft. In the final section, What You Can Do to Stop Wage Theft, we will look at what each of us can do to end wage theft.

5

How U.S. Labor Laws Fail Workers

"Teacher, which commandment in the law is the greatest?" He said to him, "You shall love the Lord your God with all your heart, and with all your soul, and with all your mind. This is the greatest and first commandment. And a second is like it: "You shall love your neighbor as yourself. On these two commandments hang all the law and the prophets."

—Matthew 22:36–40 (NRSV)

Anka Karewicz came to the United States in 2000 from Poland at the age of 20. She moved to Chicago to live with her cousin, who had been there for about ten years. Her mother had lived in Chicago for a while but has since returned to Poland.

Most Polish women new to the United States get jobs babysitting or cleaning houses. Anka didn't want either of those jobs. She tried to get construction work, but contractors laughed in her face. Finally, she got a job at a car wash chain named We Will Clean. She was upset about the working conditions but didn't know what the laws were in Illinois, how to find out, or where to turn for help.

The place employed primarily Latino and Polish immigrant workers. No one was paid very well, about $6 per hour, but Latinos were generally paid about 50 cents less per hour than Polish workers. (It is illegal to pay people on a different pay scale because of ethnicity.)

Workers had to wear uniforms. The workers were then charged for the uniforms to be sent to an outside cleaner. In reality, the uniforms were washed at We Will Clean right along with the dirty towels. (If deducting for washing the uniforms brings the wages below minimum wage, it is illegal.)

At car washes, workers make most of their money in tips. At We Will Clean, the workers were required to turn all their tips over to the managers, who then supposedly divided them equally among the workers. Workers suspected that they didn't receive all the tips. (It is also illegal for managers to take workers' tips.)

Once workers had put in 40 hours, the company would send them to work at another location in order to avoid paying them overtime, as is required after a 40-hour workweek. (If a worker puts in more than 40 hours for one employer, regardless of location and is covered by overtime, it is illegal not to pay the overtime hours.)

One worker who was injured on the job was promised the "favor" of being "hired back" once he got out of the hospital if he would not report the injury. The worker's medical bills were never covered by either the employer or workers' compensation. (It is illegal to deny someone workers' compensation if the worker is supposed to be covered by workers' compensation.)

After eight months, Anka finally left this job. A few years later she started volunteering at Arise Chicago's Workers' Center. Eventually, she was hired for 20 hours per week to help other Polish immigrants with workplace problems while she finished up her associate's degree in fine arts.

Anka's first job was with the quintessential sweatshop employer. He stole wages. He stole workers' health. He stole people's dignity. And the way our laws are structured and enforced almost guarantees that no one will ever catch up with this employer for all the ways he has stolen from workers.

If Anka had wanted to report the problems in her workplace and had known where to report them, she would have needed to contact the Department of Labor's Wage and Hour Division or the Illinois Department of Labor for the overtime issues and the stealing of tips, the Equal Employment Opportunities Commission about the discrimination against Latinos, the Occupational Safety and Health Administration about the workplace safety issues, and the state Workers Comp Commission about workers not getting workers' compensation. No worker, whether an immigrant, a community college student, a busy single mom, or the 99 percent of all workers who aren't lawyers, has the time and information needed for filing complaints with so many agencies. The laws have overlapping and confusing jurisdictions. The enforcement responsibilities are scattered. The bottom line is that the labor laws of the land are failing to protect workers against wage theft.

It may not seem that interesting to review the basic laws that protect workers in the workplace, but these laws cover the largest amount of our waking hours. It is important to have a general understanding of the variety of laws and how complicated the "system" is, in order to understand why we need to change both some of the laws and our approach to educating workers and enforcing the laws. The laws should be designed to help us treat our neighbor as we would like to be treated, and yet they clearly are falling short. Most of us spend more time in the workplace than we do sleeping, caring for our families, or anything else we do. The laws regulating how most of us are treated and paid are terribly important to our quality of life, and yet most of us have very little understanding of workplace laws. I urge the reader to learn about the basic labor laws described in this chapter in order to understand why changes are needed and what you can do to help.

The Basic Federal Workplace Protection Laws— Administered by the Department of Labor

Workers' wages are protected by a hodgepodge of federal laws. The laws were enacted at different times and usually cover slightly different groups of workers. As a result, the laws are confusing to workers and employers alike and collectively are doing a poor job in protecting workers against wage theft. Because all the laws are more complicated than the simple descriptions given here, be sure to consult the laws directly, visit a workers' center, call the Department of Labor, or meet with an attorney specializing in labor issues if you have specific compliance questions. You can also visit www.canmybossdothat.org for more information.

FAIR LABOR STANDARDS ACT (FLSA): The most significant law covering wages is the FLSA, which was initially passed in 1938, under the leadership of Secretary of Labor Frances Perkins (see Chapter 9). Currently, FLSA covers 130 million workers in 7 million workplaces. This law establishes the principles of minimum wage, overtime, restrictions on child labor, and recordkeeping. Obviously, this law has been updated since then, but its core components remain the same. They are as follows:

Minimum wage. All workers covered by FLSA must be paid the federal minimum wage or the state minimum wage, whichever is higher. There are special rules that apply to workers who earn tips. *Overtime pay.* Many workers are eligible for overtime pay, which is 1.5 times the FLSA regular rate of pay for hours worked above 40 per week. Figuring out who is and is not covered by overtime is complicated. Most workers covered by FLSA are eligible for overtime if they earn less than $23,660 per year ($455 per week), regardless of their title or position. This is called the minimum threshold. Most workers who earn more than $100,000 per year are not eligible for overtime. Workers who are covered by overtime are called "nonexempt" workers. Workers who are not covered by overtime are called "exempt" workers, meaning they are exempt from overtime. The general categories of exempt workers are executive, administrative, and professional. In addition, more than thirty categories of jobs have been defined as exempt from overtime. Many of these jobs categories are only "exempt" because employer groups have lobbied successfully to have them made "exempt," rather than because there is some intrinsic reason the workers in the category shouldn't be provided overtime pay. The following workers are some of those exempt from overtime pay:[1]

- teachers and academic personnel in elementary and secondary schools
- outside sales employees
- some computer-related employees
- employees of certain seasonal amusement or recreational establishments
- certain commissioned employees of retail or service establishments
- auto, truck, trailer, farm implement, boat, or aircraft sales workers
- parts-clerks and mechanics servicing autos, trucks, or farm implements, who are employed by nonmanufacturing establishments engaged primarily in selling these items to ultimate purchasers
- employees of railroads and air carriers
- taxi drivers
- certain employees of motor carriers
- seamen on American vessels
- local delivery employees paid on approved trip rate plans

- announcers, news editors, and chief engineers of certain nonmetropolitan broadcasting stations
- domestic service workers living in the employer's residence
- employees of motion picture theaters
- farm workers

Child labor. The FLSA has strict rules governing the hours children under 16 can work and the types of jobs children under 18 can do. In addition, most states have child labor laws.

Recordkeeping. Under FLSA, employers must keep records about hours worked and wages paid. Some states have additional laws giving workers access to their own records.

MIGRANT AND SEASONAL AGRICULTURAL WORKER PROTECTION ACT (MSPA): Although farm workers are covered by some of the FLSA provisions (minimum wage, recordkeeping, and less stringent child labor protections, but not overtime), additional provisions in MSPA address problems farm workers face. This law requires that employers disclose the terms and conditions of employment in writing, post worker protection information, pay workers when due and itemize various deductions, ensure that housing (if provided) meets federal and state standards, require that vehicles used for transportation are safe, and keep records for three years.

DAVIS-BACON AND RELATED ACTS (DBRA): These laws are commonly referred to as "prevailing wage." It means that workers are covered by regional customary wage rates, instead of just the minimum wage, when federal tax dollars finance various kinds of construction projects, such as building highways, post offices, or military facilities. Originally passed in 1931 during the height of the Depression, the law was (and is) intended to make sure that government projects help maintain good wages rather than driving down wages. The main law is the Davis-Bacon Act, but there are approximately sixty different government laws that include prevailing wage-type language, such as the Housing and Community Development Act. The secretary of labor determines these wage rates by locality and by occupation. The wage rates are posted on the Department of Labor website (www.dol.gov). Most of these wage rates apply to various types of construction workers.

MCNAMARA-O'HARA SERVICE CONTRACT ACT (SCA): Passed in 1965, this Act provides prevailing wages for service workers employed under government service contracts. Again, wage rates are given by occupation and locality. This law ensures that when government dollars are spent in a community, the dollars support and uplift area wage rates instead of undermining them.

FAMILY MEDICAL LEAVE ACT (FMLA): This fairly new law, passed in 1993, allows workers who have been employed for at least twelve months and have worked 1250 hours and are employed in workplaces employing fifty or more workers to take up to twelve weeks of *unpaid* leave to care for themselves, a new child, or a sick family member and return to a job similar to the one they left. This means people can take leaves from their jobs without fear of losing their jobs. This has been a very popular law with workers, incurring small financial costs for business.

OCCUPATIONAL SAFETY AND HEALTH ACT (OSHA): Many people have heard of OSHA, which administers the Occupational Safety and Health Act and fifteen other health and safety laws that affect the workplace. Safety and health working conditions in most private industries are regulated by OSHA or OSHA-approved state systems. Twenty-seven states run their own OSHA programs, at least for some workers. Most employees are covered, except for self-employed workers and workers who are covered under other safety laws, such as miners (covered under the Mine Safety and Health Act). Under the laws, workers have the right to know about dangerous conditions, be trained, complain about dangerous situations without retaliation, get problems addressed, and refuse to work if something is terribly dangerous. OSHA does not allow a "private right of action," which means that workers cannot file private lawsuits to enforce the laws on health and safety.

Other Significant Federal Laws Protecting Workers

Although many other laws affect workers and workplaces, let me mention three important federal ones that are *not* enforced by the Department of Labor:

EQUAL EMPLOYMENT OPPORTUNITY (EEO) LAWS: The primary antidiscrimination laws are administered by the Equal Employment

Opportunity Commission (EEOC). It is illegal to discriminate against workers based on their race, color, religion, sex, age (over 40), national origin, or disability (if it doesn't affect one's ability to do the job). Again, there are some exceptions in terms of who is covered by the laws.

NATIONAL LABOR RELATIONS ACT (NLRA): Passed in 1935 in the midst of great labor unrest, this law, also called the Wagner Act, protects the rights of most private sector workers to organize a union, bargain collectively, and strike when necessary. The law is administered by the National Labor Relations Board (NLRB). According to the NLRB, Congress enacted the law "to serve the public interest by reducing interruptions in commerce caused by industrial strife. It seeks to do this by providing orderly processes for protecting and implementing the respective rights of employees, employers, and unions in their relations with one another. The overall job of the NLRB is to achieve this goal through administration, interpretation, and enforcement of the Act."[2] Most people in the labor movement believe that this law and its enforcement are woefully inadequate to protect workers' rights to organize and join unions.

WORKER ADJUSTMENT AND RETRAINING NOTIFICATION ACT (WARN): Enacted in 1988 in the midst of an upswing in plant closures, this bill requires companies that plan to close or lay off large numbers of workers to give the workers and communities at least sixty days' notice. Most workplaces are covered if they employ one hundred or more employees. This law is not enforced by any government administrative agency. It can only be enforced in federal courts. As was mentioned in Chapter 2, approximately two-thirds of employers covered by the WARN Act violate the law.[3]

State Laws

In addition to the federal laws protecting workers, every state has unemployment and workers' compensation laws:

UNEMPLOYMENT INSURANCE: Often called just "unemployment," unemployment insurance provides money to help unemployed workers when they lose their job through no fault of their own (as determined by various state laws). This assistance is provided only for short periods of time following the end of employment, usually twenty-six weeks or less, although during times of high unemployment extensions are often given. Unemployment insurance must follow federal guidelines, but it is administered by states and paid for primarily through taxes on employers.

WORKERS' COMPENSATION INSURANCE: If an employee is injured on the job, he or she is probably eligible for coverage for the health costs related to the injury and for some wage replacement to cover the time off from the job. If an injury is a permanent one, such as a worker loses a hand, there are state-determined cash lump sums paid to the worker for the loss. Each state has its own laws determining eligibility, rates, and processes for workers' compensation.

Thousands of additional state laws affect workers' wages and working conditions. Some states have tried to fill in the massive gaps in basic protection and enforcement in the federal laws. These are some of the main types of additional laws:

Minimum wage. Most states have a minimum wage law that covers more employees than those covered by the FLSA. In addition, many states have minimum wages that are higher than the federal minimum wage.

Last paycheck. Many states have passed laws requiring employers to pay the last paychecks, given the widespread abuse of employers stealing the last paycheck.

Breaks. Eight states have laws about rest periods, and nineteen have laws about meal breaks.

State prevailing wages. Most states have state prevailing wage laws that cover state contracts.

Child labor laws. Most states have additional limits on hours for child labor and certifications needed.

Payday requirements. Most states have laws about how often workers must be paid.

Are you overwhelmed and confused by all this? Well, these are just a few of the laws. Imagine if English isn't your first language. Very little information is available in languages other than English, and hardly any of it is compiled for workers in an easily understandable form.[4]

The Laws Aren't Working

Even though there are many laws designed to protect workers, especially if one includes all the state laws, the laws don't work together in ways that ensure workers are protected against wage theft (or anything else). For most workers and small employers, the basic laws are confusing, in large part because there are so many different ones. In addition, the combination of laws has gaping holes in coverage, and many of the laws passed fifty to seventy years ago do not adequately address today's workplace problems. Below are some of the most important ways in which the laws are failing to protect workers against wage theft:

MANY WORKERS AREN'T PROTECTED BY THE FAIR LABOR STANDARDS ACT (FLSA): The main federal law, FLSA, only covers employees of certain enterprises. As advocates in the workers' centers describe it, there are two coverage tests: the size test or the interstate commerce test. Although it is frankly a bit more complicated than this, the size or interstate commerce test is a good simple summary. In order to be covered by FLSA, you must work in a place that has annual gross sales or business done involving at least $500,000 per year, or you must do something that is involved in interstate commerce. Engaging in interstate commerce can be as simple as sending e-mails out of state or producing a product that gets shipped out of state. So, there's the size test and the interstate commerce test. But lots of workers don't fit either of those tests.

If you wash dishes in a small restaurant, you may not be covered. If you are a residential construction worker for a small contractor, even if you work on homes being built by the nation's largest home builders, you may not be covered. If you work for a small franchise of a multi-billion dollar corporation, you may not be covered.

And because of the complicated definition, a great deal of Department of Labor staff time (as well as advocates') is spent assessing whether or not a worker is covered by the law.

EACH LAW COVERS DIFFERENT GROUPS OF WORKERS: The FLSA covers workers using the size or interstate commerce test. The Family and Medical Leave Act covers workers in worksites with more than fifty workers if the employees have worked there for twelve months and for at least 1250 hours. Title VII of the Civil Rights Act covers anyone who works for an employer with at least fifteen employees. WARN covers workplaces with one hundred full-time employees. COBRA (which allows workers and their families to continue health coverage for a period of time after leaving an employer) covers private employers with employees' total hours equaling twenty full-time workers.

STATE MINIMUM WAGE LAWS PROTECT SOME MORE THAN OTHERS: Some states have a minimum wage that is higher than the federal minimum, covers more workers, and is well enforced by state agencies. If you live in Illinois, you are covered by the state minimum wage of $8.25 in 2011 if your workplace has four employees. If you live in Indiana, the minimum wage is only $7.25 in 2011, the same as the federal minimum wage, but you are covered if your workplace has more than two employees.

On the other hand, if you live in Alabama and are not covered by FLSA, you aren't guaranteed any minimum wage at all. There is an Alabama Department of Labor, but it can't do much. If a worker hasn't been paid, the worker will be required to file a notarized wage claim form. Then the Alabama Department of Labor asks the employers to pay voluntarily. If the employers don't pay, the Alabama agency cannot help the workers get the pay they are owed.

But at least Alabama has an enforcement agency. In 2004, Florida voters approved a constitutional amendment that set the state minimum wage. By 2008, the Florida minimum wage was $6.79, which was higher than the federal minimum wage, which was raised to $6.55 on July 24, 2008. According to the Florida law, the Florida minimum wage applies to everyone covered by the federal minimum wage. That sounds good, but there is no one to enforce the law. In 2002, the Florida Legislature passed a bill closing down the Florida Department of Labor and Employment Security, effective June 30, 2002. Theoretically, lawyers could pursue minimum wage cases, but for workers in low-wage jobs, the amounts of money involved aren't of much interest to attorneys. Collecting a few hundred dollars matters a lot to a poor worker, but is not very enticing for attorneys to invest many hours in trying to recover those wages. The Florida state website says that the state attorney general may bring an enforcement action to enforce the minimum wage, but when Anne Janks, creator and director of Can My Boss Do That, the best worker-focused online website around (www.canmybossdothat .com), called the Florida attorney general's office to ask about enforcing the minimum wage, the staffer with whom she spoke seemed surprised to learn that the attorney general had this enforcement authority.[5] Needless to say, the Florida minimum wage law is not being enforced. Workers in Alabama and Florida need higher wages, coverage of more workers for minimum wage, and strong enforcement as much as workers in Illinois and Indiana do. The variances in coverage and enforcement do not serve to lift up all workers.

OTHER STATE WAGE LAWS ARE EVEN MORE OF A MISHMASH: Eight states require paid rest periods; most states require 10 minutes of paid rest time for every 4 hours, although in Illinois hotel attendants in large cities get 15-minute rest periods. Some states have requirements on when paychecks should be paid; others have no requirements.

MANY LOW-WAGE WORKERS ARE EXCLUDED FROM FEDERAL OVERTIME COVERAGE: In 2004, the Wage and Hour Division of the Department of Labor under Tammy McCutchen's leadership conducted a major overhaul of one of the overtime regulations designed to lift the minimum threshold below which workers would automatically be covered and simplify the definitions for other higher-wage workers. Lifting the minimum threshold below which workers are automatically eligible for overtime (if they are covered by FLSA and not otherwise exempt from overtime coverage) was great. Unfortunately, the overtime regulations are still confusing, many large groups of workers are excluded from overtime, and many exempt (salaried) employees are being worked ridiculous hours for very little money. Of the more than thirty categories of workers who are excluded from overtime, many are the kind of low-wage workers who seem deserving of overtime pay, such as the two million farm workers who grow and harvest our food, often at extremely low wages and at risk of injury and long-term health problems. So, too, do home health aides and domestic workers. Many managers or assistant managers of fast-food restaurants or gas stations, who make just above the minimum overtime salary threshold, are forced to work 60 or 70 hours a week in ways that don't seem fair either.

FIVE FEDERAL DEFINITIONS FOR AN EMPLOYEE VERSUS AN INDEPENDENT CONTRACTOR: The FLSA, the NLRA, Title VII and related civil rights statutes, the Employee Retirement Income Security Act (ERISA), and the Internal Revenue Code all use different definitions of who is an employee versus who is an independent contractor. In addition, many states also have their own definitions for workers' compensation and unemployment. No wonder there are misclassification problems. Just one fair federal definition would make it simpler for employers and workers to understand and agencies to cooperate in enforcing the laws. The FLSA standard of "economic reality" would be the most favorable to workers.

MULTIPLE JURISDICTIONS FOR WORKPLACE ENFORCEMENT: As described previously, although the U.S. Department of Labor has the largest responsibility for federal workplace enforcement, the Equal Employment Opportunities Commission has jurisdiction over discrimination issues, and the NLRB has responsibility for workers' right to organize. Within the Department of Labor, the Wage and Hour Division, which enforces the FLSA (and others), seldom coordinates with the Occupational Health and Safety Administration. Coordination between the federal agencies and the state agencies is spotty at best.

What Can Be Done?

Given the confusing array of laws with their gaping worker protection holes, no wonder workers and some employers don't understand the laws and who enforces them. When workers are confused about the laws, they don't feel confident about standing up for their rights. When employers don't understand the laws, they can fail to properly compensate workers.

We must begin to build a new national consensus about basic workplace standards that we want as a society. How do we codify the core principle of ensuring just treatment of one another? How do we put in place laws that ensure that employers treat each worker as we ourselves deserve and want to be treated? Wage and workplace standards aren't the dream. They are the bottom-line minimum below which no workplace should fall.

The standards should broaden and simplify coverage, reduce the disparities between states (by raising the bar, not lowering it, of course), and streamline enforcement. The standards should help workers and their families achieve a decent standard of living based on working a reasonable number of hours. As a nation, we should agree on the core principles for standards and then work through a collective process to develop those standards. We must seek a set of wage and workplace standards that:

- Cover almost all workers without complicated tests.
- Bring more uniformity between states.
- Simplify and streamline enforcement, allowing federal and state staff to work cooperatively.
- Support and encourage decent wages for reasonable hours of work.
- Create and enforce significant disincentives for breaking the law.
- Help all of us treat our neighbors in the workplace as we want to be treated.

Fortunately, laws are not static. The laws, though confusing and in-adequate for protecting all workers, can be changed and improved to serve the needs of society more efficiently and effectively. If the laws are not serving the public good, we must collectively fix them and create new ones that serve workers and employers in today's workplaces.

Part II

Vehicles for Stopping Wage Theft

6

Organizing to Stop Wage Theft: Why Unions Matter

But the king of Egypt said, "Moses and Aaron, why are you taking the people away from their labor? Get back to your work!"

—Exodus 5:4[1] (TNIV)

Mercedes Herrerra grew up in Veracruz, Mexico. She came from a hardworking family. As she says, "My mom instilled in me a desire to stand up for people." Mercedes and her husband have four children, one granddaughter, and one grandson.

Mercedes came to Houston in 1994. She first started cleaning houses in 1996. Then she moved to cleaning downtown buildings and sports facilities, working primarily for staffing agencies. She and her coworkers were frequently victims of wage theft.

She was never paid for overtime. Her employers would tell her, "There is no overtime. After 40 hours you work for someone else." (This is not legal.)

After Hurricanes Katrina and Rita, Mercedes was hired by a cleaning firm contracted to clean the Reliance Center. She was in charge of keeping the bathrooms clean. Her staffing agency charged her $100 per week for her shoes, gloves, masks, cleaning supplies, and shuttle rides to the center. She wasn't told when she was hired that such charges would be taken from her paycheck. As a result, her hourly wage fell significantly below minimum wage. (This is not legal.)

Frequently, employers would just not pay her for all the hours she worked. Mercedes would always complain and try to get all the wages she was owed, but most of her colleagues didn't feel comfortable standing up for themselves.

For many of the cleaning firms around town, Friday was a rush day. Workers would be told they had to clean the same number of rooms they regularly did in 4 hours in only 3, so that the managers could get off early. After 3 hours, the worker would be required to clock out and then finish the work on his or her own time. (Yes, this too is illegal.)

Perhaps worse for Mercedes than the wage theft was the treatment she received. Managers would scream at her and her colleagues. Some would tell workers they were old and worthless.

In 2005, Mercedes took a position cleaning buildings in the Galleria for ABM, a national janitorial firm. Although ABM always paid her, before the workers organized, she only earned $5.15 an hour and she had no vacation days, no sick days, no health insurance or pension, and lots of work. She was only given 4 hours of work a day. She had to clean eighteen large restrooms in 4 hours per day.

When one of the organizers came to her door to talk about organizing a union, she knew it was right. Mercedes says, "I had so much anger built up from years of exploitation." First she went to a rally at a building to support other janitors. Then she went to some meetings for training. Next she began talking with her coworkers about joining the union. She got people's names and addresses and tried to motivate them to get involved.

When she got involved, the organizing had already been going on for about a year. It took almost two years total to win a union contract.

Things have changed a lot since the Service Employees International Union (SEIU) worked with the 5300 janitors in Houston to negotiate a union contract. Now Mercedes makes $8.10 per hour and gets a raise every year. She gets one week of vacation after one year and two weeks after five years. She gets six paid holidays. She regularly gets 6 hours of work per day. Even though she doesn't yet get paid for sick days, she doesn't fear losing her job because she takes a sick day. Workers receive individual health coverage for $20 per month at a health clinic the union opened at the end of 2008.[2] The workers want lots more in their contract (higher wages, family health care, pensions, paid sick days), but they know it will be difficult to win until more of Houston's janitors are represented by the union.

Wage theft has been wiped out for the unionized janitors. Anytime there is a problem on wages, workers call the union hotline and someone helps them work out the problems.

Unions not only raise wages, benefits, and working conditions, they stop wage theft. Unions are one of the most effective wage theft deterrents around.

Unions are critical institutions to support and strengthen in the overall campaign to stop wage theft in the nation. Particularly because so many younger people do not know much about unions, this chapter helps explain how unions help workers and improve society overall.

A Little Union History

A union is a formal, structured way for workers to collectively work together to address wages, benefits, and working conditions within a workplace.

Workplace organizing is not new. Labor and community organizers claim that Moses was the first organizer. He probably wasn't—there were surely many organizers before him seeking justice in the workplace. Nonetheless, he clearly helped organized the Israelites to fight the oppression of the Egyptians against the slaves. Moses proposed a three-day strike, which infuriated the Pharaoh. Organizing for better working conditions and even striking are not new. The earliest unions in U.S. history were the craft guilds. During colonial times, groups of craftsmen (and sometimes women) organized themselves to share skills and make sure that they weren't competing with one another in driving down wages. The Carpenters Company of Philadelphia was founded in 1724 and set wages and working conditions for carpenters in the region. In 1741, the Journeymen Caulkers of Boston issued a statement about how they wanted to be paid.[3] By the end of the century there were organized shoemakers, tailors, painters, printers, cabinet makers, shipbuilders, and many others.[4] These craft guilds were the forerunners of many of the building trades unions, such as the painters, roofers, and carpenters unions.

The first factories in the United States were textile mills, which emerged in the early 1800s. These were soon followed by iron factories, which enabled the growth of machines for manufacturing and railroads. As factories expanded throughout the 1800s, so too did groups of workers within factories seeking to improve wages and working conditions, although through the first half of the century, the formal organizations of workers were still skilled craftspeople (mostly men). The second half of the century saw more formal unions organized in factory settings and many strikes and campaigns to improve wages and limit working hours. By the end of the nineteenth century, unions were organizing themselves to function locally, by state, and nationally. Labor unions pushed not only for improved wages and benefits locally, but also for state and national standards on wages and limits on working hours.

Labor history is the story of workers' organizing and their great struggle for recognition. Workers did not organize unions for some vague ideological belief in unions. Rather, they organized unions because they thought they would have a better chance to improve their working conditions if they joined with their colleagues than by doing things on their own. Most large employers, and certainly the captains of industry, vehemently opposed unions. Workers who stood up for their rights were often fired or beaten, and sometimes killed.

Relations between unions and employers became so contentious in the midst of the Depression that it was hard for the nation to prosper, which finally prompted Congress and President Roosevelt to intervene. In 1935, Congress passed the NLRA, known as the Wagner Act, which outlined labor's rights to organize and bargain union contracts. The NLRB was established to make sure employers treated workers fairly when they tried to organize unions.

The passage of this law gave a huge boost to labor organizing. From 1935 to 1937, a total of five million workers joined labor unions (one in six workers). The religious community supported this expansion of unions. From 1935 through 1955, Catholic parishes and orders ran nearly two hundred Catholic labor schools, which taught workers how to organize unions. An interesting article in *Time* magazine from 1951 describes one such school in Manhattan:

> In his eleven years as director of Manhattan's Xavier Labor School, Father Philip Carey has become a familiar figure to thousands of working men & women. He is a mild and scholarly Jesuit whose students are electricians, scrubwomen, plumbers, bus driv-

ers, pipe fitters, and wire lathers. The lesson Father Carey teaches them: how to build strong and effective unions.

Last week, as the first term of the academic year ended at Xavier, 150 men & women were enrolled. But these were only a fraction of the school's real student body. This month, while New York's dock strike raged (see NATIONAL AFFAIRS), Xavier's assistant director, Father John Corridan, was devoting full time to a steady stream of longshoremen coming for advice. The school never takes sides in such disputes; its influence is felt only indirectly. But over the years, union men all over the East have come to realize that Jesuits Carey and Corridan are as wise about labor problems as any men alive.

The school's formal course lasts two years, and students of every faith are welcome. Tuition (which is often waived): $5. There are night classes in public speaking and parliamentary procedure, labor ethics and law, in economics and trade union methods. Xavier's volunteer faculty (three lawyers, ten union officers, two businessmen and the two priests) translates its subjects into down-to-earth problems. Students study contracts, sample constitutions, hold mock conventions and negotiation meetings. Sometimes, actual union problems come before their "grievance clinics," with representatives of management on hand to talk things over with the union. Since 1936, Xavier has turned out 6,000 alumni from the big, sprawling schoolbuilding on West 16th Street.[5]

The Catholics weren't the only ones actively supporting workers organizing unions during this union expansion period. The Presbyterians organized the Labor Temple in New York City. The Methodists supported mineworkers in their rural congregations. The Congregationalists trained, and the Episcopalians nurtured Frances Perkins (Chapter 8 describes her life in some detail). The Jewish Workmen's Circle organized Labor Lyceums. (See more on the Catholic labor schools and the Workmen's Circle in Chapter 7.) African American ministers E.B. McKinney and Owen Whitfield led efforts to organize Mississippi Delta sharecroppers into the Southern Tenant Farmers Union (STFU).

The engagement of the religious community in supporting workers' efforts to organize unions extended to a broad range of religious bodies—Catholic, Protestant, Evangelical, Jewish, and others. Why did unions receive such extensive religious support? Unions were seen as effective vehicles through which workers could improve their wages, benefits, and working conditions. Unions were an effective way to stop wage theft and lift workers and their families out of poverty.

In 2011, governors and legislators in many states waged attacks on workers' rights to organize under the guise of budget cuts. The fundamental rights of workers to organize unions and engage in collective bargaining had been challenged. This is indeed a moment to understand and recognize the important contributions unions make in stopping wage theft and raising standards for all workers.

Unions Stop Wage Theft

Unions are still the best and most effective vehicle for stopping wage theft, for the following reasons:

Unions train workers about their rights in the workplace. As was explained in Chapter 4, the basic laws protecting workers are confusing, and consequently most workers are unsure about their rights and where to turn for help. Unions train local leaders about their rights in the workplace. When workers know the laws and their rights, they are much more vigorous advocates on their own behalf.

Unions have attorneys available to answer questions and file lawsuits. Whenever questions about the legality of some payment arrangement arise, unionized workers can ask their union's attorneys to answer questions. If problems can't be resolved at the worksite, the attorneys help workers file claims, grievances, or lawsuits.

Unions provide workers a structure for expressing concerns. With a union contract comes a structure for addressing problems in the workplace. Usually, each workplace has one or more shop stewards who support workers in addressing problems in their workplace. If workers aren't being paid correctly, the shop stewards will work with the workers to make sure problems are corrected through a grievance procedure.

Unions protect workers who complain. One reason many workers don't file complaints with government agencies about problems on the worksite, even if they know there is a legal violation, is that they are fearful that their employers will retaliate against them. Because union contracts outline clear procedures for how workers can and can't be fired and for how unions will challenge unfair practices, workers feel safe about raising concerns.

Unions create a counterbalance to management's control in the workplace. In most workplaces without a contract, workers have little real power to influence decisions. Unions create a counterbalance to management's control. When employers steal wages, or are tempted to steal wages, unions challenge them and hold them accountable to paying workers based both on the labor laws and the contract. If situations aren't clear, they will usually get clarified in the next contract negotiations.

Unions maintain relationships with community allies and resources. Unions usually have relationships with newspaper reporters, social service agencies, religious organizations, politicians, and others who can join workers in pressuring their employers (if needed) to do the right thing.

Industries that have high percentages of workers represented by unions (referred to as high "union density") almost never have significant wage theft problems. The unions aggressively enforce their contracts and enforce the nation's labor laws. Unions provide a strong "pushback" force against the forces that might be tempted to steal wages.

How Else Do Unions Help Workers?

In addition to stopping wage theft, unions play important roles in improving working conditions for workers. Unions help workers secure the following:[6]

Better wages. Workers in unions earn more money than workers doing the exact same job in nonunionized workplaces. According to the Bureau of Labor Statistics, in 2010 the union pay advantage was 28 percent higher for all workers, and it is even larger for people of color and women. Janitors in Chicago and janitors in Houston were doing the same jobs for the same companies, but unionized janitors earned twice as much.

Benefits. Unionized workers are more likely to have health insurance. Union members are also more likely to have health plans that include dental, prescriptions, and eyeglass coverage. In 2010, 84 percent of union workers were covered by health insurance through their jobs, compared with only 55 percent of nonunion workers.[7] Many unions are fighting to preserve or establish affordable co-payments for health insurance.

Unionized workers are more likely to have short-term disability benefits as well. Janitors in Houston would never have had health care without the union.

Retirement benefits. Unionized workers are more likely to have retirement benefits. Most union members, 87 percent, have a pension plan, compared to 49 percent of nonunion workers.[8]

A voice in decisions. All workers want to be involved in decisions that affect their working lives, and yet many find themselves and their suggestions routinely ignored or rejected. Workers want to do good quality work, and they often use their union contracts as a way to improve the overall quality of work provided. The early labor guilds were formed in order to improve members' quality of work, and those values still hold in the building trades unions. Teachers often bargain over ways to improve the quality of teaching for children. Nurses bargain over patient care. Public sector workers bargain over how to serve their clients or the public better.

Workers want a voice in decisions about work, but many feel that they are denied the right to talk and think when they enter the workplace. Too often, management, which controls workers' basic livelihood, discourages workers' participation in the company decision-making process. This is especially frustrating to workers when issues such as the scheduling of hours, workloads, and ways to make the work more effective are decided. Unions help workers have a voice in the decisions.

Safe working environments. If you work in a place where workers routinely get injured or some have even been killed, you will probably want a union to help negotiate safe working conditions. Take the case of those whose jobs involve working in trenches—working in manholes or any confined space below ground level. Between 1985 and 1995, 522 workers in the United States were killed in trench-related mishaps, only 60 of whom worked for union shops. The other 462 were employed by nonunionized firms.[9] Recent tragedies in nonunion coal mines also highlight the stark difference in safety standards between union and nonunion shops. In 2006, twelve miners died from an explosion at the Sago mine, owned by the nonunion firm, International Coal Group. The company was cited by the Mine Safety Health Administration for multiple violations, but got away by paying just $24,000 in fines. A union presence would have helped ensure that safety standards were met. In 2010, twenty-nine miners died at a Massey-owned nonunion mine that had repeatedly had health and safety violations. Had these miners been represented by a union, they would have been better able to refuse to work in dangerous conditions. A union in the mine would probably have saved those miners.

Job security. As companies outsource, downsize, and shift from permanent to contingent employees, workers have grown concerned about their job security. People want assurance that companies won't outsource their jobs to some cheaper group, another state, or even another country. Unions can't guarantee complete job security, but contracts negotiated by unions attempt to create some job protections when at all possible. In addition, unions protect workers from bosses who fire workers without cause. Almost all states in the nation are "at will" states, meaning that workers can be fired for any reason that isn't protected under various laws. So you can't be fired for being a certain faith or a certain race, but you can be fired because the boss doesn't like your "attitude" or you didn't come to work when your child was sick, for example. Union contracts ensure that there is "just cause" and a fair process before firing someone.

Fairness. Workers want to know what the rules are, what the consequences are for breaking those rules, and what the appeal (grievance) process is for alleged rule violations. Some personnel policies clearly outline them. Most don't. Too often workers follow the policies while the employers do not. Without a personnel policy that acts as a binding contract, or a union contract that makes the rules and procedures clear, workers feel, and often are, vulnerable to the whims of supervisors. Promotions, raises, penalties, and dismissals often seem random and unfair. Minorities and women benefit from union contracts that enshrine nondiscrimination language and ensure that all union members, no matter their race or gender, are paid, promoted, and treated based on their abilities to do the job.

Are Unions Perfect?

I have never given a presentation about religion–labor partnerships or about wage theft and not been asked a question about problems with unions. Let me share the typical questions and some of my responses.[10]

AREN'T UNIONS CORRUPT? Unions, like religious bodies, are made up of human beings with all their flaws and frailties. There is some corruption in unions, as there is some within religious institutions. We also know from the near financial meltdown in 2008 that there is greed and corruption on Wall Street. Wherever corruption or greed is uncovered, it must be cleaned up. For that purpose, most unions have rigorous procedures to combat corruption. When a local union is found to be corrupt, the national leadership will take over control until it can be cleaned up and an election of new leaders held. As wrong as union corruption is, it is unfortunate that it receives so much front-page media attention in comparison to the important justice work done by unions to improve wages, benefits, and working conditions for workers in low-wage jobs. By the way, did you see the stories about the Presbyterian treasurer who stole money, or the Episcopal treasurer who stole $2 million, or the National Baptist president who stole $102,000? Corruption is part of the human condition and is neither unique nor even particularly prevalent in unions.

The perception of unions as corrupt is reinforced by many mainstream newspapers that refer to union leaders as union "bosses," using a mob connotation, even though union leadership is mostly democratically elected by union members. Most of the union leaders I know are hardworking, ethical men and women who are seeking to improve conditions for their members and other workers in society. Corporate CEOs aren't called corporate bosses by the press, so why should union leaders be given that name?

AREN'T UNIONS VIOLENT? Unions advocate legal and peaceful means for achieving social gains. All national union leaders abhor violence and teach their members to practice and preach nonviolence. Nonetheless, when workers are locked out, their jobs are moved overseas, or their economic livelihood is threatened, a handful of workers may act out their anger in inappropriate ways. Unions do not condone or in any manner support the behavior of a handful of workers who may resort to violence. Despite knowing that unions don't condone violence, when union-busting consultants want to denigrate unions, they describe them as violent and show photos of violence on a picket line. Violence is wrong, whether it involves workers on a picket line, security guards harassing picketers, or companies causing economic violence (stealing wages) against workers.

AREN'T UNIONS RACIST OR SEXIST? Like corruption, racism and sexism are sins shared by unions, the religious community, and the society at large. A key goal of the leadership of the AFL-CIO and Change to Win is ensuring full participation for all in work, in society, and in unions. Although work still needs to be done, the AFL-CIO has made significant progress in making its leadership more closely reflect its membership. Part of this may be due to a change the AFL-CIO made to its constitution, which was meant to significantly develop the race and gender diversity of its leadership. Upon its establishment in 2005, Change to Win instituted three positions on its leadership council specifically designed to further race and gender diversity on the council.

DON'T UNIONS DRIVE COMPANIES OVERSEAS? Unions themselves do not drive companies overseas. Nonetheless, it is true that companies often choose to move to other countries or other parts of the United States in search of lower wages and more vulnerable workers. Manufacturing firms and increasingly service and financial firms that operate in the global economy often look for alternative production locations where labor or resource costs are lower. Unions are very sensitive to industry concerns about competitiveness because they want jobs to stay with their members. As a result, most unions are willing to bargain around ways to keep a company competitive, but the unions must also be convinced that the company is willing to invest in its workers and to invest in adequate research and product design.

Why Aren't Unions Stronger?

Given the crisis of wage theft in the nation and the effective role unions play in stopping wage theft, one would think that unions would be growing by leaps and bounds. In fact, many workers would like to have a union in their workplace—53 percent of all working Americans who are not currently represented by unions would vote to join a union if they had the opportunity to do so without risking their jobs.[11] However, many workers are afraid.

Whenever I am speaking with a group about unions, I always ask, "What would happen if you tried to organize a union at your workplace?" Every single time the response is the same: "I would get fired." Whether or not it is true that someone would get fired, the collective wisdom and understanding in the society is that if you try to organize a union, you will get fired. Needless to say, this puts a decided chill on organizing. Who can afford to lose a job unexpectedly?

The weak laws alone are bad enough for those who choose to organize. Adding insult to injury, a sophisticated, multimillion dollar industry has developed to consult and advise employers on how to oppose unions and frighten workers. More than 80 percent of companies faced with union organizing efforts hire these consultants and law firms to wage antiunion campaigns. No other industrialized nation has such a powerful union-busting industry or weaker labor protections.

U.S. labor law related to unions is mainly governed by the NLRA and the Taft-Hartley amendments. The original NLRA was passed in 1935 to improve workers' living standards by increasing the power of unions. Over the course of the next sixty-five years, the intent of the law has been changed through amendments to the Act, and various judicial and administrative decisions have weakened the unions. The Taft-Hartley amendments to the NLRA, passed in 1947, increased managers' abilities to oppose unions. The amendments permitted the employers to campaign against union representation as long as there was "no threat of reprisal or force or promise of benefit." Workers repeatedly express feeling under attack when employers oppose unions.

What happens to workers who attempt to organize?

1. Ninety-one percent of employers require employees to attend a one-on-one meeting with their supervisors where they are told why unions are bad and why they should vote against a union.
2. Fifty-one percent of employers illegally coerce union opposition through bribes and favors.
3. Thirty percent of employers illegally fire pro-union employees.

4. Forty-nine percent of employers illegally threaten to eliminate all workers' jobs if they join a union.[12]

Most of this antiunion activity occurs after the workers have signed cards indicating they want to be represented by a union and before the official NLRB-supervised election. If the point of an election is to determine what workers really want, then it would seem that both sides—union and management—should be able to present their cases fairly. But given the laws, the antiunion campaigns, and the control that employers have over workers' lives, the cases are not presented evenly. In effect, the time between signing union cards and holding an election appears to be a time to scare workers into voting against unions. Given how demoralizing the current system is for most workers, some unions have begun avoiding NLRB-supervised elections altogether and instead pressuring companies just to recognize the union based on the signed cards.

Given the organized workplace opposition to unions and the historically lax enforcement of the NLRB, as well as the societal shift from manufacturing jobs (highly unionized sectors) to service jobs (fewer sectors organized), union membership dropped to less than 12 percent of workers in 2010.[13] More public sector workers (7.6 million) now belong to unions than private sector workers (7.1 million),[14] which is why many worker advocates believe that there have been such virulent attacks on public sector workers in 2011.

Whether there is an NLRB-supervised election, card-check recognition, or a community-sponsored election, the principles of fairness and respect for one another must be maintained by all parties, employees and employers alike.

Unions Helping Fight Wage Theft

Unions, recognizing the crisis of wage theft facing workers, are stepping up their efforts to help workers understand wage payment laws and recover underpaid wages. The issue of wage theft is serving as a galvanizing issue around which to organize new workers into unions.

The International Brotherhood of Teamsters (called just "Teamsters") started an ambitious organizing program in 2006 and since then more than thirty-five thousand school bus drivers have joined the union. Most school bus drivers are women and a large percentage are people of color who work part-time and are paid ridiculously low wages for important work—transporting our children to and from school. Many school bus drivers and monitors are routinely cheated out of their wages.

The wage theft of school bus drivers' wages happens in several common ways. The most common form of wage theft is that workers are not paid for all the time they actually work, such as the time it takes to fuel and clean the bus or the time it takes a driver to inspect the bus before and after the trip.

Phillis Hodo started work for Jones Bus in Grayslake, Illinois, in 2004, working 42.5 hours a week driving school buses. In the hours in between runs, she put her previous experience running her own construction business to good use, keeping the facility safe and clean, helping to repair buses, and on Saturdays washing the bus exteriors and cleaning the interiors.

When Durham School Services purchased Jones Bus in October 2005 it stopped paying for her work in between school runs, leaving Phillis on greatly reduced wages. When she complained, the General Manager asked her to transfer to another depot in Lake Villa, promising a guaranteed 45 hours a week, working to the previous agreement.

Phillis was a "standby driver" filling in for missing drivers and certified to drive all types of buses, including those for special needs children and covering all the hundred or so routes operated by the depot.

Phillis soon found, however, that she was being worked 50 to 60 hours a week, often missing out on her lunch breaks. To make matters worse, she was told that she would not be paid for the work in excess of 45 hours but would have to "bank" those hours, taking them as paid time off. This agreement continued for several years until Phillis was abruptly informed in 2009 that she could no longer bank hours and would have to be paid up what she was owed. Despite working long hours for several years, and just using one day of banked hours, she was told that she only had *nine* banked hours owed to her.

Phillis realized that not only had she been "robbed" of hours, but that her worked lunch break hours had not been banked, and all the time over 40 hours had not been calculated as overtime. In desperation she called the company's human resources manager, who asked her to be patient while her claim was investigated. The initial result, though, was an immediate reduction in her hours from a guaranteed 45 to just 20 hours and the loss of all summer school vacation driving in 2009.

The effect on Phillis was devastating—forcing her to live on just $200 weekly. She was unable to afford the near-$100 a week required for single-person healthcare insurance.

After waiting for nine months, Phillis finally approached the Illinois Department of Labor, which recovered $6,300 owed to her from 2008. But as Phillis says, "I gave the company an opportunity to make good on their promises to me. Now I have to fight a legal battle to try and recover the outstanding two-and-a-half-years wages stolen from me by Durham School services."[15]

The Teamsters are helping workers understand how much money bus companies are stealing from them and helping them recover it. The Teamsters have developed a wage-hour survey and workers from fifteen different bus yards have completed the surveys. The surveys ask a variety of questions about working hours and conditions, including questions designed to identify wage theft. The Teamsters are helping workers get the legal help they need to file wage claims and lawsuits to recover the back wages and stop wage theft in the future. In labor contracts, the Teamsters are making sure that contract language addresses situations that rob workers of their hard-earned wages. For further information about organizing efforts, visit www.schoolbusworkers united.org.

The International Brotherhood of Electrical Workers (IBEW) is organizing satellite dish installers. There are only two satellite dish companies in the nation, Dish Network and DIRECTV. For the most part, neither of these companies directly hires workers who install the satellite dishes, but they clearly structure the entire industry. Both companies have a network of regional providers who actually do the installation, although on DIRECTV's website, it refers to the people doing the installation as "our" installers, even though only a small percentage actually work directly for DIRECTV.

The regional installation companies are squeezed by the two big highly profitable conglomerates, and then they in turn squeeze their workers.

Satellite installation is tough physical labor. Workers climb up ladders, across roofs, and are in and out of trucks throughout the day. Until IBEW began organizing workers and encouraging the U.S. Department of Labor's Wage and Hour Division to investigate, Star West Satellite, one of the regional installation companies for Dish Network, paid workers by piece rate (which is legal), but provided no overtime for hours over 40 (which is not legal). In fact, according to IBEW organizer Bob Brock, the company simply prepared workers' timesheets to show that each worker took an hour off for lunch and then only worked 40 hours each week. In reality, workers didn't take time out for lunch. And in the summer, workers often worked from 7 A.M. till well after 9 P.M., 14-hour days, five days a week—that's 70 hours, not 40 hours, per week. Most installers in Montana and Idaho earn around $25,000 per year. Brock estimates that the workers lose about $10,000 per year in unpaid overtime. "Installers in Montana are all native-born workers," says Brock, "but the treatment isn't much better than immigrant janitors receive."[16]

IBEW is helping workers keep track of all the hours they work, filing complaints with the U.S. Department of Labor and organizing workers to demand that they be paid for all their hours. For more information about the campaign, visit www.satellitechs.org.

The American Federation of State, County and Municipal Employees (AFSCME) represents primarily public sector workers. Unfortunately, sometimes there is even wage theft within government agencies. In Arkansas, prison guards have organized their own AFSCME local to address workplace problems. Across the nation, prison guard jobs are solid middle-class jobs: workers earn approximately $40,000 per year. Unlike for most workers, hours are figured on an 80-hour period over two weeks, instead of a 40-hour workweek, in order to give the prison management more flexibility in scheduling. Workers are paid a regular hourly wage for the first 80 hours. For hours 81 through 86, workers are paid the regular hourly rate and the pay is "banked," and then (at least theoretically) workers can either get paid for the time or collect the time in comp time. For hours 87 and up, workers are paid time-and-a-half overtime pay.

In the last few years, because of staff shortages, most guards have worked holidays and extra hours, so the state has been "banking" lots of money for the workers. When workers tried to get the "banked" money, they couldn't get it. In 2011, AFSCME helped the correctional guards attend a state hearing to push the state to pay workers the $16.1 million they were owed. They managed to get a commitment of $1.4 million from the Department of Corrections to begin paying off the debt owed to workers. AFSCME has pledged to keep fighting for the workers' pay.[17]

Unions Are Vital to Society

The above efforts are typical of what unions do and have always done. They show that unions are vitally needed in U.S. society. When unions represent most workers in an industry, wage theft is virtually eliminated. Given the prevalence of wage theft, it would be useful if all workers in the garment industry, poultry plants, nursing homes, agriculture, restaurants, hotels, and retail stores were represented by unions. Many unions are focusing their organizing efforts on workers in these industries. Their campaigns are worthy of support.

Unions and collective bargaining contracts are one of the best ways to help U.S. families reach the American dream of middle-class wages, benefits, and working conditions. In the past, unions have turned low-paying, sweatshop jobs in manufacturing and construction into good-paying middle-class jobs. This effort is still needed in manufacturing and construction and must be extended to retail jobs as well. Unions help companies share their wealth with the workers who help create the wealth.

Unions also improve working conditions for large groups of workers by advocating laws that set national standards and by promoting the general welfare of all workers. Unions are leading advocates for national health care, paid sick days, pension protections, and a host of other standards that would improve conditions for Americans.

The Israelites in Egypt needed to organize. Mercedes Herrerra in

Houston needed a union. Phillis Hodo needed a union. Millions of workers around the nation need protection against wage theft.

There is no better vehicle for protecting against wage theft than unions. If you want to fight poverty, encourage unions. If you want to improve your life at work, join unions. If you want to stop wage theft, support unions.

7

Workers' Centers:
Front Lines against Wage Theft

Who rises up for me against the wicked? Who stands up for me against evildoers?

—Psalm 94:16 (NRSV)

In this prayer for deliverance, the Psalmist is asking God for help in fighting injustice. Workers' centers are a front-line defense against the modern-day injustice of wage theft. Workers' centers serve as worker-led organizing groups that can challenge an entire industry's treatment of workers. They offer a hands-on way that advocates, people of faith, unions, and social service agencies can stand with and support workers who are not represented by unions. Workers' centers can also be a valuable outreach and enforcement partner with government labor agencies.

Agata and Elzbieta[1] started working at Bright Star Cleaning Service in June 2006. The job was a "live-in" arrangement. They both lived in the same room and were charged $300 per month *each* for rent and utilities. The two women shared a small room with only a closet, a small chest of drawers, and two beds. They also shared a bathroom, with one toilet and one sink, with six other women who lived on the same floor. There was another building with eight other women who worked for Bright Star Cleaning Service.

At the beginning of their employment, Agata and Elzbieta were required to attend training for which they never got paid (an illegality). Every day they were driven to various houses by the employer or by a driver employed by the service. They would leave their dormitory around 7:00 A.M. and return between 5:00 and 6:00 P.M. They cleaned two to three houses per day. They worked with hazardous chemicals, but didn't know if they needed any protection. They usually worked six days a week, for 10 to 11 hours a day. On Saturdays, they worked a shorter day. They were always paid a flat rate of $7 per hour, no matter how many hours they worked throughout the week (another illegality). Agata and Elzbieta claim there was only one week in which they worked less than 49 hours, and they were never paid for overtime.

When Agata and Elzbieta quit in September 2006, they were not paid for their last week's work, nor were they paid several months' worth of overtime. Agata and Elzbieta had kept detailed notes on all their work. They repeatedly contacted their employer to receive their money, but the employer avoided any contact with them.

In January 2007 after making many attempts to get their final paycheck, the women sought help at the Arise Chicago Workers' Center from Anka, the young woman whose first job was at a car wash (see Chapter 5). Initially, Anka sent the employer a letter on behalf of the former employees requesting the workers' unpaid wages. The employer ignored the letter. Several weeks later in February, Anka mailed letters to customers using the services of Bright Star Cleaning Service asking them not to use the company until the employer paid Agata and Elzbieta.

March 2007 was a busy month. Early in the month, Anka talked with the employer. She admitted that she did not pay Agata and Elzbieta, and for this she offered three reasons: (1) They were her friends and they had "special arrangements"; (2) Agata and Elzbieta should have been more grateful for a job and place to live—in fact, perhaps they should really have paid her for helping them get settled in a new country; and (3) Agata and Elzbieta were independent contractors and not eligible for overtime. The employer offered to meet with the former employees as long as no one else was present. Agata and Elzbieta refused to meet with her unless there was at least one witness.

Because things seemed stalled, Anka contacted the Wage and Hour liaison with the Chicago Area Worker Rights Initiative, a government and community partnership that Arise Chicago had helped convene. An official complaint for the last paycheck was filed with the Illinois Department of Labor, and a complaint about health and safety issues was filed with OSHA.

Instead of paying the workers their money, the employer hired an attorney who sent a letter accusing Anka of "unlawful actions" and threatening a libel suit. A volunteer attorney with the workers' center sent a response letter explaining that "truth is an absolute defense against the claim of defamation."

At the end of March, the employer decided she would pay the workers. She brought the checks over to the workers' center and gave them to Agata and Elzbieta, who subsequently dropped the charges with the Illinois Department of Labor. Meanwhile, the OSHA complaint was forwarded to the Aurora office for processing. The employer, who was clearly still angry—perhaps because of the OSHA complaint—left a threatening voice mail on the workers' cell phones after she paid the money.

Anka also checked to see if Bright Star Cleaning Service had workers' compensation coverage, as required by law. The company had only gotten it as of February 2007 and so did not have it the previous summer when sixteen cleaning women had been working for it.

Finally in June 2007, the employer agreed to pay an OSHA penalty of $420 for failing to provide information about hazardous chemicals or training in how to use the hazardous chemicals, and for not keeping safety data sheets.

The workers got their money, and the employer finally purchased workers' compensation insurance. Perhaps the employer will be a bit more careful about chemicals in the future (although it is doubtful that $420 is much of an incentive to do the right thing). The workers learned that they could get employers to pay their wages. Agata and Elzbieta now work for themselves. They still work hard, but nobody takes advantage of them. They have both become members and active leaders in the workers' center, helping other women like themselves.

Workers' Centers Build on Historic Labor Support Efforts

Even though the current versions of workers' centers are relatively new models for helping workers who are being exploited in the workplace, the idea of safe centers where immigrants and native-born low-wage workers can get help and learn organizing skills is not new. Workers' centers are in the long tradition of community and labor centers that support workers challenging wage theft and other forms of exploitation and advocating unions, ethical legislation, and public understanding of worker issues.

SETTLEMENT HOUSES: The settlement houses established at the turn of the twentieth century were early versions of workers' centers. According to Kathryn Kish Sklar, more than one hundred settlement houses, like the famous Hull House in Chicago, helped immigrant workers in urban areas. Like the workers' centers of today, the settlement houses offered educational programs for immigrants, directly challenged unjust employers (and landlords), advocated and passed progressive legislative initiatives, and connected middle-class people of conscience with immigrants struggling to make ends meet.

Jane Addams of Hull House is the best-known settlement house leader, but an equally important reformer from Hull House was Addams's colleague, Florence Kelley. In 1893, Kelley was appointed the first chief factory inspector of Illinois. With a team of twelve investigators, Kelley publicized factory working conditions and then helped lobby for the nation's first legislation limiting women and children to 8 hours of work per day, although the bill was soon overturned. The Illinois Association of Manufacturers was formed in 1894 with the sole purpose of repealing the law.[2] Kelley then became the first executive secretary of the National Consumers League, which mobilized public support for labor legislation, and she was the woman who introduced Frances Perkins to labor issues when Kelley spoke at Mount Holyoke College, where Perkins was studying.

Some of these settlement houses still exist today. Most have become large social service agencies, serving both immigrants and other low-income families. They conduct English as a second language (ESL) classes and general educational development (GED) classes, run Head Start programs, and operate soup kitchens and shelters. A few, such as Erie House, helped start workers' centers, which then became independent entities, reclaiming the early work of the settlement houses.

LABOR LYCEUMS AND THE (JEWISH) WORKMEN'S CIRCLE: The Workmen's Circle became a national organization (with three New York chapters) in 1900. It was organized for mutual aid and education for Jewish immigrants and for social justice for the broader society.[3] By 1910, it had 450 branches that ran a variety of programs, including Sunday schools for children, cultural groups such as choirs and orchestras, and insurance programs (death, funeral, burial, and health care insurance).[4] The Workmen's Circles were instrumental in developing many of the nation's *labor lyceums*. These lyceums, built or rented by the Workmen's Circle chapters, were centers where labor unions and workers met for education and planning on labor issues. Given the strong Jewish immigrant involvement, the lyceums were decidedly pro-immigrant. More than one hundred communities had labor lyceums by 1925,[5] which were clearly forerunners of the current workers' centers.

Although the Workmen's Circle still exists, it no longer organizes labor lyceums or workers' centers. According to the website (www. circle.org), "The Workmen's Circle/Arbeter Ring fosters Jewish identity and participation in Jewish life through Jewish, especially Yiddish, culture and education, friendship, and the pursuit of social and economic justice."[6]

THE CATHOLIC LABOR SCHOOLS: From the 1930s through the 1960s, Catholic parishes, dioceses, orders, and universities sponsored Labor Schools. In a May 17, 1945, letter to James Carty of Chicago Theological Seminary, the Reverend George Higgins (later made monsignor) explains the purposes of the Catholic Labor Schools as "a) to teach Catholic social ethics as expounded in the social encyclicals of the Popes b) to teach certain allied subjects of a more secular nature which will put the ethics course in its proper context and will enable the students to participate in union affairs in a more intelligent and more enlightened way: for example, labor history, labor legislation, collective bargaining, parliamentary laws and public speaking, etc."[7] These schools were clearly designed to strengthen Catholic involvement in the labor movement. They had the solid support of the church leadership, as demonstrated by the letter Father John Ryan sent to Catholic colleges in the country in 1936 asking them to organize Catholic Labor Schools. According to newspaper articles from the period, there were more than one hundred Catholic Labor Schools (see Chapter 5), but I suspect it was closer to two hundred. (See Appendix C for a list of 140 parishes and sites that operated Catholic Labor Schools.) The list was compiled from files in the "workers' center" box at the American Catholic History Research Center and University Archives.[8]

There are two remaining workers' centers that are direct descendants of these Catholic Labor Schools. The Labor Guild in Boston is the only continuously running Catholic Labor School in the nation. The Labor Guild's website describes the group's history: "In the early 1940's members of the machinists and IBEW unions from Watertown Arsenal formed an association called the '409' Club. This group enlisted the help first of a Jesuit priest and then of Archdiocesan priests to give lectures on labor matters. This educational effort was interrupted by the war, but in 1946 the group reunited and gained the approval of the new Archbishop Cushing to form the Catholic Labor Guild of the Archdiocese of Boston. Fr. Joseph A Robinson was named Chaplain. Meetings were held in various parish sites. This newly formed Catholic Labor Guild held Communion Breakfasts and several classes in Public Speaking and Parliamentary Procedure."[9] From 1970 to 2007, Father Ed Boyle, a Jesuit priest known for his support for workers and unions, served as the Labor Guild's chaplain. Father Pat Sullivan is its current executive secretary.

The other direct descendant of Catholic Labor Schools is the Comey Institute of Industrial Relations, which is an outreach program of Saint Joseph's University. In 1943, Reverend Dennis J. Comey, S.J., founded the Saint Joseph's Institute of Industrial Relations in Philadelphia to support workers in Philadelphia's manufacturing sector. Later renamed after him, the Institute still provides training, applied research services, and technical assistance to Delaware Valley workers and their organizations.[10]

FARM WORKER SERVICE CENTERS: Low wages, dangerous working conditions, poor housing and transportation, and child labor have long characterized farm work in the United States. The National Farm Worker Ministry was established in 1920 to engage the religious community in helping farm workers. Although its early work focused primarily on providing social services, the mission for the work matured and recognized the power of standing with and supporting farm workers when they organized and fought for justice. The farm workers and the religious community partnered in developing farm worker service centers where farm workers could learn their rights and new skills, connect with attorneys for filing wage claims, organize with one another to challenge injustice in the fields, and advocate more just policies.

The United Farm Workers Service Center began in 1966 to provide working families with services that would enrich their lives and serve to meet crucial community needs. The service center and related programs that it developed provide housing, education, workers rights and immigrant rights training, and other needed programs. The Coalition of Immokalee Workers operates a strong and active service center in Immokalee, Florida. Pineros y Campesinos Unidos del Noroeste (PCUN) operates a service center in Woodburn, Oregon. The Farm Labor Organizing Committee (FLOC) operates service centers in North Carolina and Ohio. In addition, independent farm worker service centers that are essentially workers' centers have been established in many communities around the nation. All these centers do work similar to that of the new workers' center movement.

The Workers' Center Movement Today

Today's workers' centers have emerged out of a long line of social reformers, faith-based worker advocates, and immigrant-led centers. Nonetheless, there is a new upswing in the development and expansion of centers focused on stopping wage theft and improving working conditions. These centers have sprung forth rapidly, in large part due to the national epidemic of wage theft, the relative weakness of unions in society today, and the failure of the Department of Labor to protect workers. Often struggling to fill the gap on a shoestring, workers' centers play important roles in the community. For the most comprehensive and thoughtful description and history of the workers' centers, be sure to read *Workers' Centers: Organizing Communities at the Edge of the Dream* by Janice Fine.[11] In 2006, Fine identified 137 workers' centers, although more form every year. (A list of organizations that help workers with wage theft problems, including workers' centers, is in Appendix D.)

The largest number of workers' centers are affiliated with the National Day Labor Organizing Network (NDLON).[12] These centers serve primarily day laborers. The second largest network of workers' centers is coordinated by IWJ.[13] These centers are known for their connections with both the labor and religious communities. A third network of workers' centers is coordinated by Enlace, which works in the United States, Mexico, China, Indonesia, and some European nations.[14] National People's Action and Jobs with Justice both have some workers' centers affiliated with them. Some workers' centers are not affiliated with any network and operate completely independently.

In the last few years, several new sector-based networks have emerged. Restaurant Opportunities Centers United (ROC United) has workers' centers in eight locations that are addressing concerns faced by restaurant workers. Domestic Workers United is a network of immigrant domestic worker organizations in New York that came together in 2000 and passed the Domestic Workers Bill of Rights in 2010. The organization is now building ties with other groups around the nation organizing domestic workers.

In some cities, like Boston, San Francisco, Los Angeles, and Chicago that have multiple workers' centers, the centers have joined in informal networks to coordinate their efforts within the cities. There is an enormous amount of crossover between centers and networks, all trying to learn from one another and push forward standards for workers in the society.

In addition, there are a dozen or so legal clinics that focus primarily on worker issues and view their work more like workers' centers. They were generally started by attorneys, but the staff understands the need to involve workers in creating solutions, complement legal strategies with direct action approaches, and engage the broader community in policy changes.

The core mission and work of workers' centers is to help workers improve conditions in their workplaces. They address both what is legal in the workplace and what is just. The centers accomplish their mission by:

Educating workers about their rights and organizing skills. Given the mishmash of laws that exist (see Chapter 4), all centers conduct worker rights education programs in multiple languages. They also train workers in core organizing skills, such as how to develop strategies and appropriate tactics for challenging illegal and unjust behavior in the workplace. These training sessions, usually conducted utilizing popular education methodologies, are held in the centers themselves, in congregations, in social service agencies, on street corners, and in union halls.

In the fall of 2004, a workers' rights advocate was conducting a series of workshops in Chicago's South Side. Immediately after a 3-hour-long session, a worker approached the advocate to inquire about what the law had to say about someone who had been severely burned on the job. When the advocate asked what happened, the worker lifted his left shirt sleeve to reveal what appeared to be a third-degree burn. The advocate, amazed that the worker had patiently sat through the entire presentation, immediately drove the worker to the emergency room. The next day a group of workers from the same workplace came to the workers' center. They reported that they were not being paid overtime and not being paid for all hours worked, and they were also asked to do dangerous tasks without proper equipment, including asbestos removal and electrical work in flooded basements. Workers had been injured but didn't know they had any recourse. When the workers heard their options, they immediately decided to file complaints with OSHA, the Wage and Hour Division of the Department of Labor, and EEOC. Using their newly learned organizing skills, they also engaged in work stoppages and mobilized community support to pressure the employer, a well-connected real estate mogul, to stop breaking the law and do the right thing. After less than a week, the employer signed an agreement promising to obey all workplace laws dealing with paying people, keeping workers safe, and not discriminating, and he also agreed to raise wages and offer health insurance. Through knowing their rights and learning organizing skills, the workers addressed both the illegal workplace behavior (wage theft and injuring workers) and the unjust treatment (low wages without benefits).[15]

Confronting employers who have stolen wages. Workers' centers have learned that one of the fastest ways to recover workers' wages is to confront employers directly. In August 2007, Francisco was fired from Outdoor Escapes, a landscaping company where he had worked for four months. On the day he was fired, he asked for his unpaid overtime pay. His employer told him, "We don't pay overtime."

Francisco went to the CTUL workers' center in the Twin Cities to see how he could retrieve his stolen wages. Francisco had carefully kept all his check stubs showing that he had been paid regular wages for all of the 15 to 20 overtime hours he had worked each and every week. CTUL's staff and Francisco began by analyzing what power or leverage the worker and allies had to make the employer pay the back wages and made a plan together.

First, Francisco and the CTUL staff wrote a letter to the employer informing him that if the wages weren't paid within ten days, the group would take further action and the employer would begin to accumulate default wages. Minnesota law states that if wages are owed to a worker and the worker is fired and asks for his or her money, the employer has 24 hours to pay the wages or else default wages can accumulate using the average day's pay for up to fifteen days.

When the employer did not respond, the workers' center staff called him to make sure he had received the letter and asked to negotiate with him. The employer claimed that Francisco had damaged some property on the job so he wasn't going to pay him.

Workers' centers always try to move problems from an individual to a collective level. Francisco talked with other workers who had also worked many overtime hours and not gotten paid. Several workers who had been employed for over four years were interested in getting their back wages and showed up at an organizing meeting. When the employer heard that many workers were claiming they were owed overtime wages, he called to indicate his interest in negotiating.

Initially, the employer sent a check for Francisco's overtime hours, but it did not include the default wages. Nor would the employer discuss paying the overtime owed other workers. Francisco said it was not enough.

Together, the group of workers decided to contact Outdoor Excapes' clients about the company's refusal to pay overtime. The workers sent letters to clients, with copies to the employer, and asked them to call the employer. The employer called demanding that they stop sending the letters and indicating that his attorney would be in touch.

After several conversations with his lawyer, another round of letters to more clients, and mediation, Outdoor Excapes paid all the workers what they were owed—over $40,000 in overtime back wages plus the default wages. Even more important, the employer now pays overtime to all workers.[16]

Filing complaints with government agencies. Workers' centers help workers navigate the alphabet soup of government agencies (Department of Labor, OSHA, EEOC) and know where and how to file complaints. Sometimes they also push government agencies to take workers' cases.

A group of workers came in to the Northwest Arkansas Workers' Center from Christian Brothers, a well-known construction company. The owner provided all workers with social security numbers and was not paying taxes on these fake numbers. Some workers were paid for their work, but others were not. Those who were paid had money deducted from their checks for "workers' comp insurance" (employers are required to pay this, not workers). The workers decided to file charges through the Department of Labor's Wage and Hour Division. The local staff member hesitated to investigate the case because of the "amount of time it would take to calculate how many hours the employer owed the workers." Quickly thereafter the workers' center organized workers to file charges together in small groups and personally walk into the Wage and Hour office in Bentonville. The staff was persuaded to initiate an investigation and was assisted step-by-step by the workers' center staff. In the end workers got back over $100,000 in back wages.[17]

Holding government agencies accountable. Workers' centers try to tap into all the existing resources and agencies that can help workers. As a result, they often end up realizing how agencies are failing to use the power they have and failing to create systems that are effective in helping workers recover their unpaid wages. Workers' centers have been pushing leadership in police departments, district attorneys, the U.S. Department of Labor, state departments of labor, local licensing agencies, and others to do more to help workers whose wages have been stolen.

Linking workers with ethical attorneys. The private bar is important in protecting workers in general, but is especially important in handling most workers' compensation cases (i.e., when workers are injured on the job and need help). State workers' compensation laws are complicated, and most state systems are hard to maneuver without an attorney. Many workers' centers organize legal clinics on a regular basis, drawing on the expertise of attorneys in the community. Some of the workers' centers have their own legal staffs, and others draw completely on colleagues who support the centers and are interested in helping workers.

Encouraging workers to organize. Workers will be best protected against wage theft if they organize a union, so workers' centers encourage workers to organize with a union if they so choose. The centers usually have strong connections with local union leaders, especially since the AFL-CIO has signed affiliation agreements with workers' centers[18] and can help refer workers to unions that organize in their sectors. In addition, sometimes the centers assist workers in forming an independent association and signing agreements with their employers.

In February 2003, a group of workers came to a training offered by the Chicago Interfaith Worker Rights Center. The workers, a mix of African Americans and Latino immigrants, worked at a local window factory that was cheating them of overtime pay and pitting the African American workers against the Latinos. African American workers were told by their supervisors that they worked too slowly and that for each one of them there were one hundred Latino workers waiting to take their jobs. Latino workers were told that African American workers resented their presence and wanted them replaced. At the training, the African American workers were asked to talk about what the civil rights movement meant in their lives, while the Latino workers were asked why they were forced to emigrate. In the end, all the workers realized their common self-interest and drafted a plan to organize a union in their workplace. In less than a year the workers had a contract that stopped the wage theft of overtime pay and provided them with significant pay raises, health care benefits, and paid vacations.

Some workers are organizing worker committees in workplaces, even without the support of unions. Somos un Pueblo Unido in Santa Fe, New Mexico, has helped build twenty committees in workplaces. Workers themselves are putting in place structures to stop abuse and improve conditions.

Challenging sectors that have rampant wage violations. The Twin Cities-based CTUL launched its Campaign for Justice in Retail Cleaning in 2011 after the organization helped retail cleaning workers recover more than $30,000 in stolen wages the previous year. According to organizer Brian Payne, "The race to the bottom in wages and working conditions for retail cleaning workers exists because of the incredibly competitive nature of the industry. Giant corporations like Target and SuperValu leverage their size to pit dozens of cleaning companies against each other, each underbidding the other in order to gain the contract. As the cleaning companies constantly lower their bids, the workers suffer the consequences: ever increasing workload, drastically lowered wages, and often wage theft."

So the CTUL members decided to change this reality through the Campaign for Justice in Retail Cleaning. Workers called on Cub Foods (a supermarket chain that is part of SuperValu) to play a leadership role in ending wage theft in retail cleaning by meeting with workers to establish a code of conduct guaranteeing fair wages and working conditions for the workers who clean their stores. After nearly a year of attempting to open a dialogue with Cub Foods through letters, petitions, and many other communications, workers called for a hunger strike.[19]

Passing pro-worker legislation. Workers' centers, like the earlier settlement houses and farm workers' service centers, have helped lead the nation in pushing for worker-friendly legislation. YWU,[20] based in San Francisco, was a major leader in the citywide coalition that mobilized to pass the nation's first Paid Sick Days legislation. Arise Chicago mobilized workers' centers and allies throughout Illinois to pass the Day and Temporary Labor Services Act, the nation's first and strongest legislation regulating day labor agencies. Many of the workers' centers have played active roles in community and state efforts to pass living wage ordinances, raise the minimum wage, or enact wage theft bills.

Engaging allies in supporting workers. In September 2007, four African American workers from Rumpke Recycling stopped by the Cincinnati Interfaith Workers' Center complaining of low wages, lack of bathroom facilities, and horrible working conditions. The workers' job, sorting through garbage passing by on a conveyer belt to pull out recycling materials, would be difficult in the best of situations, but was made worse because the employer didn't seem to care one iota about working conditions. Despite having a large contract with the city of Cincinnati, Rumpke Recycling was not paying its workers the state-required minimum wage of $6.85 per hour. Rumpke Recycling claimed that its workers were not covered by the Cincinnati Living Wage ordinance because its workers were temporary, not permanent, workers.

As bad as the wages were, the workers were equally upset about the freezing cold conditions and the lack of a restroom nearby. The Cincinnati Workers' Center filed complaints on the wages with the Ohio Wage and Hour Division and began building support from the broader community. The center arranged for several workers to speak at the Interfaith Justice and Peace Center in Cincinnati to members from four Cincinnati-area Catholic parishes that were participating in the Just Faith[21] program. As luck (or God's providence) would have it, several members of the congregation who heard the workers knew Rumpke family members. Almost immediately, the workers got a bathroom and heaters on the line.

The workers and their community and religious allies then pressured the Cincinnati City Council to pass a motion on May 21, 2008, that required companies like Rumpke Recycling, which do business with the city of Cincinnati, to pay living wages, as defined under the city's Living Wage Ordinance, to temporary workers as well as permanent ones.[22] Workers' centers offer not only a safe space for workers to meet, but also places where more affluent but caring members of the community can meet and build relationships with workers who are struggling. These personal relationships enable cross-class and cross-race/ethnicity coalitions that are essential for changing the direction of the nation. Too few Americans really understand the crisis of wage theft in the nation. Anyone who spends even an hour at a workers' center will learn about the crisis through workers' stories.

The Houston Interfaith Worker Center has engaged congregational youth groups in outreach and educational efforts. Tapping the desire of youth to provide service in the community, the Houston Center invited youth groups to spend a day helping reach out to construction workers. First, the young people heard from worker leaders and the center staff about working conditions in Houston. Next, the volunteers pasted information about the worker rights center to plastic water bottles (not good for the environment, I'm sure). Then the young people delivered the bottles to construction workers at worksites throughout the city. Young people saw for themselves the working conditions and got the opportunity to talk with workers. The young people were shocked to learn about unsafe working conditions and stolen wages. In addition to radically educating these young people, the outreach informed workers about the center, and quite a few visited as a result.

Providing other social services. Because the workers' centers are meeting places for workers, they offer a variety of social services and additional programming, such as ESL classes, voter registration drives, and financial literacy classes. When the nation finally passes a comprehensive immigration reform creating a path to citizenship, many of the workers' centers will serve as citizenship centers as well.

Creating worker-owned cooperatives. The Workplace Project, one of the nation's first workers' centers, helped launch UNITY Housecleaners, Long Island's first domestic workers' housecleaning cooperative. To become a member, workers must complete a four-week course covering the essential components of running a successful cooperative and a training class on housecleaning skills. Providing a full range of housecleaning services, UNITY members earn between $15 and $16 per hour for work gained through the cooperative. Ten percent of the money earned by each member is contributed back to the cooperative to help cover operating expenses and build a self-sustainable organization. Several other groups of housecleaners affiliated with workers' centers are building similar cooperatives.

The Madison Workers' Rights Center helped form the Interpreters' Cooperative of Madison (ICM), which provides "quality, affordable interpretation services to make community, academic and governmental events and meetings more inclusive and accessible." Bilingual community leaders are able to get paid for the services, a small fee is collected for the Workers' Rights Center, and community groups are encouraged to be more inclusive. It is a win-win cooperative.

In our nation's history, whenever large numbers of workers have been exploited, new civic structures and institutions have emerged to support the workers and challenge unjust structures. The civic institutions, be they settlement houses, Catholic labor schools, farm worker service centers, or today's workers' centers, combine direct help for the workers being exploited in addressing the immediate problems they face with longer-term education and advocacy to level the playing field. The expanding crisis of wage theft demands both immediate responses and long-term societal changes. The workers' centers are doing both. They are meeting the needs workers are facing right now, as best they can with limited resources, and they are pushing the nation to look anew at how it is protecting workers in low-wage jobs against wage theft. Workers' centers alone can't enact the changes we need as a society to stop wage theft, but together with unions, religious organizations, community allies, and revitalized labor enforcement agencies, they can play a significant role in mobilizing local communities to challenge and end wage theft.

8

Business Leaders Challenge Wage Theft

As each has received a gift, employ it in serving one another, as good managers of the grace of God in its various forms.

—I Peter 4:10

Stan Marek

"Wage theft is our industry's dirty little secret. But it is not little and not really secret," says Stan Marek, president and CEO of Marek Family of Companies, a set of large building and construction firms operating primarily in Texas. Richard Shaw, president of the Houston Federation of Labor introduced me to Stan Marek. Richard told me, "Stan's company is not union, but he is a really good employer."

Stan Marek and the other leaders at Marek Family of Companies are like many ethical employers. They pay people well, offer family benefits (health care, paid sick days, vacations, pensions), insist on safe workplaces, and share profits with workers. They seek to build a highly skilled and stable workforce.

Stan's family business was organized as a sheetrock business by three Marek brothers in the late 1930s. The company closed when the brothers went to war and then started up again at the end of World War II. Throughout the 1950s and 1960s, the company grew and expanded, becoming a full-service construction company and supplier of materials as well as labor.

Stan was raised in the construction business where he was trained as a union carpenter. He moved into leadership roles in the 1980s, a time of economic turmoil in the construction industry. Tough decisions were made to scale back workers and restructure companies.

Business started picking up in the 1990s and continued into the new millennium despite the brief setback created by the events of September 11, 2001. The Marek Family of Companies expanded and grew. However, the industry had changed. While previous workers were mostly Caucasians coming off Texas farms or from the North, many of the workers of the 1990s and later were Latino, both American born and immigrants. There was an ample supply of workers for the industry that depressed wages.

As Stan explains, "The immigrants especially (some of whom were illegal working with fake documents) weren't worried so much about the wages; they were just happy to have a job." Construction jobs in particular were easy to come by, so Stan found himself competing in an industry that was ripe for worker exploitation. Some of Stan's competitors paid low wages, offered little training, and ignored basic safety measures.

But Stan resisted the temptation and continued to offer better-than-average wages, engaged in sharing profits through a bonus program, and provided training—especially in the safety arena—believing in a solemn duty to protect his workers from harm in the workplace.

"We could see what was happening, but felt helpless to do anything about it, so we resigned ourselves to take care of our own" says Stan. "There was plenty of work—the practice of some of our fellow contractors wasn't having a direct impact on us, so we just focused on doing things right by our people."

Somewhere along the way, Stan's concern about the worker exploitation problem broadened. Perhaps it was the fact that it soon began having an impact on his business. More likely, though, it was because the problem itself had widened.

As Stan describes it, "1099 contractors were popping up in lieu of hourly workers—in other words—contractors found that by calling their workers 'independent contractors,' they could escape many of the state and federal taxes as well as minimum wage and overtime requirements. With no employees, they could also avoid the need for having to purchase group health insurance or workers' compensation coverage. This instantly made them more competitive on bid day." This payroll fraud was wage theft and worker exploitation in its purest form. No longer could Stan stand idly by and watch the industry he grew up in go in this direction.

So, Stan and the other leaders at Marek decided it was time to stand up and push the industry. As they say about their vision for 2011: "The standard we want to be judged by when this year is finished is not whether we endured at any and all cost, but whether we succeeded by not wavering from the values and principles that have always been a part of the Marek difference."[1] The company says its core values are as follows:

We value people. Each team member will be given the opportunity to develop to their fullest potential.

We value integrity. Doing the job right the first time is essential. We insist on quick response and quality results because these are the things our customers deserve.

We value safety. Our management is dedicated to providing you a safe working environment. We expect you to be equally dedicated to working safely.

We value profit. Making a fair profit on good work is the only way we can continue to provide growth and opportunity to the Marek Family of employees.

We value our customers. Customers, too, are part of our family and we insist they be treated honestly and ethically. They are our life's blood, both today and tomorrow.

We value sharing. We recognize our community has needs, too. By sharing profits with our employees and sharing resources with our community, we contribute to a better future for all.

We value competition. Competition is the fuel that drives us to deliver excellence. By always striving to be the best, we all become winners.[2]

Stan and other company leaders are devoting part of their time and talent to pushing the industry. They are as follows:

• *Making candid presentations about the problems.* At a 2010 presentation at Texas A&M to 250 construction science students and 20 faculty members, Stan laid out the problems in the industry: "We have rampant wage theft and misclassification characterized by low wages, folks paid as independent contractors or in cash or as day laborers, no overtime pay, folks working 60–80 hours per week with no days off, no medical benefits (70 percent of construction workers are uninsured) and no retirement. If we care about our workers, we've got to see that folks are paid better."[3]

• *Engaging major construction associations.* They are trying to get contractor members to embrace higher principles and to speak out about the problems.

• *Running ads touting values.* Instead of touting its low prices, Marek is touting its values and standards.

• *Promoting values on the company website.* All the core values are listed and discussed on the website.

• *Investing in job training.* Not only does the company invest in its own workforce, it partners with nonprofits that are trying to bring people into the trades.

• *Creating a website, Construction Citizen, to promote values.* Stan wants to change the industry. The website is a forum for discussing ethical issues in the construction industry.

• *Advocating a rational immigration program.* Stan regularly flies to Washington, D.C., and advocates with elected leaders for comprehensive immigration reform.

Instead of changing their values, Stan and his colleagues have decided to take on the industry—to challenge the industry to clean up its act. And he is part of a growing number of business leaders who are pushing for a rational immigration program so that hardworking employees can come out of the shadows.

Ethical employers who operate in sectors like construction that are notorious for wage theft need to do more than just treat their own workers fairly. They need to follow Stan's lead and work to clean up the industry. As Stan says, "The government can't do it. Unions aren't strong enough to do it. Business leaders must clean up the industry."[4]

Jennifer Piallat

Jennifer Piallat grew up in the restaurant industry. For twenty-five years she worked in restaurants. She never had health insurance. She never had sick days. She, like most of her coworkers, felt disrespected. As she aged, she struggled with the physical backbreaking aspect of restaurant work. She worked one place for four years and the owner didn't know her name.

In 2005, she had the opportunity to purchase Zazie, a French bistro in the heart of Cole Valley in San Francisco. She had been a manager at the restaurant for five years and loved the location and the patrons.

Jen wanted to treat people better than she'd been treated most of her career; she also had a hunch that if you treated people better, they would be better employees. According to Jennifer, 30 percent of restaurants that close do so because of employee theft. She says, "People steal because they are treated poorly. They feel like they deserve something from the place." She believes restaurant owners can't set up mechanical systems to stop employees from stealing, because it is way too easy in restaurants to steal. But you can make people not want to steal by treating them fairly.

The first change she made when she took over was to offer health care, dental care, and chiropractic care (an important benefit given the physical demands of the job). All employees have employer-provided health care if they work one shift or more per week. Then a year later, she offered a 401k plan with a 4 percent employer match after one year on staff. She provides two weeks of paid vacation, two weeks of paid sick days, and bonuses based on sales (a profit-sharing arrangement). Workers are allowed to eat for free.

Jen has thirty-two staff members. Only two employees are on a salary—ones that should be, compared to the standard industry of paying dishwashers "on salary," so they end up working 70 and 80 hours without overtime. The rest of her staff are paid hourly, decent wages and overtime for hours over 40. When asked about the common industry practice of paying people in the kitchen as independent contractors, she scoffed. "That's bunk," she said.

Her approach has paid off. She has low staff turnover. She has had the same kitchen staff for six years. In the last two years, she has only had to hire two servers and two bussers.

Her staff doesn't steal. They feel treated with respect, and they want the restaurant to succeed. If someone is tempted to steal, the other employees won't permit it (or they report the person).

Her staff is responsible. They watch if food comes in that is not good quality. They complain if food boxes are half full. They make sure that the food is stored properly. Consequently, there is less food loss.

Her customers are treated well because her staff is experienced, happy, and healthy.

Jennifer received consulting services from AOC SF, which provides consulting services for independent and multi-unit restaurant operators, particularly for those in the start-up phase. Of the 900 restaurants receiving consulting services from AOC SF, Jennifer's restaurant provides the most benefits for workers *and* has the highest profit margins! In 2010, not the best year for many restaurants, she had a 27 percent profit margin, which is high for the restaurant industry, even in good years. Her approach to staff, combined with great food and atmosphere, has made her business popular and profitable.

Other restaurants have begun to hire Jen to consult with them on her business model. She says, "I don't try to convince them that it is the right moral thing. I tell them it is good for your bottom line to treat your staff well. It's smart business."

Unfortunately, she says most restaurateurs aren't yet convinced. They claim, "My staff isn't reliable like yours. My situation is different. It won't work here. I can't afford it."

Jen is convinced that her approach is best and that it would work for others. It is legal. It is fair. And, it is profitable.[5]

Check out Zazie next time you are in San Francisco (www.zaziesf.org).

Lindsey Lee

Lindsey followed his wife to Madison, Wisconsin, where she was doing research in the University of Wisconsin Biology Department. Lindsey couldn't find the job he wanted. Because he'd grown up in retail (his dad owned Hale Hats in Flint, Michigan), he decided to go back into retail.

When he himself was in graduate school, he had a friend who would hang out nonstop in a fancy coffee shop. The friend and others paid a lot for coffee. Lee looked around Madison and there weren't very many nice coffee shops on his side of town (the near east side) at the time. Certainly not nearly as many as there are now.

He also figured that starting a coffee shop didn't require huge start-up costs. He could do his own construction and rehab, and he only needed one week's worth of stock to get started. He started Ground Zero Coffee in 1998. He began with just five employees. It has now grown to two locations and twenty employees—still a small business, but a relatively stable one.

Lindsey has always tried to pay people fairly well and fairly. All employees get paid sick days, and some full-time employees get health insurance. He struggles to give people better benefits than most, but he says it is tough. "The system feels like it is set up to punish the folks who do the right things," says Lindsey, "It is a competitive business, and the marketplace seems to reward folks who don't offer health insurance or sick leave."

In 2006, Madison had a big debate on a Paid Sick Leave bill. When Lindsey first heard about the proposal, he viewed it as just one more thing he was going to have to do. But then when he reviewed the bill closely, he realized that it really did make sense for employers to provide sick days, especially in the restaurant industry. Who wants workers coming to work sick? The bill did not pass, but Lindsey decided to go ahead and offer paid sick days. It made sense to him.

Most of the restaurateurs did not support the bill. As he says, "Small-business folks are not particularly conservative or particularly liberal. We're practical. But we're independent. We don't like to be told what to do." After the debate, several small businesses decided to offer paid sick days. To them, paid sick days made sense and were affordable, and the benefits outweighed the costs.

Lindsey explained that the way to get all restaurants to treat people right is to pass standards and reasonable regulations that apply to everyone. "The bad wage payment practices in restaurants is a systemic issue," says Lindsey. "We need standards and we need them enforced. You cannot always count on the marketplace to reward good employment practices and discourage bad ones."

He added that when the FMLA was first proposed, businesses claimed it would ruin them and cripple the economy. They predicted that workers would abuse it. And most small businesses aren't even covered by the law. Now, twenty years later, allowing workers to take leave to care for family members is the norm. It is not an undue burden, even for small businesses that choose to follow the law even if they are not required to do so.

Similarly, six years ago, smoking was banned in the bars in Wisconsin. Some bar owners said they would have banned smoking years ago if they could have, but they needed a standard policy for all. At the time, the ban was controversial. Now it is not.

The problems with wages and benefits for restaurant workers are serious. "We are lucky in Madison to have the Worker Rights Center to help keep folks honest," says Lindsey, "But we really need reasonable standards that can make sure workers are paid fairly and level the playing field for businesses trying to do the right thing."[6]

Ron von Paulus

Ron, a Miami native, went into the Navy straight out of high school. When he got out, he had a variety of jobs. He delivered pizzas. He worked in restaurants. He worked at a hotel. Sometimes he had two restaurant jobs simultaneously in order to make ends meet. Only in two of his jobs did he ever have health care, paid vacations, or paid sick days. "I was an employee for twenty years," says Ron, "I saw lots of bad managers and I wanted to be different."

Eventually, he went to school for hospitality management. "In school, they'd tell us 'this is the law,' but on the job they'd say, 'Yes, but here's how we operate.' That usually meant no overtime or falsifying payroll records."

After Hurricane Katrina, which damaged trees in South Florida, he began helping with clearing up the tree debris and realized that some trees survived better than others depending on how they'd been cared for. He became very interested in tree management and eventually became a certified arborist.

In 2003, he began Big Ron's Tree Service. He liked working with trees, liked working outdoors, and wanted to have his own business. Unfortunately, the sector in which he works is rife with wage theft.

"Lots of folks are paid under the table, in cash. That's wrong," says Ron. "Landscape employers stiff workers all the time. They're pirates."

The prevalence of wage theft makes it hard for Ron to compete. His competitors' labor costs are approximately 30 percent less because they don't pay employment taxes and insurance. Most of his competitors commit payroll fraud, not claiming workers as employees. Some employers want to be able to show a workers' compensation policy when they bid on jobs so they will carry workers' compensation on one or two employees and then pay everyone else in cash and not cover them.

According to Ron, the workers who get taken advantage of the most are undocumented immigrants. Employers threaten to deport people if they complain. "Some of the hardest workers you'll ever meet are undocumented," says Ron. "Lots of times they don't get paid. It's wrong."

Ron is a member of the International Society of Arboriculture (ISA), which promotes safe and environmentally responsible ways to care for trees. The organization indirectly addresses the problem of wage theft in landscaping by suggesting to consumers that they "ask for certification of personal and property liability insurance and workman's compensation. Then phone the insurance company to make certain the policy is current."[7] Although this may help individual consumers hire ethical contractors, it does nothing to challenge unethical employers in the sector.

And for most consumers, this message about certifications for insurance and workers compensation is not clear enough. Consumers don't understand that if the price is very cheap, the employer is probably stealing from workers.

Broward County has established tree-trimming landscaping standards that require consumers to hire licensed landscapers. The licensing process requires employers to be qualified to do the work and to provide workers' compensation on all their employees, which means they can't be paid under the table. This not only helps the trees, but also the workers.

Ron believes there needs to be standards that are enforced, as in Broward County, or there needs to be basic enforcement of the labor laws, which is why he supported the Dade County Wage Theft Ordinance passed in 2010.

Currently, Ron has four full-time employees. They are paid from $9 to $12 per hour. If they work more than 40 hours per week, they get paid overtime. He'd like to pay them better and would like to provide more benefits, but he can't because he competes primarily with employers who cheat workers and commit payroll fraud.

At times, Ron has had to pay his mortgage late in order to pay his employees on time. As he says, "If they do the work, you got to pay them." He explains that running a business involves risks. "The employer takes the risks. If things go well, you get the profits, but you can't transfer the risks to the employees and not pay them. They didn't sign up for that."

Ron doesn't consider himself a perfect guy. He says, "I cuss too much and tell a dirty joke occasionally. But I know what's really wrong—stealing wages from workers."[8]

If you need tree service or landscaping in South Florida, check him out at www.bigronstreeservice.com.

Fabian Loera

Fabian grew up working in the fields in California. His parents were migrant workers. His father died when he was young. His mother was very religious. She raised a family of eight and instilled in all of them the value of caring for those less fortunate. As a child, he remembers his mother packing his daily lunch with an allotment of homemade tacos to feed an army so he could share with his coworkers who had just arrived from other countries in pursuit of their dreams. Working in the fields, he saw lots of abuse, but his mom raised him to be a "giver," someone who wanted to help people instead of take advantage of them.

After high school, Fabian went into the U.S. Navy. For the first six years he was a boiler technician. Then he was handpicked to work as a corrections specialist (in the military prison) for four years. In 1990, a year before he was going to finish his tour of duty, Fabian and a friend decided to form a janitorial business, Sunrise Floor Systems, in order to have work when they got out of the service in 1991.

The janitorial industry was a lot better then than it is today. At that point, most firms were paying around $5.25 per hour. His firm was paying people between $7.50 and $8.00 per hour, with raises every six months, holiday and sick pay, health insurance, and pension. The market supported decent wages and benefits. The company began cleaning offices and then shifted into supermarket work, which is a bit more specialized. Throughout the 1990s, he built the company by getting contracts with supermarket chains. By the end of the decade, he had almost four hundred employees.

In 2000, the market changed abruptly. Supermarkets refused to renew contracts with ethical employers and began looking for the lowest-cost bidders. Janitorial contractors were hired that did not have licenses and paid workers below the minimum wage. His competition, paying workers half what he was and without benefits, took his jobs. He went from four hundred employees to zero. His fellow ethical contractors experienced similar problems.

The SEIU saw many of its union contractors paying decent wages and benefits be undercut like Fabian. The year before Sunrise Floor Systems fell apart, in 1999, SEIU convinced a group of ethical contractors to form the Maintenance Cooperation Trust Fund (MCTF). Funded by contractors, MCTF defines itself as "a California statewide watchdog organization working to abolish illegal and unfair business practices in the janitorial industry." Even though California has one of the better state enforcement operations, like most other state departments of labor, it is woefully underfunded and understaffed. MCTF was formed to help "expose unlawful operations, encourage accountability, promote responsible business practices, and help level the playing field in the interest of clients, employers, workers and the general public."[9]

Fabian left the janitorial industry in 2003 and went to work for the IRS in 2005 working for the Small Business and Self Employed Division. During the time Fabian left the industry, one of the major events that contributed to steering the industry back toward ethical contracting practices was a major lawsuit in the supermarket industry. The MCTF, SEIU, a team of lawyers, and activists were involved in the lawsuit *Flores v. Albertsons* in which workers won $22 million in stolen wages from the major grocery chains including Albertsons, Vons, and Safeway. Over time, many of the larger chains put in place ethical contracting guidelines that created more of a level playing field for ethical employers.[10]

In 2008, Fabian returned to the industry after standards had risen to their prior levels, creating a space for Sunrise Floor Systems and other ethical employers to flourish. He really loved the idea of helping provide good jobs and a career for people. According to Fabian, "For many workers, being a janitor is not just a job, it is a career. They take it serious and want to do quality work." When he restarted his business, almost all his employees were people who had worked for him five years earlier.

Now he has 120 employees. Workers start at $8.65 per hour and wages go up to $12 per hour. Everyone gets vacation—up to four weeks depending on seniority. He provides full family health insurance, paid holidays, pension, and overtime pay for holidays and over 40 hours a week (of course). As a result, he has very low turnover in staff. He provides a lot of health and safety training, so people don't have as many injuries as other firms, which keeps his workers' compensation rates reasonable. If workers have an opportunity to move to higher-paying jobs and careers, he encourages them to do it.

Fabian is angry when he talks about the industry. "Nationwide, the industry is set up to abuse workers," he says. "The underground market is huge and nobody is watching. Probably 80 percent of the janitorial companies are not paying workers and not paying the government. Without decent enforcement of labor standards ethical employers can't compete."

Fabian is doing his part to clean up the industry. He is active in leadership with MCTF. He has formed a coalition of ethical employers to focus on paying workers better and reducing turnover. He gives seminars for other contractors on how to treat workers fairly. He gives seminars for workers helping them know their rights.

Fabian recognizes that some contractors don't want to be responsible, but he believes that others do want to treat workers fairly, but they have gotten themselves locked into contracts that mean you can't pay workers legally. Fabian is clear, "Employers need to commit to paying workers fairly, but the only real long-term solution is consistent government enforcement to level the playing field."[11]

If you need janitorial services in Southern California, contact him at www.sunrisellc.net.

Tom Henry

Tom and his brother Peter were raised in Exeter, New Hampshire. Like many brothers, they had similar values—but different gifts—and went in different directions after high school. Peter went off to Brown University as an economics major, and after graduating began working as a mechanic at Landry's Bicycles in Taunton, Massachusetts. Tom went to Oberlin College and ended up doing theater work in Baltimore.

In 1975, Peter and Tom's father, John, took a second mortgage on his house to help Peter purchase Landry's Bicycles, a firm originally started by the Landry brothers in 1922.

Tom remembers his father telling him when he was young that one day he'd be a psychologist or a minister, and so, after the breakup of the theater group in Baltimore, Tom moved back to Boston and decided to try theology. He went to Andover Newton Theological Seminary from 1979 to 1983 and received his master's of divinity degree. During this same time, Tom and his wife, Karen, founded the Boston Theater Group, which rehearsed in the church where Tom was also doing his "in care" ministry. To "make ends meet" and to keep his feet on the ground, Tom worked part-time in his brother's bike shop first as a bike assembler and mechanic and later as a salesperson and manager.

After graduating from seminary, instead of becoming an ordained minister, Tom continued the theater work and took on some additional part-time work as the sexton of the church where he had been "in care." Under the influence of a professor at Andover Newton with whom Tom had taken a course on the "ministry of the laity," Tom began to question why the pastor's work was considered sacred and others' work—the secretary's and sexton's, for example—was not. He struggled over the church's view of vocation and ministry, and, frankly, its limited vision for how one conducts a ministry in the world. Deeply questioning the role of the pastor in the church and in the world, Tom decided to devote himself full time to the bike business.

In 1987, Tom became a joint owner of the bike shop along with his brother Peter and Peter's wife, Jeanne. "The bicycle business seemed full of the sacred," says Tom. Specifically, Tom saw the power of hospitality to transform the world.

The Henrys have been running Landry's now for thirty-five years and have a lofty vision of Landry's Bicycles becoming the best bike shop *for* the world. To do that, they believe they must have the best staff-team to deliver the Landry's experience to customers. "The Landry's experience is a seamless flow of love," says Tom. "Customers should feel something different when they walk in the door."

In order to have the best staff, the owners believe in paying people enough to make a career. According to the annual National Bike Dealers Association Survey, the average Landry's hourly wage is approximately 40 percent higher than what is typical for comparable bike shops. The company offers a 4 percent 401K match, paid vacations (two weeks a year if you take vacation in season or three weeks if you take it in the off-season), and paid holidays. Landry's pays 75 percent of individual or family medical insurance for those who work 32 hours or more per week and matches up to $1500 on the employee's health savings account (HSA). The company also has a profit-sharing plan, and the owners recently created an Employee Stock Ownership Plan (ESOP). The Henrys expect that over the next ten to fifteen years, the company will become 100 percent owned by the ESOP, which will have been funded entirely by company contributions. The Henrys are excited about this succession plan.

Figuring out the "right" way and amounts to pay people has been a struggle. During a few rough years in 1991–1992, when everyone, including the owners, was making $11 per hour, all were cut back to $9 per hour. As the company has grown, the leadership has grappled with creating a payment structure that rewards people for their contributions and yet maintains a degree of internal equity. Although the spread between lowest-and-highest paid employees is wider than at the beginning, there is still a commitment to trying to create good-paying middle-class jobs with which members of Landry's staff can raise families. "If the company prospers, the employees should have the opportunity to prosper," says Tom. "We want to build a culture which helps us all get over the mountain together."

Landry's Bicycles has grown and prospered. It now operates a family of four retail stores. It employs forty year-round salaried people and adds another thirty-five to forty hourly positions in the warm weather. The bicycle business in cold regions typically loses money in the off-season and has to be incredibly efficient and successful in the warm season. Landry's Bicycles uses the off-season to focus on staff development, leadership training, and process improvement so that they can be a "wildly efficient team" in season. Again, according to the National Bike Dealers Association Survey, Landry's staff produces approximately 40 percent more sales per hour per person than the national average in spite of keeping people on through the slow winter season. This higher efficiency is largely what allows for the higher pay.

This better-paid, well-trained, and more efficient team creates a profitable company because the employees listen well to customers, channel their energy into smooth processes, have clarity about standards, and work together. The company has little employee turnover. "A great retail sales team performs like a jazz dance group," says Tom. "We don't walk; we dance across the sales floor."

In addition to its internal work, Landry's Bicycles is active in bicycle advocacy. It sponsors over forty charitable bike events a year. It sends staff to Washington, D.C., to lobby for bike paths and other bike-friendly policies. It recruits people to sign postcards supporting biking. Tom believes that everyone in the company is a "missionary" for cycling.

Tom estimates that there are four thousand to five thousand specialty bike shops in the nation, and he often imagines what a force for good they could be. Unfortunately, not all bike shops are like Landry's Bicycles, though Tom says there are a number of great shops that do have some of these same attributes.

"I can't help wondering if some of the shops that discount their prices to the public the most aggressively pay for it through shirking responsibility to their employees, decreasing the level of service to their customers and maybe even engaging in some form of tax manipulation or some other form of neglect of service to the common good." When asked what should be done about the problem, Tom says businesses should view themselves as "good citizens—supporting workers and the communities where they work." He believes we need to start with education of young people. For example, he believes that business schools and economists need to recognize and teach a more holistic theory of what motivates a business. "Profit as the sole or primary motivator of a business is a flawed theory that leads to mistrust among customers, suppliers, government agencies and other businesses—a mistrust which often undermines the very profitability that businesses seek. It is strange to me that we have one set of core cultural values in our nation—enshrined in the Declaration of Independence and the Constitution—but then we have a reduced set of values for our businesses. Business institutions make up one of the most powerful underlying forces in our world and they need a set of values worthy of that power. I reject a one-dimensional business value system. For Landry's a deep, wide and capable love of self, neighbor and community (undergirded with financial sustainability) is the prime mover."

If you are in the Boston area, buy your bicycle from Landry's Bicycles (www.landrysbicycles.com).

Carl Agsten

When I told Larry Rubin, the communications director for the Mid-Atlantic Regional Council of Carpenters, that I was profiling ethical business leaders, he told me to check out the website for Agsten Construction. So, I did.

The description of the company on the front page of the Agsten website reads, "Agsten Construction Company is a commercial and high end residential contractor based in Charleston, West Virginia. We employ the states' most skilled union workers. Our commitment to excellence in commercial construction, residential construction and construction contract management has earned us the reputation of one of the leading construction companies in West Virginia."

Also on the front page of the website is a quote from owner Carl Agsten. He says, "We have worked hard over the years to build relationships on solid foundations of trust and integrity, just as stated in the Golden Rule. We strive to treat each client, no matter how large or small the project, with the same consideration and attention to detail. That is the way we always have done business and it's the way we will always do business." The mission statement is even clearer in its values and commitments to workers. It reads, "Our company was formed to provide a vehicle for putting to use our knowledge, skills, reputation, respected family name, and true Christian principles such as the Golden Rule, in providing construction services to owners with a need for quality, timeliness and value, while earning a reasonable profit. The company would also provide good paying jobs for others with good construction skills, or the desire and ability to learn them, who also share our goals and values."

I was eager to talk with someone who proudly acknowledged using union labor and mentioned the Golden Rule on the front page of his website. I wanted to understand where his values came from and get his thoughts on the construction industry today.

Carl was born during the Depression. His grandfather came from Germany, got into construction, and did very well. The family settled first in Pittsburgh, Pennsylvania, and then moved to Charleston, West Virginia, where he started H.B. Agsten and Sons. The company was always union. There was never a question about using union labor and paying people decently. Carl's dad, his dad's two brothers, and a nephew all worked with H.B. Senior. Over time, his dad and one other left and started their own construction companies.

Carl was raised in a Baptist church and home. As he tells it, the brand of Baptist was pretty strict—no dancing, no cards, no drinking, no mixed swimming pools (that is, boys and girls in the same pool). His parents taught him and showed him how to care for his neighbors.

As Carl grew up, it never occurred to him that he would do anything but construction. Back in the early 1950s, if you were going to college and wanted to be in construction, you either got an engineering or an architecture degree. Carl got a degree in architecture. He then went into the Navy and spent four years as an officer in the Civil Engineer Corp.

When he returned to his family in Charleston, he began working for his dad's construction firm. That company dissolved in 1974 and Carl formed Carlton Inc., named after his daughter. The company grew and prospered—always union. There was lots of work. Carl did well and so did his employees. He sold the company to a larger corporation in 1992, but stayed with the new buyers and their successors for about seven years. Carl wanted to keep working, but liked the freedom to set priorities and values that comes from running your own business. Thus, in 2000 he started Agsten Construction. The company did really well for a while. He focused on commercial projects. For several years in the mid-2000s, Agsten Construction did $25–30 million worth of business a year, employing 80 to 110 union guys and twelve to thirteen office staff.

Then in late 2005, he took a huge concrete job that almost killed the company. There were numerous problems with the job, the company lost money, and he struggled to keep the company together. Soon thereafter, the economy collapsed and construction jobs dried up. The business dropped to seven people in the office and only fifteen union guys in the field.

By coincidence, while Carl was doing commercial work near a large resort hotel, he had the opportunity to get involved in high-end residential jobs building very large homes. The residential market was a bit of a shock to him. "In commercial jobs, most of my competitors were union companies. We all worked under the same rules," says Carl. "But things were totally different in residential. Most of the industry is nonunion, workers are paid very little, and most have no health care or safety training. Lots of the subcontractors were paying people under the table or calling workers independent contractors."

In order to bid jobs in residential construction, Carl had to negotiate a "residential rate" with the laborers and carpenters—a rate that was lower than commercial rates but would still pay a decent rate and provide health care. "I don't want guys working without health care," says Carl. Agsten Construction also does drug testing, which is almost unheard of in residential work.

He says the other problem in residential construction is the lack of safety training and protection. He regularly sees guys working on roofs without any fall protection.

When Carl and his first wife were raising their kids, they attended a variety of churches. After his first wife died, he remarried and together they joined a Lutheran church where Carl's spiritual life grew and deepened.

Carl has needed that faith during the last few years. He quoted James 1:2–3 to me, "Consider it pure joy, my brothers, whenever you face trials of many kinds, because you know that the testing of your faith develops perseverance." Carl's business and many ethical business leaders in construction are facing trials. Carl feels a little like Job—he has tried to do the right thing for his employees and customers, but he is battered by unethical companies around him.

And like Job, he sees folks claiming to be people of faith, but cheating workers and cheating customers. He says, "They talk the talk, but don't walk the walk. Money becomes another God."

Carl and other ethical construction contractors are troubled by companies that are driving down standards in the business. Not only are there problems in the residential construction side, but in the commercial side. Some commercial guys bid prevailing wage jobs and then classify skilled crafts as laborers.

Carl has been active in the Kanawha Valley Contractors Association. The association negotiates wages and works together with the building trades unions to maintain standards in the industry. In past years he served as its president. Members of the association have tried to educate customers about unethical contractors. Carl explained that there was a car dealer who was considering hiring a company to do a job that was notorious for cheating its workers. The ethical contractors sent a letter to the car dealer explaining what was going on and urging him to reconsider a more ethical contractor. He did.

When asked what is needed to address the problems, particularly in residential construction, he says, "We need consistent enforcement of labor laws."

Carl has always played by the rules—the nation's rules and the Golden Rule. He will continue to run his business both legally and ethically, but its getting harder to do. Carl needs a level playing field.

If you need a contractor in West Virginia or nearby states, contact Carl at www.agstenconstruction.com.

Supporting Ethical Business Leaders

All seven of these business owners operate in sectors that are rampant with wage theft. They vary from relatively large to very small business owners, but the lessons from them are clear:

• *Employers have choices about how to pay people.* Even in sectors in which wage theft and payroll fraud dominate, ethical employers can choose to go in another direction.

• *Ethical employers should push their sectors.* It is good to pay your own people fairly and legally, but in sectors dominated by wage theft, ethical employers need to speak out and challenge others to do better. Pushing others to also follow the law can help level the playing field, removing the financial advantages held by employers who commit wage theft and payroll fraud.

• *Treating workers fairly has economic benefits.* Employers who treat workers fairly experience less staff turnover, less employee theft, improved productivity, and loyalty to the company and the work. Nonetheless, ethical employers in particularly competitive sectors can be at a competitive disadvantage with unethical employers who steal wages.

• *Employers need reasonable standards that are enforced across the board to level the playing field.* It is not fair that ethical employers have to compete against wage thieves.

There are a few employer associations that talk about fair payment issues including wage theft and payroll fraud, but not enough. One important association in the construction industry is the National Alliance of Fair Contracting that supports fair treatment of workers and strong enforcement of labor laws to level the playing field for ethical employers. (Learn more about the National Alliance of Fair Contracting at www.faircontracting.org.) It would be helpful if other general business ethics networks, such as Businesses for Social Responsibility and Business Alliance for Local Living Economies, would engage their members in these issues.

Some of the nation's largest employer networks are completely silent on these issues, even in sectors that have rampant wage theft. For example, the National Restaurant Association offers no leadership on wage theft in the restaurant association. The American Hotel and Lodging Association is concerned about diversity and "green" issues, but not wage theft. The Associated Builders and Contractors groups has a policy on the FLSA touting flexibility, but nothing about wage theft and payroll fraud, clearly important problems for workers in the construction industry. These industry associations could play an enormous role in reducing wage theft and payroll fraud if they would lift up the issues in conferences, through publications, and on their websites.

Dr. Patricia Werhane, managing director of DePaul University's Institute for Business and Professional Ethics, is convinced that wage theft is a problem business leaders should address. Her board of directors, composed of leading Chicago area business leaders, was shocked to learn the scope of the problem, when she arranged for a presenter to talk about it. Dr. Werhane is working on a documentary on wage theft aimed at educating the business community on the issue and a "case study" on wage theft that can be used to lift up the issues in business schools. "Wage theft is a serious ethical problem for the business community," says Dr. Werhane, "What's more important for workers than getting paid?"

Workers' centers are seeking ways to honor and affirm ethical business leaders. YWU in San Francisco introduced me to Jennifer Piallat. The organization first met her when she spoke out in favor of the paid sick days bill. Since then, her restaurant, Zazie's, is regularly featured in the organization's *Dining with Justice: A Guide to Guilt-Free Eating*. Check out the guide before you eat in San Francisco at www.youngworkers united.org.

The Tompkins County Workers' Center in Ithaca, New York, initiated the Living Wage Employer Certification Program in 2005 to publicly recognize and reward those who pay a living wage. Any employer in the private, public, and nonprofit sectors is eligible to apply. Employers who are certified are provided with a "Living Wage Certified" emblem for display, promoted via the workers' center's publications and website, and recognized at public events. Seventy-two employers have been certified. According to Pete Meyers, the coordinator of the Tompkins County Workers' Center, "The program enables us to compliment good business and challenge others. If Autumn Leaves Used Books can pay a living wage, why can't Barnes and Nobles? If GreenStar Food Coop can do it, then why can't Wegman's, Tops and P&C?"[12]

In order to stop and deter wage theft, ethical business leaders must provide leadership in cleaning up sectors in which wage theft has become commonplace. Stan Marek's memo to his leadership team about 2011's challenges should serve as a rallying cry for all ethical businesses: "This year will be more challenging than most...our industry is not willing to change unless the government starts enforcing the wage and hour laws or there are major changes in the immigration issue....Leveling the playing field would do wonders for our bottom line! We'll be asking more from each of you this coming year. It's not about survival, we'll survive. It's about supporting the principles that got us where we are—treating people fairly and working as a team."

Stan Marek, Jennifer Piallat, Lindsey Lee, Ron von Paulus, Fabian Loera, Tom Henry, Carl Agsted, and hundreds more are standing up to wage theft and treating people fairly. Ethical employers are Jewish, Muslim, Christian, from other faiths, and some with no particular faith. But all talk about values and put those values into practice.

But to stop wage theft, we'll need tens of thousands of ethical business leaders. Courageous business leaders brought women and people of color into leadership roles. Courageous business leaders helped end child labor. Courageous business leaders reduced their environmental footprint. Today, ethical businesses can and must help stop wage theft by modeling good behavior, challenging others to behave more ethically, and supporting enforcement initiatives that level the playing field.

Part III

Strengthening Enforcement

9

Leadership Matters:
Lessons from Frances Perkins

The righteous considereth the cause of the poor: but the wicked regardeth not to know it. Where there is no vision, the people perish: but he that keepeth the law, happy is he.

—Proverbs 29:7, 18 (KJV)

The Department of Labor building in Washington, D.C., is named after Frances Perkins, the most illustrious secretary of labor in the nation's history. Her leadership shaped the labor future of the nation. Challenging the scourge of wage theft in the nation and addressing the decline of jobs that pay a living wage require leaders like Frances Perkins. Having her name on a building is not enough. The nation needs leaders throughout the U.S. Department of Labor, throughout state enforcement agencies, and even in local agencies that claim to share her vision and commitment to workers.

Perhaps because too few of us paid attention in history classes, most Americans have no idea who Frances Perkins was, despite her significant leadership role in crafting and passing the core legislation establishing social security, minimum wage, child labor protections, and unemployment insurance. People my mother's age know her. Many people of my generation have heard the name, but don't quite know why. Most of the young staff at IWJ never heard of her.

Frances Perkins was the secretary of labor from 1933 to 1945.[1] She was the first woman to serve in a president's cabinet. I have her picture with a quote hanging by my desk that says, "I came to Washington to work for God, FDR, and the millions of forgotten, plain common workingmen" (thanks to a great bookmark given to me by Gerry Shea and made by the AFGE local that represents DOL workers for an anniversary event celebrating Perkins's leadership).

Frances Perkins was raised in a middle-class family in Massachusetts. Hers was a loving Congregationalist family, and her faith informed her work. According to her biographer, George Martin, "Her religion was the source of her strength."[2] It was during her time at Mount Holyoke College that she was introduced to the struggles of working people. She attended a presentation about sweatshops by Florence Kelley, the national secretary of the National Consumers' League, that Perkins later claimed "opened my mind to the necessity for and the possibility of the work which became my vocation."[3] Also influential was a course on industrial society in which the professor sent the students to visit factories and report on the living and working conditions of paper and textile mill workers. Perkins was shocked at what she discovered. (A side note: This should encourage teachers to get students out of the classroom!)

After graduating, Perkins took a job as a substitute teacher, but began to throw herself into volunteer work at her Congregational church. After visiting the homes of factory workers, she organized a club for teenage girls working in factories, which offered classes on cooking and sewing. When the hand of one of the girls was cut off by an unguarded machine and the company shirked its responsibility, Perkins spearheaded a public protest and forced the company to compensate the girl with $100 for the loss of her hand. (Another side note: Our religious volunteer work transforms us even as it helps others.)

Two years later, Perkins took another teaching position, which required a move to Chicago. While in Chicago, she became an Episcopalian. Although her weekday work was spent in a well-to-do suburban school, her weekends and holidays were spent at Chicago Commons, a settlement house in a poor neighborhood. Dr. Graham Taylor, a clergyman and social worker who founded Chicago Commons, introduced her to labor unions. "It was Dr. Taylor who first explained unions to her as a social force that could help to improve the living conditions of workers and their families."[4]

Through Chicago Commons, she met Jane Addams of the Hull House (another settlement house, a forerunner of today's workers' centers), who would become a lifelong friend. Eventually, Perkins quit her suburban teaching job and moved into Hull House as an unpaid but full-time resident worker. At Hull House, she organized community residents to address problems and spent more time with people struggling to earn a living. Although she was only there for six months, the organizing experience clearly influenced her. (And yet another side note: Those six-month interns may change the world.)

Perkins moved back east to take a position at the Philadelphia Research and Protection Association as its sole staff person. Her mission was to help immigrant white girls from Europe and black girls from the South who arrived in Philadelphia looking for work and were often exploited by unscrupulous employers or prostitution rings. She visited rooming houses where the girls lived and employment agencies for which they worked. She wrote detailed reports on the living and working conditions of these young girls and launched a successful public campaign to clean up conditions and regulate both rooming houses and employment agencies. While in Philadelphia, she took classes at the Wharton School of Finance and Commerce at the University of Pennsylvania, which brought her to the attention of Dr. Simon Patten, who recommended her for a fellowship to study for her master's degree at Columbia University in New York City.

While studying at Columbia, she conducted tenement studies in a rough neighborhood in mid-Manhattan appropriately called Hell's Kitchen. Her thesis emphasized that dealing with poverty requires more than giving food to children. Rather, society must provide "adequate incomes and adequate education to all its workers." Perkins was hired as an investigator and then was appointed the executive secretary at the New York Consumer's League, a group that focused on improving wages, hours, and working conditions by mobilizing consumer pressure on employers (sounds like IWJ).

As part of her job with the New York Consumer's League, Perkins began lobbying in Albany advocating a 54-hour workweek law for women. To support the bill, she conducted investigations of various industries such as laundries, nut factories, and bakeries. She also started a study on industrial accidents when the Triangle Shirtwaist fire occurred on March 25, 1911. Perkins happened to be there that day and looked on in horror as many young women jumped to their deaths because they couldn't get out of the building—a scene she never forgot.

The New York Committee on Safety, a small independent organization, was formed in response to the fire, and Perkins was hired to staff it. Perkins soon made herself an expert on factory safety so that she could lobby for reforms in Albany. The state passed a bill forming the New York State Factory Commission. Perkins was loaned from the Committee to the Commission to help with investigations. She and Commission members conducted drop-in investigations in factories throughout the state, through which she learned firsthand what kinds of reforms were needed. Eventually, thirty-six new state laws were passed to protect industrial workers, as well as a modified version of her 54-hour bill.

In 1913, Perkins married Paul Caldwell Wilson, a reform activist and researcher in New York City at Grace Episcopal Church in New York City.[5] She continued to use her maiden name, much to the chagrin of many. They had a baby daughter, Susanna, which curtailed her work for a few years.

In 1917, Perkins became the director of the New York Council of Organization for War Service. She then worked on Al Smith's campaign for the New York governorship, organizing women into the campaign. When Smith became governor, he appointed her to serve as one of the five members of the New York Industrial Commission. She faced huge opposition to her confirmation from manufacturers and merchants, and even some party faithful and organized labor leaders, but eventually she was approved by a large margin in the New York Senate.

Perkins served workers in New York as a labor consultant and Industrial Commission member under Governor Al Smith (1919–1920, 1923–1928) and then as labor commissioner under Governor Franklin D. Roosevelt (1929–1932). She gained experience in bringing workers and employers together in strike situations, establishing and enforcing labor codes, adjudicating workers' compensation claims, supervising a large staff, organizing an emergency jobs service program, convening labor and business leaders to fight unemployment, assembling and using research data, crafting a program for unemployment insurance, and testifying before the U.S. Congress in support of worker-friendly legislation.

When Franklin D. Roosevelt became president in 1933, he appointed Perkins as his secretary of labor, the first woman cabinet member in the history of the nation. She was not appointed as a token female, however. Indeed, she had incredibly strong credentials for the job, and her skills and perseverance had been tried and tested. But again, not everyone thought she should have the job, including some in organized labor. Before she would accept the position, she outlined her vision. "She proposed federal aid to the states for direct unemployment relief, an extensive program of public works, an approach to the establishment by federal law of minimum wages and maximum working hours, true unemployment insurance and old-age insurance, abolition of child labor, and the creation of a federal-state employment service."[6] Now that's a vision!

Perkins spent the next twelve years in her cabinet position, during which time she played major leadership roles in creating:

- The Civilian Conservation Corps, which put six hundred thousand young men to work in camps working on conservation projects planned and supervised by the National Park Service (March 31, 1933).
- The Wagner-Peyser Act, which reestablished the U.S. Employment Service (June 6, 1933).
- A Senate resolution authorizing U.S. membership in the International Labor Organization (June 19, 1934).
- The Federal Emergency Relief Administration, which provided grants to states and public relief agencies for distributing $4 billion to families during the Depression.
- The Civil Works Administration, which provided jobs for more than four million jobless men and women, and then the Works Progress Administration.
- The National Industrial Recovery Act, which established labor and business standards during a time of economic crisis.
- The National Labor Relations Act to "promote equality of bargaining power between employers and employees and to diminish the causes of labor disputes" (July 5, 1935).
- The Social Security Act, which created a retirement insurance program for senior citizens, perhaps the most important antipoverty legislation ever passed, as well as an unemployment insurance program (August 14, 1935).
- The Fair Labor Standards Act, the most important set of labor protections ever passed (June 25, 1938).
- Health supervision in plants holding government contracts.

When Frances Perkins was asked what she was most pleased about, she didn't mention this long list. Rather she talked about the impact she had on state labor laws by the regular conferences and meetings she convened between federal and state labor officials. There are many remarkable aspects of how Perkins operated, but let me mention one particularly unusual one, at least in today's world. During her twelve years in a national leadership position, she spent one day a month in silent retreat at the All Saint's convent in Catonsville, Maryland.[7] Her faith undergirded her vision and practical approaches.

So why was Frances Perkins probably the most effective secretary of labor ever? Following are some of the important characteristics of Frances Perkins's leadership that should be sought by all those in key federal, state, and local enforcement roles:

Commitment to improving conditions for workers. Commitment is demonstrated by how one lives life, not by words in a confirmation hearing. Frances Perkins demonstrated her commitment to working men and women long before she was asked to serve as the secretary of labor.

Hands-on experience with exploited workers. Perkins's surveys of working conditions, visits to workers' homes, and personal conversations with workers gave her a deep understanding of the problems and instilled a drive for solutions. Her concern for workers wasn't just an intellectual or ideological perspective. It gave her righteous indignation—an anger in response to injustice. She brought a "view from the bottom" that affects how you see solutions. As I told Mr. Paul DeCamp when he was first appointed as Wage and Hour administrator in the George W. Bush administration and brought no personal experience with low-wage worker issues, the view from the top and the view from the bottom are different.[8] No matter how nice, smart, or concerned you are, experience with exploited workers affects how you view situations.

A desire to find goodness in everyone. Even though Perkins was an advocate for workers, she sought to find goodness in all political leaders and employers. She believed that we must find common ground in the nation and work across political party lines to improve conditions for workers in low-wage jobs. She believed that the vast majority of employers do care about their workers and want to comply with the law.

Pragmatism about getting things done. Perkins would drive forward her vision, but she worked with people and compromised when necessary to get things done. Pushing progressive ideas without accomplishing anything doesn't help workers. She was both driven and pragmatic, a powerful combination.

Toughness born from struggle. Perkins was accustomed to opponents attacking her, allies not agreeing with her, or some calling her names or poking fun at her. Her early years of work standing for workers had prepared her for the rough and tumble of national politics. She did not take things too personally, and she did not allow the attacks or criticisms to slow her down. She kept going even when a highly politicized Congress sought to impeach her in 1939 over her handling of the Harry Bridges hearings. Perkins refused to condone the anticommunist hysteria and deport Harry Bridges, the head of the International Longshoremen's and Warehousemen's Union and West Coast Director of the CIO, without just cause. The Judiciary Committee dismissed the impeachment resolution.

Willingness to speak and write about workers' concerns. In order to move an agenda forward, Perkins had to speak and write about it in public. She did so ably, giving hundreds of talks to worker, employer, religious, and civic groups. She used her bully pulpit for worker concerns. Early in 2008, I reviewed on the DOL website six months' worth of speeches given by George W. Bush's Secretary of Labor Elaine Chao: never once in a speech did she push an employer group to raise wages, improve benefits, or reduce workplace injuries. Chao used every speaking opportunity to talk about what a wonderful job the Department of Labor was doing and how wonderful the economy was under the current administration. What a waste of a bully pulpit.

Unfortunately, many state and federal labor department leaders use their bully pulpits to laud their agency's accomplishments and their bosses' administrations (the president's or the governor's) rather than to educate people about the problems, challenge employers to do better, and galvanize advocates to help. Enforcement agency leaders need the courage to help push the nation, not just defend their agencies.

In contrast, Perkins used her speaking engagements as opportunities to lift up the workers and advocate improvements. Even after she retired, she continued to teach at labor centers, passionately speaking to the concerns of working men and women and lifting their spirits. The nation needs someone who will talk publicly about the real problems facing workers and will challenge both employers and public officials to improve conditions, particularly for workers in low-wage jobs.

A constant advocate for workers. Perkins also pushed the president to speak about the issues. In his message to Congress on January 3, 1938, Roosevelt spoke of seeking "legislation to end starvation wages and intolerable hours."[9] He made the case to the American people about the importance of the FLSA. I can't imagine that Frances Perkins didn't help him with the language and the arguments. Workers need the U.S. secretary of labor to help the president address wage theft and workers concerns and the state enforcement agencies to help governors consider how they could do more to protect and support workers.

Vision for the Department of Labor. Frances Perkins came to the job with a vision of what she wanted to accomplish. She believed in the fundamental mission of the department and advocated strongly for its staff and resources. Too many state enforcement leaders passively accept reductions in the staff and budgets. All federal and state enforcement leaders must reinvigorate their staff members, many of whom are demoralized through the constant attacks and budget cuts of the last three decades, especially the last decade.

A clear plan. Frances Perkins only agreed to take the job as secretary of labor after the president agreed to help her accomplish her goals. She came to her position with a clear sense of ways she could help workers. She was flexible with her plan, but she moved it forward. A few years ago, I met with a new state labor director and asked what her vision was for leading the agency. She seemed stumped by the question. State and federal enforcement leaders must have clear plans and must be determined to move them forward.

Relationship and support from "the boss." The secretary of labor cannot move major programs and legislative initiatives without strong support from the president. Frances Perkins had that support. State agency leaders cannot move things without the governors. If the agency leaders don't have the relationships and support they need, they must figure out how to build it. Workers need them to get the additional leadership support essential to moving programs.

Steadfastness. Frances Perkins remains the longest serving secretary of labor in U.S. history. By serving for twelve years, she was able to accomplish a lot. If you assume that it takes at least a year, perhaps two, to even understand a leadership role, it is important that leaders stick around. Although Secretary Elaine Chao served both terms under President George W. Bush, she had four different Wage and Hour administrators. By the time the Wage and Hour administrator began to learn the job, the person was gone. Perkins gave a speech at the end of her senior year in college that ended with the verse from I Corinthians in which the Apostle Paul says, "Therefore my beloved brethren, be ye steadfast, unmoveable, always abounding in the work of the Lord, forasmuch as ye know that your labor is not in vain in the Lord."[10] The U.S. Department of Labor and state departments of labor need leadership that will remain continuously steadfast in fighting for working people.

Administrative skills. Being smart and committed to worker justice is good, but not enough. Leading a state agency, and certainly leading an organization as large and complex as the Department of Labor or even a division such as Wage and Hour or OSHA requires leaders with administrative and management experience.

Willingness to listen to the public. Many representatives from workers' centers, universities, religious organizations, unions, and lawyer groups have experience combating wage theft. Perkins listened to people such as these and learned from them. So too should state and federal leaders.

Connections with worker advocacy groups. Frances Perkins knew the leadership at the National Consumers League, the primary national advocacy organization for the minimum wage, and made efforts to know other labor leaders as well. She knew many of the state factory inspectors and labor agency leaders. She knew people who could help push an agenda. In order to move anything in Congress, the secretary of labor and other Department of Labor leaders must call upon and work with worker advocacy organizations around the country. Having connections with those groups would be helpful. Similarly, state enforcement leaders should get to know those concerned about workers in their states.

There are probably few in the nation who could be as prepared for her leadership role as Frances Perkins was. Nonetheless, state agencies and the U.S. Department of Labor should seek people for leadership roles who have at least some of the preparation, characteristics, and vision she had. As Timothy Reardon, a retired regional administrator with Wage and Hour shared with me, "Leadership at the top makes a difference. It frees people to be creative and shakes things up."

The nation's workers are in crisis. Workers deserve strong leaders fighting on their behalf. Combating wage theft requires strong leadership. Leadership matters.

10

The U.S. Department of Labor: More Important Than Ever

And if you give yourself to the hungry and satisfy the desire of the afflicted, then your light will rise in darkness And your gloom will become like midday. Those from among you will rebuild the ancient ruins; You will raise up the age-old foundations; And you will be called the repairer of the breach, the restorer of the streets in which to dwell.

—Isaiah 58: 10,12 (NRSV)

In 1996, when a group of religious leaders and I first started IWJ, my colleagues and I would regularly get calls from workers about their problems in the workplace—they hadn't been paid, they'd gotten fired, or they were being cursed at regularly. The workers would tell us that their pastors suggested they call us.

My initial instinct and practice was to refer workers to unions representing workers in their industries. Occasionally this worked, but not often. Unions weren't interested in representing workers in two- or three-person shops and were focused on strategic approaches in key industries, something my colleagues and I supported.

My next plan was to refer them to the appropriate government agency. Well, that was easier said than done. Which one? How did one know which agency covered what?

As any good employer, I had the minimum wage poster hanging in my office. At the time, the poster read: "Call the Wage and Hour Division of the Department of Labor." I looked in the Chicago phone directory. There was no such listing. Being a fairly resourceful person, I called all the numbers listed under the Department of Labor. I finally found the Wage and Hour Division—it was listed in the Chicago phonebook as "Farm Labor Compliance." I don't know if you've visited Chicago recently, but we don't have too many farms. When you actually reached the Division, you were told, in English only of course, to leave a number where someone could call you back between 9:00 A.M. and 5:00 P.M. Imagine working in a sweatshop and trying to leave a number where someone from the Wage and Hour Division could call you back during working hours.

There was no listing for the Wage and Hour Division in the phone book. If you managed to find the correct telephone number, no one was home to take your call. The chance that a low-wage worker whose wages had been stolen could find help? Zero. So much for being easily accessible.

Another problem—even if a worker knew about and could locate the Wage and Hour Division, how would he or she know if the Division would collect his or her last paycheck? Or should he or she seek help from the Illinois Department of Labor? What was the difference between the two?

Next, I looked for a workers' rights manual that explained the state and federal worker protections laws, who enforced them, and where a worker could go for help. Surely some union, advocacy group, or agency had created such a guide that I could distribute. Wrong. In the great labor city of Chicago, there was no comprehensive workers' rights manual.[1]

I assigned a Lutheran Volunteer Corps intern a project of preparing a small workers' rights manual, which I thought would take a couple of weeks. Wrong again. This small project turned into a six-month ordeal, but catapulted me and my colleagues into the world of workers' rights education and enforcement, or the lack thereof.

Thankfully, the Wage and Hour Division of the Department of Labor has made it much easier for workers to complain. It now provides a toll-free number for workers to call that links people with someone immediately, and the Wage and Hour Division is now listed in the Chicago phone book. The Department of Labor's website is getting easier to navigate, but I still prefer to refer advocates and workers to the Can My Boss Do That website (www.canmybossdothat.com) because it uses clearer language and integrates the state and federal protections.

Over the years, I've had many opportunities to work collaboratively with the Department of Labor. IWJ affiliates have created dozens of workers' rights manuals for various states and in various languages. This is all fine and good. Nonetheless, in a period in U.S. history in which wage theft is rampant, unions represent less than 12 percent of the workforce,[2] workers' centers are expanding but struggling with inadequate resources, and far too few ethical employers are stepping forth, a strong, aggressive, and vocal U.S. Department of Labor is critical, indeed more important than ever. A strong and effective U.S. Department of Labor, allied with community partners, is the best hope for many workers in low-wage jobs.

In the initial version of this book, I had three full chapters on the U.S. Department of Labor, but things have changed in the last couple of years. The Department of Labor, with its excellent new leadership, has implemented some of the suggestions made in the previous edition and developed other outstanding approaches to thorny problems. State and local enforcement campaigns have mushroomed. And several excellent new resources have been developed that offer detailed recommendations for changes at the Department of Labor. Two resources are particularly important to note:

Improving Workplace Conditions through Strategic Enforcement: A Report to the Wage and Hour Division by David Weil offers a thorough analysis of how the Division can use its resources more strategically to stop and deter wage theft in industries that routinely steal wages. Download this publication at http://www.bu.edu/phpbin/news-cms/news/?dept=644 &id=56366.[3]

Just Pay: Improving Wage and Hour Enforcement at the United States Department of Labor is a compilation of recommendations by the Just Pay Working Group, convened by the National Employment Law Project. The Just Pay Working Group is composed of twenty-seven legal and community experts on wage theft. This resource is available from www .nelp.org.[4]

Consequently, this new edition eliminates many of the recommendations that have already been implemented. And though I am aware that some of the recommendations still included are being considered, I want to add my voice to those advocating changes. But before outlining a set of recommendations for how the Department of Labor can strengthen its enforcement, it is important to understand the history and core functions of the agency. As the author of one book about the Department of Labor says, "Although enumerating these activities may make dull reading, behind them lies the struggles, hopes, and achievements of tens of millions of workers."[5]

Understanding the Department of Labor

The executive branch of the U.S. government is divided into fifteen departments, each of which is headed by a secretary. These secretaries form the president's cabinet, which directs overall policy and administers government agencies. The Department of Labor is the largest government agency designed to help the nation's workers.[6] Originally, the issues of labor were lumped into the Department of Commerce and Labor, which was created in 1903. The labor side of this department focused primarily on research and reports on working conditions. Labor unions and the settlement house movement believed there needed to be more focus on improving working conditions. Finally, in 1913, the American Federation of Labor pushed through a bill sponsored by Representative William B. Wilson of Pennsylvania creating a separate Department of Labor.[7] Representative Wilson was appointed the first secretary of labor. The purpose of the Department of Labor is as follows:

> To foster, promote, and develop the welfare of the wage earners, job seekers and retirees of the United States; improve working conditions; advance opportunities for profitable employment; and assure work-related benefits and rights.

From day one, this new agency was short on resources and long on responsibilities. Congress allocated only $4 million for its first year to cover two thousand Department of Labor employees. Almost seventeen hundred of these employees were in the Bureau of Immigration, which was then assigned to the Department of Labor. The remaining staff members were in Labor Statistics, Naturalization, and the Children's Bureau.[8] Many of the core functions for which the Department of Labor is now known, enforcing wage standards and health and safety standards, were not initial responsibilities because there were no federal standards.

A few years later, in 1917 when the United States entered World War I, the Department of Labor became the federal agency that mobilized industry and labor to support the war effort. (The Department of Labor played a similar role during World War II.) The Department's role in job placement emerged during this period as it opened more than four hundred local offices to recruit and place workers in war industries.[9]

After World War I, the responsibilities assigned to the Department of Labor expanded. The Railway Labor Act (passed in 1926 and then amended to include airline workers in 1936) defined terms for bargaining, arbitration, and mediation between railroad workers and employers. The Norris-La Guardia Act (1932), known as the "anti-injunction" law, outlawed courts from supporting agreements that required workers to give up their rights to a union as a condition of employment. It also withdrew federal power to issue injunctions in nonviolent labor disputes. In addition, job training and placement programs were dramatically expanded during the Great Depression. In 1933, Frances Perkins was appointed secretary of labor by President Franklin D. Roosevelt.

Although there have been many excellent secretaries of labor since Frances Perkins, both Republicans and Democrats, no one did more than she to shape the role of the Department of Labor as an agency that did both job training and placement and labor standards enforcement. As you learned in the previous chapter, she drafted, lobbied for, and then began implementation of the FLSA. Passed in 1938, the FLSA was clearly the most significant labor standards bill that Congress had ever approved.

Over the years, Congress added many more job training, job placement, and workplace enforcement responsibilities to the Department of Labor. And perhaps inevitably, the responsibilities for program and enforcement were added in a piecemeal fashion, without careful thinking about how they all would fit together. As a result, the agency has responsibility for enforcing hundreds of laws and dozens of programs that don't quite mesh and that actually overextend its ability to be effective.

Department of Labor Divisions

The Department of Labor is a relatively small federal agency with approximately eighteen thousand employees and a proposed FY 2011 budget of almost $14 billion. Most of its budget goes to benefits and training programs, not enforcement activities. As it is currently configured, the Department of Labor has four primary functions.

First, it oversees state benefit programs (unemployment insurance) and federal benefit programs (workers' compensation for disabled minors, longshore workers, nuclear workers, and federal employees). In FY 2011, under the president's budget, the Department of Labor would oversee the distribution of approximately $92 billion in benefits to workers.

The second function is to give out grants. Most of the grants are for employment and training programs and are handled by the Employment and Training Administration. In FY 2011, under the president's budget, the Department would give out approximately $4.1 billion in grants, 71 percent of which are provided via formulas to the states.

The third function is producing statistics. The Bureau of Labor Statistics provides regular information about the nation's workers that is used by Congress, researchers, other government agencies, and the Department of Labor itself.

The fourth function is the enforcement of labor laws. Although the bulk of the Department's money goes into benefits and grants, half the agency's staff (nine thousand employees) are focused on enforcement. In FY 2011, under the president's budget, $1.5 billion of the Department of Labor's $14 billion operating budget will be devoted to enforcement activities. There are a variety of enforcement divisions that are responsible for enforcing a wide number of worker protection laws for all 150 million workers and 8 million workplaces in the country. The following divisions have primary enforcement responsibilities—key departments within the Department of Labor (DOL) are as follows:

The *Employee Benefits Security Administration* protects private sector employee pension, health, and other benefit programs.

The *Wage and Hour Division* is the most important department relative to our concerns about wage theft. This division enforces many laws, including the FLSA, which addresses minimum wage and overtime.

The *Occupational Safety and Health Administration* is responsible for enforcing workplace health and safety laws and educating workers and employers about best practices to ensure safe workplaces.

The *Mine Safety and Health Administration* enforces the laws covering mines and some mills. Most of the department is focused on coal mines, but it also covers other kinds of mines and mills.

There are also a variety of offices and divisions that support the secretary of labor and support these programmatic functions. The Office of the Solicitor, the DOL legal office, is one support division that is particularly important for fighting wage theft. In order to stop wage theft, the agency needs an aggressive and well-staffed Solicitor's Office that can back up the Wage and Hour Division and litigate cases when reasonable settlements can't be reached quickly with employers who have stolen wages.

More Cops Are Needed

The Wage and Hour Division, the main Department of Labor division that enforces wage protection laws, needs more cops on the job, both to recover stolen wages and prevent more theft. When bank robberies rise in a region, the FBI shifts enforcement staff. When drug dealing increases in a neighborhood, local police shift officers. When there is a national crisis, such as occurred on 9/11, the nation responds by setting up a new agency and hiring thousands more staff dedicated to addressing the problems. Think of the thousands of workers now employed at airports to guard against terrorism.

Wage theft demands similar attention and focus. The nation faces a wage theft crisis with abysmally low staffing levels in both the federal Wage and Hour Division (the primary federal division that addresses wage theft) and state labor enforcement agencies. If we are serious about recovering workers' wages, deterring future wage theft, and recovering unpaid taxes, we must make ending wage theft and payroll fraud a national priority. When the FLSA was passed in 1938, the Wage and Hour Division was created to enforce the law.[10] The division is composed of investigators, essentially front-line cops who ferret out wage theft, and their administrative support personnel. These investigators actually have police powers. They have the right to go into workplaces and demand to see records. They have the right to interview managers, supervisors, and workers. They have the right to immediately stop illegal child labor. They have the right to stop the shipment of goods produced by workers who have not been paid in compliance with the FLSA (using the "hot goods" power used mostly in farm labor and garment cases). They are not research-type investigators. They are detective-type investigators, hence the term "cops."

By June 1941, the Wage and Hour Division (WHD) had 1769 employees "stationed in the field"[11] who were charged with enforcing the FLSA. At the time, it was responsible for protecting 15.5 million workers covered by the law and monitoring the three hundred sixty thousand workplaces in which they worked. That works out to about one investigator for every nine thousand workers. Even then, it was quite an undertaking. Those investigators conducted 48,449 physical inspections of the establishments the WHD was responsible for covering. WHD investigators inspected 12 percent of the establishments covered by the law.[12]

Well over half of those inspections were focused on companies that the investigators thought might be breaking the law, not in response to complaints. Today, we call those investigations "targeted" investigations. Then, these inspections were called "routine" investigations or "industry drives." In 1941, the WHD found 31,493 employers in violation. Fifty-four percent of them came from these routine investigations and industry drives.

In 1968, 60 percent of the WHD investigations were targeted investigations, not complaint-driven ones. The investigators focused on places "that violations are likely to be found."[13]

Over the years, many additional labor laws have been added to the WHD's enforcement responsibilities. The 1960s saw a flurry of bills passed that were assigned to the WHD for enforcement, including the Contract Work Hours Standards Act, the Equal Pay Act, the McNamara-O'Hara Service Contract Act, and the Age Discrimination in Employment Act.

In 1983, the Migrant and Seasonal Agricultural Worker Protection Act became law. This law is designed to protect farm workers, but has never had the teeth or the number of investigators assigned to adequately do the job.

In 1993, Congress passed the FMLA, and the WHD became responsible for enforcing the act. This important law allows workers to take unpaid leave time to deal with medical issues affecting themselves or their family members. Unfortunately, this law piled enormous amounts of work on the investigators, but the department hired no additional investigators. One former regional administrator estimated that a quarter to a third of his investigators' time was spent on enforcing the FMLA. This was a huge work addition, with no additional staff.

Today, Wage and Hour investigators are responsible for enforcing wage laws covering more than 130 million full- and part-time workers, working in approximately seven million workplaces. Even though the Obama administration added investigators to Wage and Hour, bringing the total investigators up to approximately one thousand, the Division continues to be woefully understaffed. One investigator is responsible for more than one hundred thirty thousand workers and seven thousand workplaces.

The overall crisis in terms of investigators means that any vulnerable subset of workers is inadequately protected. The Child Labor Coalition estimates that the Department of Labor has the equivalent of only twenty-three full-time employees assigned to conducting child labor investigations,[14] even though there are one hundred forty-eight thousand youths illegally employed in an average week and over two hundred thousand injuries to youth (and an average of sixty-seven deaths) per year.[15] The Farmworker Justice Fund estimates that the equivalent of only twenty full-time investigators are focused on enforcing the Migrant and Seasonal Protection Act, which covers farm workers. And in 2005, only twenty-five of the 1780 child labor investigations conducted involved agriculture employers, even though agriculture is one of the most dangerous industries for children.[16] The Child Labor Coalition sums it up: "There is no justification for investigating such a dangerous industry so infrequently."

No wonder we have a crisis of wage theft and payroll fraud in the nation with so few cops on the job and so few investigators focused on industries commonly known to steal wages from poor workers and revenues from public treasuries. As one current Wage and Hour investigator told me, "We're just doing triage with cases." Most of the recommendations advocates offer to the Department of Labor suggest how the Division can use its limited resources more effectively. Although it is critically important that the Division conduct more targeted investigations and work more collaboratively with allies, the Division still needs to get more cops on the job. The Department of Labor leadership and the advocacy community must continue to make the case that the nation faces a crime wave of wage theft and payroll fraud that demands a doubling or tripling of Wage and Hour investigators. We can get more cops if we make the case for them clearly—and loudly. In the early 1990s, when one neighborhood in New York City, Washington Heights, was wracked by violence and corruption, the mayor and police commissioner committed an additional 110 police officers to that one neighborhood.[17] When Mayor Antonio Villaraigosa was elected the mayor of Los Angeles in 2005, he pledged to add one thousand police officers to the city's police force. By March 2008, despite budget shortfalls, he was halfway toward meeting his pledge. Regardless of whether or not one agrees with these police force expansions, they demonstrate that leaders can advocate and successfully increase enforcement staff, by significant numbers, when there is a crisis and the political leadership to make this happen.

The most dramatic national mobilization of additional enforcement staff came after 9/11. Only two months after the attack on the Twin Towers and the Pentagon, Congress passed the Aviation and Transportation Security Act establishing the Transportation Security Administration (TSA). One year later, the new department had received 1.4 million applications and hired fifty-three thousand new airport screeners.[18] There was enormous political will. Money was found. Staff was recruited, hired, and trained.

Because of the important role the Solicitor's Office (the Department of Labor's attorneys) plays in backing up the Wage and Hour Division, we must also ensure that there are enough attorneys to adequately support the fight against wage theft. In 2010, there were 6825 FLSA suits filed in federal court. Only 151 of them were filed by the Department of Labor. If the Wage and Hour Division can't get employers to pay workers, the Solicitor's Office must file suits in court to get the money back.

Don Sherman of the Cincinnati Workers' Center helped eleven workers file a wage claim against Masonry Structures Inc., based in Rogers, Arkansas, in September 2007. These workers had helped the company build Wal-Mart stores in Iowa, Pennsylvania, and Maryland. The workers had been offered $13 per hour but were never paid. The workers and Don believe they are owed more than $15,000 from the company. In March 2008, a DOL Wage and Hour investigator in Arkansas informed Don that an agreement had been made with the owner of the company, David Crowell, to pay the wages back on a monthly installment plan. In June 2008, after the workers complained about not receiving any money, the investigator informed the workers that the employer had reneged on paying and that the Department of Labor was considering whether or not to pursue the case in court.[19] What's the question? The workers didn't get their money, and they have put their trust in the Department of Labor. The case should be pursued. The Solicitor's Office must assign or hire more attorneys to work on wage theft cases. If the investigators aggressively pursue wage theft cases, there must be staff and resources to file the cases in court if quick settlements don't occur.

As this second edition of the book goes to press, Congress is slashing budgets for enforcement agencies under the guise of fiscal discipline. Instead of hunkering down and trying to protect an already inadequate number of enforcement personnel, the Department of Labor and its allies should broadcast the dimensions of the crime wave, advocate increases in cops on the job, and make the case that increased enforcement personnel will rebuild families, level the playing field for businesses, increase tax revenues, restore trust in government, and stimulate the economy. A good offense is the best defense.

Wage theft is at epidemic proportions. We clearly need more cops on the job.

Create a Community Enforcement Model

Workers need the Department of Labor's Wage and Hour Division to work more collaboratively with community partners.

Remember the story in Chapter 2 about Tin Oo, Aung Bee, and Dah La Klee, the Karen refugees in Indianapolis who had been given bounced checks for their construction work in 2007? First Exodus, the refugee settlement agency in Indianapolis, called the employer and asked him to pay. He didn't. Exodus then asked Reverend Bob Coats, a retired American Baptist missionary who had worked with the Karens in Thailand (and my father-in-law), if he could help. Bob interviewed the workers (in Karen of course) and got all the details about what happened. He then helped the workers file a complaint with the Wage and Hour Division of the Department of Labor. After three months, a Wage and Hour investigator called to say she had been "put on the case," but she recommended that Bob just take the case to small claims court. She also said that he "shouldn't be surprised if the case takes a while." Six months later, neither Bob nor the workers had heard anything. Bob was not asked to translate for the investigator. Exodus was not asked whether other refugees had worked for this same employer. The workers weren't asked to gather additional information to help with the investigation. The investigator took some information and then was never heard from again.[20]

The workers needed help, but so did the investigator. The workers, Bob Coats, and the investigator should have been a team working together. The crisis of wage theft in the nation requires a rethinking of how workplace standards are enforced. We can no longer rely on a handful of highly trained workplace cops to protect the nation's workforce from what has become an epidemic of wage theft.

Instead, we must create a community enforcement model. We must draw from the lessons and experiences of community policing, which "redefines the philosophy and work of police to include problem-solving partnerships with the community."[21]

The Center for Problem-Oriented Policing, a nonprofit organization comprising affiliated police practitioners, researchers, and universities dedicated to the advancement of problem-oriented policing, outlines that community policing:

- Focuses on crime and social disorder through the delivery of police services that includes aspects of traditional law enforcement, as well as prevention, problem solving, community engagement, and partnerships.
- Balances reactive responses to calls for service with proactive problem solving centered on the causes of crime and disorder.
- Requires police and citizens to join together as partners.[22]

Although elements of community policing have existed for centuries, the modern community policing movement initially emerged in the 1960s in response to concerns about rising crime rates and unfair treatment of African Americans and then again in the 1980s during a period of rising crime rates and worsening police–community relations. The traditional mode of police officers intervening in situations, often in discriminatory fashion, completely on their own, was not only alienating community residents, but was not effective. As a result, police departments began to shift their approaches, seeking ways to partner with community groups and solve community problems.

The Wage and Hour Division and its leadership around the nation are interested in creating community-policing-type partnerships to reach out to workers. Nonetheless, most partnership initiatives have been hampered by a lack of resources, bureaucratic control from Washington, D.C., and staff changes. In addition, there are obstacles to investigators sharing information with other enforcement agencies, advocates, and even workers themselves. It is useful, however, to understand the existing partnerships from which new models and approaches can develop.

One of the most significant community partnerships in recent years was Justice and Equality in the Work Place, referred to as JEWP, the dream child of Betty Campbell, who was the DOL assistant district director and district director during the start-up phase, and strongly supported by the Wage and Hour administrator, Tammy McCutchen. The initiative, launched in Houston in 2001, brought together U.S. labor-related agencies, including the U.S. Department of Labor Wage and Hour Division, the Office of Federal Contract Compliance Programs (OFCCP), the Occupational Safety and Health Administration (OSHA), the U.S. Equal Employment Opportunity Commission (EEOC), foreign consulates, such as the Consulate General of Mexico and the Consulate General of El Salvador, local religious and community agencies, such as Catholic Charities, and state and local agencies, such as the Texas Workers' Compensation Commission and the Police Department—Office of Community Affairs. When she was promoted to deputy regional administrator for the Southwest Region, Campbell launched a similar group in June 2003 in Dallas. In both cities, the groups agreed to "work together through information sharing and mutual support toward promoting justice, safety and equality in the workplace."

Both groups developed educational outreach programs for Latino workers to make them aware of their rights and responsibilities in the workplace, met regularly to review their public awareness programs, distributed Spanish-language resources developed by the partners, conducted public educational forums, and created a workers' rights "hotline" where Spanish-speaking workers would be encouraged to call. According to a Department of Labor press release in 2003, the Houston Justice and Equality in the Workplace Program, in its first two years, helped the Wage and Hour Division to recover over $1.3 million in back wages for nineteen hundred workers as the result of investigations initiated by referrals from the partnership. Nearly 70 percent of all calls at the Houston program were referred to the Department of Labor.[23]

Unfortunately, the Houston program did not have sustained staffing. When Campbell moved to Dallas and other local partners changed, the program fell apart. By the time IWJ started a workers' center in Houston, there was no one answering the hotline, despite the number being plastered on billboards around the city. The workers' center was able, after several meetings, to convince the group to allow it to answer the hotline calls so that workers would be able to speak to someone.

Campbell's commitment to pulling people together to jointly address wage theft problems in the community is the right direction and should continue to be built upon. The experience of how the initiative was allowed to fade away demonstrates the importance of having the right career and political leadership in place.

In 2000, the Interfaith Committee on Worker Issues helped create the Chicago Area Workers' Rights Initiative (CAWRI), which brings together staff from the DOL Wage and Hour Division, the DOL Occupational Safety and Health Administration (OSHA), the Equal Employment Opportunity Commission (EEOC), the Illinois Department of Labor (IDOL), the Illinois Workers' Compensation Commission, and community workers' centers and legal clinics. The group developed a uniform complaint form that could be filled out by workers (through workers' centers) and accepted jointly by the various agencies. One person from the government agencies reviews the complaints and forwards them to the appropriate agencies. CAWRI has undertaken a couple of industry initiatives focused on both education and enforcement, but without dedicated staff for the collaboration and strong endorsement from top agency leaders, the collaboration doesn't begin to reach its potential.

The Employment Education and Outreach initiative (EMPLEO) was launched in Las Vegas in September 2003, as the city continued to see an increase in the number of Latino workers, mostly in the hospitality—restaurants and casinos—and construction industries. It then expanded to Los Angeles. Patterned after Houston's JEWP, EMPLEO was created to help the cities' growing populations of Spanish-speaking workers understand their workplace rights and responsibilities. EMPLEO is a joint effort between businesses and community organizations, state and federal government agencies, and the Consulate of Mexico.

Before EMPLEO, Spanish-speaking workers had little or no access to state and federal agencies handling workplace-related complaints. Most did not even know such agencies like the DOL Wage and Hour Division, the DOL Occupational Safety and Health Administration (OSHA), and the U.S. Equal Employment Opportunity Commission existed. As part of the program, a workers' rights hotline was set up through which workers can call and file workplace-related complaints. The hotline is staffed by volunteers at the Mexican Consulate, who then refer callers to the appropriate agencies.

In its first two years, EMPLEO hotline volunteers received anywhere from ten to fifteen calls a day. And, in 2007, more than one thousand current and former employees of Las Vegas-based plastering and masonry company, Desert Plastering, received close to $1.2 million in back wages as a result of a DOL Wage and Hour investigation triggered by a complaint referred by EMPLEO.

Beginning in 2007, however, the number of calls received by EMPLEO dwindled. Johannes Jacome, deputy consul at the Mexican Consulate, attributes the drop partly to the slowdown in construction activity. Still, he said, EMPLEO partner agencies continue to encourage workers to use the hotline and report any workplace-related problem.

In 2010, a new DOL and community partnership was formed in Denver, Colorado, to help community partners understand the enforcement agencies better and then to figure out collectively how to better provide educational tools and programs for immigrant and low-wage workers. "The first six months of the collaboration involved relationship and demystifying the process of helping workers recover unpaid wages," said Reverend Daniel Klawitter, Director of Interfaith Committee for Worker Justice of Colorado. Chad Frasier, the District Director for Colorado, had previously been involved with partnerships in Houston and played an important role in convening government partners. The collaboration includes representatives from the Wage and Hour Division, OSHA, Columbia Legal Services, El Centro, the Colorado Immigrant Rights Coalition, Interfaith Committee for Worker Justice of Colorado, SEIU, and others. The partnership has organized worker education events at community locations and is working on media outreach efforts, a wage theft brochure, and collaborative approaches for reaching workers in a few sectors in which wage theft is particularly rampant.

Having funding for community policing efforts matters. Although the Wage and Hour Division provided modest staffing support for the initiatives described above (possibly a tenth of one person's time), none of the collaborations identified above had dedicated full-time staff that could help move forward joint initiatives. Most serious citywide policing initiatives dedicate police officers to the effort and provide funding for community allies.

When Congress passed the antitrafficking legislation to protect workers against the trafficking of workers as slaves, it allocated money for outreach. As a result, the Department of Justice (DOJ) Civil Rights Division and Health and Human Services funded forty-two task forces to bring together state, local, and federal law enforcement with neighborhood partners. In addition, funds were available for targeted educational outreach. No such funds have been set aside to support community wage enforcement task forces, but clearly they should be.

OSHA, the division that enforces health and safety laws, seems to have an easier time collaborating with community partners than the Wage and Hour Division does. Perhaps it is because OSHA administers a grants program to work with community organizations in providing training on health and safety issues to workers. Or perhaps there is simply a different internal culture that has developed that is committed to collaborative work.

Developing a community policing model for wage enforcement makes sense, but it won't happen except as window dressing if top leadership is not driving it and resources are not committed to adequately tap the potential of community partners.

In 2011, the Wage and Hour Division created ten new positions focused on community outreach. Time will tell if these new staff positions can build deep and meaningful partnerships or if they simply do outreach presentations.[24]

With strong community partnership models, the Wage and Hour Division can:

Question more workers away from the workplace. In 2004, a group of restaurant workers visited the Madison Interfaith Workers' Center because they weren't receiving minimum wage or getting paid overtime. They were afraid they would lose their jobs or, worse, the employer would retaliate against their families in their home countries. Consequently, the workers filed anonymous complaints with the Department of Labor. Instead of asking the center staff to organize a meeting with workers at the center or at a nearby congregation, the investigator called the employer and scheduled a time to stop by the restaurant and talk with the remaining workers. The employer told the workers what he wanted them to say, and they did so out of fear of losing their jobs.[25]

Community partnerships can assist the Wage and Hour Division in questioning workers away from the workplace, especially in situations where there is reason to believe workers might be fearful of retaliation. Workers' centers, legal clinics, union halls, and congregations could be asked to serve as places where the enforcement staff could meet with workers.

Communicate more effectively with workers. Once a worker files a complaint or a worker center helps workers file a complaint about wage theft, the worker and the center often get pushed out of the investigations. Workers complain that investigators won't return phone calls, don't discuss potential settlements, and don't ask for additional information that could strengthen the cases. Part of the lack of communication is simply a workload problem. The investigators have too many cases and can't be as responsive as they should. But part of the problem is the approach. Community partners may speak the languages of the workers or have ways to communicate with them that investigators don't.

Collect better information. Even though workers may be victims of crimes, they are willing and eager to help in the process of gathering information to make their cases. So too are the workers' centers and other allies. Unfortunately, many investigators do not tap the willingness of workers and community allies to help gather information for their cases. Investigators should figure out how to educate workers and community partners about the kind of information needed.

Michael Kerr, Wage and Hour administrator from December 1999 to January 2001, and the current assistant secretary for administration and management at the Department of Labor, told me the story of his father, Thomas Kerr, who represented janitors in an antitrust case. When attorney Kerr took depositions, he did so in an auditorium thinking that people might be more comfortable doing so together. One by one, he began to get statements from the workers up on the stage. As workers listened to the questions he asked, they began to understand the information he needed. The further along the process went, the more useful information he gathered. The workers themselves were forthcoming, and they found other workers who could help with information. There's no reason why Wage and Hour investigators couldn't use similar approaches for engaging workers in information gathering.

Don Sherman, director of the Cincinnati Workers' Center, describes a typical situation in which he assisted four workers who had been cheated of wages by Capital Building Services, a Buffalo Grove, Illinois-based company that hired janitors to work at Target and Meyers stores at night. The workers filed a claim with the DOL Wage and Hour Division on August 3, 2006. The Wage and Hour Division personnel never communicated with the workers. A year later, in the summer of 2007, the case settled and the workers believe they got half of what they were owed. Perhaps the case wasn't strong enough to recover all the owed wages, but surely the case could have been strengthened with the involvement of the workers and their allies,[26] and the workers were entitled to know why this settlement was reached.

Worker Rights Education

In addition to getting more cops on the job and partnering with community allies, the Department of Labor must help educate workers about their rights in the workplace and how to address workplace problems. The Department of Labor's We Can Help campaign is a wonderful new initiative to reach underserved workers.

Some worker allies worry about the Department of Labor's focus on worker education and outreach because they believe the Department should focus on enforcement. It *should* focus on enforcement, *and* it should provide educational tools and resources for workers. Enforcement and worker education go hand in hand. Workers who know their rights and understand enforcement tools are much more likely to hold employers accountable for paying them fairly. In the 1968 DOL budget report to Congress, a time during which 60 percent of investigations were targeted toward low-wage egregious industries, the agency conducted an aggressive outreach and education program that included development and distribution of nontechnical pamphlets, national press releases, a series of questions and answers for use in newspapers, radio and television spot announcements, and hundreds of presentations.[27]

One of the best models for government-sponsored education and outreach is the Department of Agriculture's Cooperative Extension Service. This nationwide network of extension offices provides experts "who provide useful, practical, and research-based information to agricultural producers, small business owners, youth, consumers, and others in rural areas and communities of all sizes."[28] The Cooperative Extension Service was established along with the land-grant university system. Its original mission was to "teach agriculture, military tactics and mechanical arts" and to "promote the liberal and practical education of the industrial classes."[29] In its early years, the Service organized farmers' institutes, schools, and youth clubs. By 1918, a total of 2435 counties had Ag Agents, and 1715 counties had Home Demonstration agents. This grassroots educational network reached deep into communities, offering popular education programs and helping people organize to address problems. During World War I, the Service helped organize farm cooperatives. During the Depression, the agents educated people about the emergency government action programs and money management.

During World War II, the Service helped people organize Victory Gardens and scrap metal drives. The Service's education programs are practical, responsive to community needs, and collaborative with community organizations.[30]

The Cooperative Extension Service is based in the Department of Agriculture, because it serves the agency's core constituency, farmers and their families. The Department of Labor needs a strong educational outreach program focused on its core constituency, workers. Following are a few recommendations for strengthening workers' rights education and outreach aimed at stopping or reducing wage theft:

Develop a peer outreach program. Many public health programs have learned the advantage of training outreach workers to reach out to families with simple messages about health issues. Farm worker health programs recruit and train health promoters—"promotorios." Maternal and child health programs in urban areas increasingly are hiring and training community women to visit with new mothers about health issues. These programs work. The Department of Labor should develop such a workers' rights education program, training workers (including people who speak languages other than English) and sending them out to help train their colleagues. A partnership between the Department of Labor and the Corporation for National and Community Service could create a pilot program of worker rights outreach workers using the VISTA program.

Create educational outreach materials for each targeted industry. Although the Department of Labor Wage and Hour Division creates and puts on its website many excellent fact sheets, there are very few popular education-style resources designed for workers. In 2000, IWJ worked with the Department of Labor on creating a Spanish-language educational video and a photo-novella (a book with lots of pictures) in English and Spanish. IWJ then helped distribute those resources to poultry workers. These are the kinds of resources that should be created. In industries in which there are widespread health problems as well as wage problems, the materials should address both sets of problems.

Arrange for weekly radio shows on worker rights. Arise Chicago Workers' Center runs a weekly radio show called Radio Chamba on a small college radio station. The show is operated and hosted by workers who are leaders at the workers' center. Sometimes Radio Chamba interviews a government agency person talking about workers' rights. Other times it interviews an area attorney or a union organizer. Still other times, the show hosts workers who have experienced problems in the workplace and joined with others to address the problems. Workers are encouraged to call in with questions. The Wage and Hour Division could organize similar weekly national call-in shows on workers' rights in multiple languages. These should be podcast and made available on the DOL website.

Write a weekly worker rights column for ethnic media. The Wage and Hour administrator should write a weekly *Stop Wage Theft* column addressing workers' rights questions. The column should be distributed nationally to publications that reach immigrant and African American communities. Mainstream media would be invited to pick up and carry the column as well.

Show workers' rights videos at one-stops. The federal and state job training programs collaborate in running "one-stop" centers where workers can access help for finding jobs and gaining educational skills. When workers go to one-stop centers, they often have to wait. Workers' rights videos should be shown in the waiting rooms.

Create worker rights apps. In 2011 the Wage and Hour Division issued a recordkeeping app to make it easier for workers to record their hours. Other apps should be developed helping workers quickly gather information about their rights.

Create and promote a "do-it-yourself" kit. It is very difficult for workers, especially those with poor writing skills (this includes the one in five American adults who are functionally illiterate[31]), to challenge their employers. The Alberta, Canada, wage enforcement agency has a simple "do-it-yourself" kit for assisting workers in informing their employers that they are owed back wages. The Wage and Hour Division could easily create, distribute, and post on its website a similar kit for assisting workers in talking directly with their employers about back wages problems. Workers would be able to copy the basic letter with official-sounding language and put in their specific information about hours worked and wages owed. A copy of the relevant law or fact sheet should be attached.

Punish Wage Thieves

If you steal someone's cash, you will probably go to jail. If you steal someone's wages, at most you might have to repay the wages. Or maybe not. Stealing wages is unlawful, but not a high-priority crime.

If a worker steals from his or her employer, the worker faces serious consequences. The worker would most certainly be fired, losing his or her job and income, and in most states would be denied unemployment insurance. The worker would probably be prosecuted and, if found guilty, fined and/or imprisoned.

If, on the other hand, an employer steals wages from workers, it is usually a crime without consequences. Unless the wage theft is based on repeated or willful violations, the worst thing that might happen is that the employer will have to pay the worker victims what they should have been paid in the first place.

In most states, if you steal property valued at more than $1000, it is considered a felony and you could spend a year or two in a state prison. Perhaps you might get free with probation for the first offense, but if you stole more than $1000 a second time, you would almost certainly go to prison. Taking anything of value without the owner's consent is called theft or larceny. When force or intimidation is involved with the theft, it becomes robbery, which has more severe punishments. Given the kind of intimidation many workers experience in the workplace, it is appropriate to consider the stealing of wages as wage robbery, not "just" wage theft. Retail companies are very concerned about shoplifting— the intentional stealing of products from their stores. In order to combat shoplifting, stores have hired security guards and instituted policies of pushing for the arrest and prosecution of shoplifters. The retailers believe that having a strong policy of arresting and prosecuting shoplifters is the best deterrent against other shoplifters.

The same logic should follow for wage thieves. The best deterrence against those who might steal wages against workers is to impose serious consequences for those who are caught stealing wages.

Quite often, an employer gets away with paying less than is owed the workers. For example, let's assume that an employer has been underpaying workers for the last five years. When the case is settled, the back wages will probably only be for two, or at most three years, not the five years' worth of wages that were stolen. This is because federal law only permits recovery of two, or in the case of willful violations, three years' worth of back wages.[32]

Many employers who steal wages from workers do not keep accurate records. If the workers claiming underpayment of wages do not keep good records themselves on all the time worked, the government investigators may not be able to prove that the employer stole all the wages claimed by the worker. Consequently, the employer will get away with paying less than what the employer should have paid.

Given the constant turnover in many low-paying jobs, an unethical employer wishing to steal from workers can assume that many workers will move on before filing a complaint or before an investigator might get around to visiting a workplace. Again, the wage thief might very well suffer no consequence for the wage theft.

Currently, most federal workplace investigations are triggered by complaints. (This is in contrast to targeted investigations in which the enforcement staff "targets" industries that are believed to be stealing wages.) Thus an unethical employer can assume that if he or she intimidates his or her workers enough, they won't file complaints and the employer won't be inspected. Given how stretched the enforcement staff is, it is safe to assume that without a complaint there will be no unannounced "drop-in" inspection. The wage thief will probably face no meaningful consequences for either intimidating workers or stealing wages. If someone should happen to file a complaint, the most the employer will probably have to pay is the back wages the employer should have paid in the first place.

If employers who steal wages only pay workers the wages they should have been paid, employers in effect get a no-interest loan from their workers. Meanwhile, workers, especially workers in low-wage jobs who aren't paid the wages owed, must take out loans, often in the form of credit card debt or payday loans at exorbitant interest rates, to meet their basic food and rent bills. Or they might lose their homes altogether.

The lack of meaningful consequences for wage theft is clearly one of the reasons for the rising epidemic of employers stealing wages from workers. Employers know the chances of getting caught are quite low and that if they do get caught, the consequences are negligible—usually only repaying a portion of the wages the employer should have paid in the first place.

In order to stop wage theft, we must use all the existing penalties available to enforcement staff and design more effective penalties if they are not sufficient. Penalties for stealing wages should be meaningful not only for punishing those who steal wages, but, more important, to deter others who might be tempted to steal wages.

Compliance with the nation's laws relies both on general acceptance of the basic principles of law and morality and on fear of the consequences of breaking the law. There must be both incentives for good behavior and disincentives for bad behavior. Punishments must be fair and appropriate and must consider the circumstances. And punishments are most effective if they succeed in scaring people into doing the right thing and don't actually have to be used. We must publicly punish some of the worst wage thieves and make others who would dare steal wages worry about the possible consequences.

As the director of a nonprofit, I know full well that if I don't pay employer taxes on payroll and on a timely basis, the IRS will fine me and might even take my house away. If our finances are tight, we may juggle other bills, but never the IRS payroll taxes. Those of us in the nonprofit community have heard about other nonprofit organizations at which the IRS took the director's or board members' homes to pay the payroll taxes. There is a powerful disincentive looming out there. Few employers feel the same way about the Department of Labor, but they should.

Following are recommendations for punishing wage thieves. Most of them the U.S. Department of Labor has the power to do but has not used consistently. A few might require modest policy changes. The U.S. Department of Labor should:

Routinely impose civil money penalties and liquidated damages for recurring and willful offenders. The labor laws can sometimes be a bit confusing, especially with regard to the question of who is exempt and nonexempt from overtime (meaning who has to get paid overtime and who doesn't). But once a company has been reprimanded for violating a labor law and has been told how to fix it, there should be no question about the right thing to do. Willful violators, those whom the investigator can demonstrate understood the laws and intentionally violated them (such as employers who keep two sets of time records), should also be punished to the full extent possible. In addition, employers who refuse to quickly repay workers their back wages and who force the Department of Labor to take them to court should face tougher consequences.

Under current statutes, the Department of Labor has two primary tools for punishing those who steal wages—civil money penalties, referred to as CMPs, and liquidated damages. Neither of these punishments is used as often as it should be.

CMPs are assessed by the Department of Labor. As of 2008, the maximum CMPs allowed on minimum wage and overtime violations are $1100 per violation. The CMPs for a child labor violation are $11,000 per child. A child labor violation causing death or serious injury of a child may result in a maximum penalty of $50,000, which may be doubled to $100,000 for a repeated or willful violation. The Department of Labor seldom uses its fining ability, and when it does fine wage thieves, it is usually not enough to get the attention of the broad community.

The Department of Labor only issued fines in 1439 cases in 2006 and 1691 cases in 2007. Almost half the companies fined were for child labor violations.[33] (The Department of Labor seems much more willing to fine companies for child labor violations than for ongoing wage theft.) In 2006 and 2007, only 370 and 477 companies, respectively, were fined for violations of the FLSA. On average, each company was fined only $8000.[34] This figure is woefully inadequate as a disincentive to employers who steal tens of thousands and sometimes hundreds of thousands or millions of dollars from workers' wages.

The most obvious group of employers who should be fined are those who repeatedly steal wages. In 2006 and 2007, the Department of Labor issued CMPs for fewer than half of the companies that were found to have either repeat or recurring violations.[35]

	2007	2006
Cases with repeat violations	772	821
Repeat cases assessed CMPs	336	350
Percent of repeat cases assessed CMPs	**44%**	**43%**
Cases with recurring violations	479	426
Recurring cases assessed CMPs	192	179
Percent of recurring cases assessed CMPs	**40%**	**42%**

Liquidated damages is another powerful tool for enforcement. Liquidated damages is a fancy way of saying that a worker may get up to double the wages stolen. Thus, if a worker is owed $5000 in back wages, the employer would be required to pay the worker up to $10,000. When private attorneys take cases to court, they often seek liquidated damages. Because I had never heard of workers getting liquidated damages when they filed complaints with the Department of Labor, it wasn't until I was working on this book that I understood that the Department could actually seek to recover liquidated damages.

Even those employers who refuse to quickly repay workers and make the Department of Labor take them to court to recover the wages are not routinely punished with either CMPs or liquidated damages. In reviewing 294 consent decrees (court settlements) that were entered from 2002 to 2006 in federal court cases brought by the secretary of labor that resulted in payment of FLSA back wages, only twenty-eight cases (9.5 percent) were awarded CMPs and only sixty-six cases (22.4 percent) were awarded liquidated damages.

The Department of Labor should routinely seek both CMPs and liquidated damages from employers with recurring violations (they've been found guilty of the same crime before) and willful violations (the inspector knows the employer intentionally violated the laws), and those who refuse to reach a settlement agreement quickly and thus require the Department of Labor to take the issue to court (which takes time and resources away from enforcing other violations). The CMPs should be the maximum allowed—$1100 per violation involved for wage theft and $11,000 for child labor violations (more if the violations result in death or serious injury to the child). If this doesn't get violators' attention, then the fines need to be raised.

Expose recurring and willful wage thieves. If rat droppings are found in a restaurant, a public notice of that health violation is put in the newspaper or on the Internet. If I want to check out the health inspections of a Chicago restaurant, all I have to do is type in the restaurant's name on the Chicago Health Department's website and I can get full information about all the health inspections. The Wage and Hour Division should provide equally transparent information to the public about those who steal wages.

Some would argue that *all* violations should be publicly posted. Perhaps this is true, but if one assumes that some first-time violations involve misunderstandings of the laws, especially overtime exemptions (which are confusing despite the 2004 efforts to clarify them), then it seems fair to list *recurring* and *willful* violators.

The website should be publicized and easy to search on (unlike the Department of Labor's back wages search program). I should be able to type in "Target" and see if this company has violated the same laws more than once or if the company has been deemed to have willfully stolen wages.

In addition, when a company steals wages repeatedly, it should be listed in local newspapers. I suspect there are newspapers that would partner with the Department of Labor to regularly list wage violators.

Expand the use of "hot goods" provisions. The FLSA allows the Wage and Hour Division to stop companies from shipping their products in interstate commerce when the companies have violated the laws. Even though the "hot goods" provision had been used earlier, it was resurrected in the late 1990s, beginning in 1997.[36] The Wage and Hour Division aggressively used its power to force garment manufacturers to comply with labor laws by stopping the shipment of garments, which are usually sewn for just that season, in order to force quick payment of back wages and penalties.

I saw this provision used effectively once in Chicago. Arise Chicago was contacted by workers who had recently been laid off from their jobs. Not only had they not received sixty days' notice of the layoffs, but the company refused to give the workers their final paychecks. The company made suntan lotion. (You may think it odd that a Chicago company would make suntan lotion, but it is true.)

After quickly trying to figure out what was going on, we discovered that the company had huge inventories of suntan lotion. It was planning to sell the lotion and reopen in another configuration, having gotten rid of its workers and cheated them of their last paychecks. The Department of Labor used the "hot goods" provision to hold the warehouse full of lotion hostage and force the company to pay the workers money owed. This "hot goods" provision dramatically increases the economic consequences of withholding wages from workers and thus is an effective means of getting workers paid quickly.

Expand the use of "mechanic's liens." A mechanic's lien is a "hold" against your property that, if unpaid, allows a foreclosure action, forcing the sale of your property. It is recorded with the County Recorder's office by the unpaid contractor, subcontractor, or supplier. Sometimes liens occur when the prime contractor has not paid subcontractors or suppliers. Legally, the homeowner may be ultimately responsible for payment—even if the person has already paid the prime contractor.[37] So, residential construction workers who have not been paid could file mechanic's liens, but of course most low-wage workers don't know they can do this. The Department of Labor should collaborate with state agencies in assisting workers in using mechanic's liens.

In 2004, ten Austin, Texas, construction workers visited the Workers Defense Project. They had been working on building new Hilton hotels in Austin and Omaha, Nebraska. The workers claimed they were owed $15,000 in back wages from a contractor. When Hilton management was initially contacted about the problem, the management refused to pay. As soon as a lien was placed on the hotel using the Texas Mechanic's Lien law, the management quickly became involved and helped ensure that the contractor paid the workers their back wages.[38]

Aggressively punish those who fire or harass workers who file complaints. Protecting workers who file complaints with government agencies must be a high priority or else workers won't file complaints. The FLSA prohibits retaliation by employers against employees who complain about wage theft, but the Wage and Hour Division has pursued very few retaliation cases. When pursued, the Division has had some success. For example, a garment shop in New York City fired a worker who had the guts to file a complaint with the Wage and Hour Division. The Division pursued a retaliation claim on behalf of the garment worker in federal court and obtained an injunction ordering the sweatshop to reinstate the worker. Similarly, in Chicago, the owner of a Chinese buffet-type restaurant paid the back wages as ordered by the Wage and Hour Division, but then required the workers to give the money back. The Wage and Hour Division promptly dragged the owner back to court to recover the money for employees. These were great victories for the workers, but we need more cases like these. Workers who are pressured, harassed, or fired for complaining about wage theft should be "made whole" quickly. Whistleblower complaints should be investigated within 48 hours, and if there is sufficient evidence of retaliation, they should be:

- Addressed with the employer within seven days.
- Taken to court within fourteen days if the employer refuses to remedy voluntarily.
- Publicized when the worker is returned to the job.
- Remedied to the maximum extent available under the law (back wages, liquidated damages, interest, and CMPs).

Require interest payments on back wages. As noted earlier, by not paying workers their wages, employers in effect get a no-interest loan from the workers. When back wages are due to workers, employers should be required to pay the workers interest on their back wages. This would reduce the financial advantage of wage theft and increase the penalty. This relatively modest penalty should be sought for all back wages owed, regardless of whether or not the wages were stolen intentionally.

Extend the statute of limitations on payment of back wages by recurring/willful violators. In the current law, if an employer's violation is found to be "willful"—meaning the employer clearly knew he or she was stealing wages from workers and did it anyway—the Wage and Hour Division can expand collection of wages from two years to three years. Instead, the Division should be allowed to collect back wages for the entire time period for which the workers' wages were stolen.

Grant the secretary of labor the discretionary authority to require a recurring or willful violator to reimburse the Department of Labor for the entire cost of its investigation and litigation. Requiring an employer who intentionally steals wages to pay for the full costs of investigating the lawbreaking would increase the costs to an unethical employer. This strengthens the penalty for stealing wages. When cases are filed by private attorneys and settled, the employer pays workers' back wages, usually liquidated damages, and the attorneys' fees. Recovering costs for investigating cases could support further investigations.

Require recurring and willful violators to notify their employees, customers, and suppliers of their wage theft. What if unethical companies who willfully or repeatedly stole wages from workers were required to mail letters to all their workers and suppliers explaining that they had stolen wages from workers and that they were going to change their behavior? This would encourage more workers to step forward and would educate suppliers about these issues. In the same way that health departments put signs on windows of restaurants that are shut down, the Wage and Hour Division should require employers to post signs indicating that they had stolen wages. I think twice about eating in a restaurant that was shut down, even temporarily, for health violations. Posting such wage theft signs would embarrass employers, thus serving as a significant disincentive to stealing wages.

Publicly take someone's home or send someone to jail for stealing wages in a particularly egregious fashion. Underpaying someone is not good, no matter what. But some situations are significantly worse than others. When an employer has willfully and repeatedly stolen large amounts of money from vulnerable workers, perhaps causing some of them to become homeless, the employer should face serious consequences, such as the confiscation of a home to repay the workers' wages. In FY 2007, the IRS prosecuted 2837 cases against tax delinquents. Ninety percent of them were convicted and served an average of twenty-two months in jail.[39] Taxpayers know that if they don't work out a back payment arrangement, usually including interest and penalties, the IRS will prosecute and put you in jail.

When Martha Stewart lied about a stock sale, she was sent to jail for five months. The Securities and Exchange Commission is very clear that those who profit from illegal stock actions must both "disgorge" (pay back) their ill-gotten profits and be penalized. Just paying back the ill-gotten profits is not sufficient. Lawbreakers often pay significant penalties and some are sent to jail.

When Paris Hilton violated her probation (several times) by driving with a suspended license, she spent twenty-three days in jail. Lots of people go to jail for driving with a suspended license.

These high-profile cases send powerful deterrent messages to all others who might be tempted to lie about stock sales or drive with a suspended license. Can you name anyone who has been sent to jail for stealing wages? Only a tiny few employers who regularly and willfully steal wages from workers are jailed. In fact for most employers, the consequences of wage theft are minimal.

Post information about wage robbers who owe workers more than $50,000 in back wages. It would also help workers to know even first-time violators who steal substantial amounts of money. It would be another deterrent to wage theft if employers knew their crimes would be posted online in a searchable database. The website listing substantial and repeat wage violators should be updated regularly and allow easy access to information about employers who violate wage and hour laws. Those who molest children are placed on a predators list. Those who injure workers are posted on OSHA's website. Those who steal a significant amount of wages or repeatedly steal from workers should be identified.

In addition to serving as a strong deterrent to those who might steal wages, posting violators encourages workers who have had their wages stolen to complain themselves if they find that their employer has been found in violation in the past.

Require employers to distribute settlement agreements to all their workers. Employers should be required to distribute their settlement agreements on labor issues, including back wages, to all their workers, so that workers understand what was agreed to and know that their employer has had compliance problems. If problems continue and the workers complain again, the penalties can be (and should be) higher. For large cases, the settlement materials should automatically be posted online, such as is done for cases handled by the Federal Trade Commission (see www.ftc.gov) and the Securities and Exchange Commission (see www.sec.gov).

Stop the clock when workers file back wages cases. If a worker has had wages stolen, usually the Department of Labor will only collect wages for the last two years (in occasional "willful violation" situations the Department will go back three years). Changing the statutory limit to have the clock stop when a worker files a case would mean workers would recover more of their stolen wages. It would be even better to add any additional wage theft that occurred since the complaint was filed to the two-year back wage recovery. This would encourage employers to settle quickly and come into compliance.

In order to seriously confront the crisis of wage theft, the primary national wage enforcement agency, the Wage and Hour Division of the

Department of Labor, must enhance its arsenal of penalties and make public examples of those who would scoff at the nation's labor laws by repeatedly and willfully stealing wages from workers.

Each day American workers go to work expecting that their employers will comply with existing law concerning wages and hours, and that if they do not, government will hold them to account. Government must do so if it expects to retain the public's trust.

Target Investigations and Settlement Agreements

Numerous studies have shown the prevalence of wage theft in particular industries, such as restaurants, construction, landscaping, farm labor, retail, hotels, janitorial services, and homecare. Workers in these industries are particularly vulnerable to wage theft, even though they often don't file complaints. Much more focus should be placed on targeted investigations. The Wage and Hour Division should:

Devote half the investigators' time to targeted investigations. By 2007, the Wage and Hour Division was only devoting 23 percent of its resources to targeted inspections,[40] compared to 30 percent in 2000,[41] 60 percent in 1968,[42] and more than half in 1941. Some will argue that this percentage can't be raised without more investigative staff. This is wrong. Targeting is even more important to do with limited enforcement staff. Without targeted initiatives, investigators will respond to those who complain the most, who tend not to be the most vulnerable workers, and those from sectors with rampant wage theft. The secretary of labor and allies should insist that the percentage of investigators' time focused on investigations increase from its current level to at least 50 percent of investigators' time.

In order to focus this much on investigations, the agency must expand its collaborations with workers' centers and ensure that its bar-referral program, launched at the end of 2010, is working smoothly in order to make sure that workers with unpaid wages have places to turn for assistance. Providing the "do-it-yourself" resources online as proposed earlier in the chapter might help in reducing those requiring assistance as well.

Learn how industries are structured and go after those at the top of the food chain. David Weil in his report to the Wage and Hour Division on strategic enforcement explains, "The employment relationship in many sectors with high concentrations of vulnerable workers has become complicated as major companies have shifted the direct employment of workers to other business entities that often operate under extremely competitive conditions. This 'fissuring' or splintering of employment increases the incentives for employers at lower levels of industry structures to violate workplace policies, including the FLSA. Fissuring means that enforcement policies must act on higher levels of industry structures in order to change behaviour at lower levels, where violations are most likely to occur."[43] The two main satellite dish companies in the nation don't technically employ any dish installers, and yet they have influence and could help set standards for thousands of dish installers. Pulte Homes, the nation's largest home builder, doesn't hire workers directly, but again it clearly could help set standards for thousands of workers.

The Department of Labor provided a model for how this can be done in its work with the garment industry in the late 1990s. When the Wage and Hour Division found contractors who were illegally underpaying workers, the Division confiscated the products under the "hot goods" provision. The manufacturers, who had hired the contractors and needed the goods to move their work forward, agreed to compliance agreements that engaged the manufacturers in monitoring compliance with labor laws in order to recover their embargoed goods.[44]

Develop formal agreements with companies with franchises. If I decide to become a Subway franchise owner, I agree to a set look, a set menu, and a set font for materials. I pay for the look, the guidance, and the prestige. Obviously, the Subway Corporation, or McDonald's, or Hilton, or dozens more, could put in place a set of personnel and employment standards that could help stop and deter wage theft. The Department of Labor should use its leverage, especially in the midst of settlement agreements over problems, to encourage companies that have franchise agreements to include a set of standards, which if not met, would result in an owner losing his or her franchise.

Think and Work Outside the Bureaucratic Boxes

As dedicated as Wage and Hour investigators and leaders are, the agency operates in bureaucratic fashion. Perhaps this is inevitable for a large agency, but its leaders should push the agency to think and work outside the normal boxes. The Wage and Hour Division should:

Target and train a team of joint Wage and Hour and OSHA investigators. Some industries, such as residential construction and meat packing, are notorious for both their wage violations and their health and safety problems. These industries need joint investigations and people who are trained to spot both kinds of problems. Either investigative teams can be created jointly by the two divisions, or new investigators can be hired and trained to spot both kinds of violations. In most European nations, labor inspectors are assigned to regions. The labor inspectors enforce all the laws.

Gilberto worked at Genesis Fabrications from December 2007 through April 2008. He quit because of the low pay and terrible working conditions. He heard the Houston Interfaith Workers' Center might be able to help him get all the wages he was owed. Gilberto claimed that none of the fifteen to twenty workers were paid the minimum wage or overtime despite working approximately 72 hours per week. The owner's excuse was that "the company is new and everyone needs to pitch in to make the company strong." Gilberto was living at the factory and working as a security guard at night, receiving drop-off deliveries. His night duties were in exchange for not paying rent and not included in the 72 hours a week.

When the workers' center advocate, Laura Boston, heard about this company, it sounded like the typical sweatshop. As any good advocate would, she then asked about health and safety problems. Gilberto told her there was inadequate ventilation in the workroom where argon, propane, and acetylene were used, workers were provided only paper masks that were inadequate for protecting them, there was no evacuation plan, no fire detectors, no sprinkler system, exposed electrical wires looked dangerous, and the electric sanders had no guards over the blades. Other safety problems were possible, but these were the ones Laura and Gilberto identified. Gilberto's employer stole wages and put his employees in physical danger.[45]

The workers' centers have found that most employers who routinely steal wages from workers do not devote much time and money to protecting their health. "We almost never see a wage theft case in which there isn't also some kind of health and safety problem," said Adam Kader, director of the Arise Chicago Workers' Center. "Employers who will steal wages don't invest in healthy workplaces."

Wage and Hour and OSHA should consolidate resources and jointly target industries that are known to both steal wages and injure workers. Targeting and training a team of inspectors is the first step in broader enforcement collaboration.

Develop a one-stop approach for enforcement. If you are a worker with a variety of problems at your workplace, here's what happens: You might begin by calling the toll-free number on the FLSA Minimum Wage Poster (every workplace covered by the FLSA is required to post this number). Try it yourself—call 1-866-487-9243. This gets you to a person in a national call center who asks your zip code. Let's say you claim you are having wage problems, health and safety problems, and some discrimination problems. The person will then read a script about the laws pertaining to a few of the words you mention and then refer you to various government agencies. (The language on the scripts is legal "gobbledygook"—it's incomprehensible even if you are familiar with the laws.) In this situation, you would be referred to the area Wage and Hour Division, the area OSHA office, and the area Equal Employment Opportunities Commission (EEOC). The call center can give you all the numbers for the agencies and can transfer you directly to either Wage and Hour or OSHA. If you have several different types of problems, which is quite common, you have to file multiple complaints with multiple agencies.

Brenda Vasquez came into the Workers Defense Project in 2005 complaining about sexual harassment at a chain restaurant with locations in Austin, Dallas, and Houston. When the workers' center volunteers began talking with her, they quickly realized she also had wage problems. She was encouraged to bring colleagues with her to the center. Eventually, five workers filed a lawsuit seeking more than $25,000 in back wages.[46] Had the woman only called EEOC, she would never have learned about the possibility of collecting the back wages.

In the fall of 2007, another worker visited the Workers Defense Project saying she had been raped by her manager. The workers' center leaders helped her file a claim with the EEOC and the EEOC has filed a suit against the manager, but they also asked about wages. Sure enough— she too had been denied overtime. Other workers admitted that they too had not gotten overtime pay. Together, the center is helping them recover more than $10,000 in back wages.[47] Again, had the woman only called EEOC, it is doubtful that those wage issues would have been addressed. A one-stop approach would allow workers to get help with the variety of issues they face. The same employers who injure workers will steal wages. Those who harass workers will steal wages. Those who steal wages will injure and harass. If you have three different problems, you would need to meet with three different agencies, usually at three different locations. If you happened to be an immigrant without proper documentation, you probably couldn't even get into the government offices. Having multiple offices covering multiple jurisdictions does not serve the best interest of workers.

The more holistic "one-stop" approach to problems that the two hundred-plus workers' centers around the country use offers a better model for how the agency should serve workers. In most of the workers' centers around the country, workers are invited to attended workers' rights training sessions in which they learn about their rights in the workplace and get their most basic questions answered. Then the workers can meet with attorneys or workers' rights advocates who review their problems with them and help them figure out how the problems can be addressed. The worker is always in control of decisions made about his or her situation.

In 1998, Congress passed the Workforce Investment Act (WIA), which requires states and communities to bring worker training and employment services under one roof. Ten years later, most of the one-stop centers have thirteen of the sixteen mandated programs participating.[48] The Department of Labor rightly realized that it needed "one-stops" for worker training and employment service. Now it must recognize that it needs "one-stops" for workplace problems. Initially, the agency should create ten pilot clinics at which Wage and Hour, OSHA, EEOC, and state worker agencies all collaborate to assist workers with a variety of workplace problems. If workers routinely visit the center with pension problems, ERISA enforcement staff should be added. These clinics should be run collaboratively with workers' centers and community organizations. The clinics should operate in the evenings and on Saturdays in order to best serve most employed workers. The clinics should not be located in downtown government buildings that intimidate immigrant workers,[49] but rather should operate in low-income and immigrant neighborhoods in congregations, libraries, community centers, and other institutions that are accessible and welcoming.

Support and work more strategically with state labor enforcement agencies. As was mentioned in Chapter 9, Frances Perkins viewed her work with state agencies as one of her most significant accomplishments. Today, the Department of Labor nationally provides very little support for state agencies. The two primary state associations, the National Association of Government Labor Officials (www.naglo.org) and the Interstate Labor Standards Association (www.ilsa.net), are poorly staffed and have limited roles in expanding labor law enforcement initiatives.

In conversations with state labor department staff, problems also arise when state agencies want to collaborate with the federal agencies. For example, according to Bob Anderson of the Wisconsin Equal Rights Division, if Wisconsin begins investigating a case and the federal Wage and Hour investigators want to look at the situation, Wisconsin will share its files and records. If the situation is reversed, the federal Wage and Hour investigators will not share files and records with the Wisconsin investigators. As he says, "The feds operate under The Privacy Act. Wisconsin operates under the Open Records Act."[50] There must be ways to encourage collaboration for the good of both workers and the general public.

Despite the challenges of working together, some of the most creative and effective new wage enforcement approaches are being developed at the state level. The Wage and Hour Division should learn from these new approaches, facilitate sharing of best practices between states, and build alliances to push overall for more effective mechanisms for protecting workers against wage theft and payroll fraud. This will require a commitment of staff and resources to convene federal and staff enforcement staff and a willingness of senior Department of Labor leadership to lead the way in building collaborative strategic relationships.

Convene stakeholders to discuss ways to raise standards and expand coverage. The Department of Labor's primary role in fighting wage theft is to enforce the law as strongly and as effectively as possible. However, the nation's labor laws aren't nearly as strong and clear as they should be. The Department of Labor should use its national leadership to convene task forces to look at new approaches for raising standards and expanding labor protections for vulnerable workers. These conversations are multi-year ones, but they are important to begin so there is a chance of engaging a broad cross section of the American public in understanding the wage theft problems and grappling with responsible policy solutions. Perhaps we need a national Wage Theft Task Force or a Wage Standards for the Twenty-First Century Task Force. Below are some of the policies that should be considered:

Establish a penalty wage for nonpayment of wages within fifteen days. The maritime industry has what's called a seafarer's penalty wage. At the end of a voyage after the cargo is unloaded or when a seafarer is discharged, the employer (called "the master" in the law) is required to pay the seafarer within four days. When payment isn't made promptly, the employer has to pay the seafarer two days' wages for each day the payment is delayed.

Reverend Sinclair Oubre, president of the Apostleship of the Sea and former IWJ board member, says, "The penalty wage makes sure that seafarers are taken care of when they get to port. The penalties have almost eliminated wage theft."[51] Douglas Stevenson, the director for Policy, Advocacy, and Law at the Seaman's Church Institute of New York and New Jersey, describes the Penalty Wage Act as a "simple, uncomplicated and consistent deterrent to all unscrupulous ship-owners."[52]

Given the prevalence of workers not getting their final paychecks, establishing such a penalty wage for unscrupulous employers would help workers get paid. Because the penalties can become substantial fairly quickly, employers tend to pay the workers rather than risk paying the penalties. Let me give a quick example. Let's assume a worker gets $10 per hour, usually 8 hours a day ($80 per day) and that the worker was let go and owed for five days of work ($400). The employer would be required to pay that $400 within fifteen days. If the employer refused to pay, a penalty wage of $160 would be added for each day past fifteen that the employer didn't pay. So if after six weeks the employer still hadn't paid, the worker would be owed the basic back wages ($400) plus a penalty of $160 × 30 ($4800).

Minnesota has a similar approach to last paychecks referred to as the "default wage." The law says that when an employer gets rid of an employee, that worker can demand payment of wages (and commissions) within 24 hours after demanded. If the employee is not paid within this 24-hour period, the employer is considered in default. The discharged employee may then charge and collect the amount of the employee's average daily earnings for each day up to fifteen days. Like the seafarer's penalty wage, this default wage makes it expensive to withhold workers' last paychecks and thus can serve as a strong deterrent to wage theft.[53]

Require employers to pay the wage they promised. One of the major problems for workers, especially workers in low-wage jobs, is that employers don't pay them the wages they were promised. Unless the employer doesn't pay minimum wage or doesn't pay overtime, the issue is not covered by the FLSA and thus is not enforced by the Wage and Hour enforcement staff. Farm workers have to be paid according to what they were promised (under another law), but there are no federal protections for most other workers. For most workers, their primary option is to file a suit claiming breach of contract. Because workers usually learn quickly that they are not going to get paid what they are promised, the total dollar amounts stolen are too small to justify filing suit, except perhaps in small claims court. Consequently, most workers have no recourse for not getting paid the wages they were promised.

Employers should be required to pay workers for the wages they promised. This can be done by amending the FLSA or passing another law requiring employers to put in writing the promised wages and then to pay them. Either way, it is important to ensure that workers are paid all the wages they are promised. Not only should employers not steal, they shouldn't lie either.

Simplify and expand the coverage of the Fair Labor Standards Act (FLSA). Chapter 2 described the many ways in which employers steal workers wages, and Chapter 5 described how complicated the laws are. For the Department of Labor's Wage and Hour Division as well as for the advocates in workers' centers, way too much time gets wasted on figuring out whether or not workers are covered by the FLSA, rather than helping workers recover their wages.

A worker visits the Houston Workers' Center complaining of unpaid wages. The advocate then tries to find out what kind of business employs the worker in order to assess whether he or she is covered by the FLSA. Does the business do $500,000 worth of business or engage in interstate commerce? Many workers don't know the size of their employers' business, and unethical employers will deny (or hide) the fact that their businesses do this much annual volume. Workers are also covered if they personally perform activities associated with interstate commerce, such as processing a credit card or calling someone long distance.

These complicated "interstate commerce" definitions are not helpful to low-wage workers and do not make common sense to the average American. If someone works for an employer, he or she should get paid the minimum wage and be protected by basic labor laws.

The coverage requirements for the OSHA are simpler. OSHA covers all private sector workers who aren't covered by other laws, such as miners. The only exceptions are self-employed people, privately employed domestic workers who work in the home of their employer, and family members on a family farm. The FLSA would be a lot simpler if it had a comparable definition.

Most of the states have passed minimum wage laws that make it much simpler to figure out who is covered and who is not. In most states, all workplaces with two or more workers are covered by the state minimum wage. This is much simpler for workers to figure out than the complicated interstate commerce rules. The FLSA could cover all workplaces with at least two employees. That would be much simpler to administer, saving investigators and advocates time for forcing compliance instead of figuring out if someone is covered.

Given the billions of dollars in overtime wages stolen annually from workers, it would also be helpful to explore ways to simplify the overtime regulations. No matter how many times I have read the regulations, I still find them confusing. The complexity of the tests for who is exempt and who is not exempt from overtime makes it hard to educate workers and employers about the problems and difficult to enforce. In addition, it is hard to justify the exclusion of thirty different categories of workers from overtime primarily because the employers exercised their political influence to get the workers excluded from overtime coverage. Consequently, all ideas for simplifying the overtime regulations and reducing those exempted from coverage should be debated and considered. Based on past experience, revising the overtime regulations is in itself a multiyear project.

Even though colleagues who do policy work assure me there will be a huge uproar over simplifying definitions and expanding coverage some-what, this seems like a political fight worth having. Are there really that many people who think any worker should work for less than minimum wage? Wouldn't it be better for workers and employers to have an over-time law that we could all explain simply?

Develop a uniform (minimum) labor code. Because every state has different labor laws on a wide variety of topics and very few states do much out-reach about the laws, the result is that most workers are clueless about many of their rights in the workplace. For businesses trying to operate in multiple states, making sure that the businesses are complying with such a wide variety of laws is both confusing and expensive. Thus, it is in the interest of businesses, workers, and the society at large to develop a uni-form minimum labor code.

Laws reflect our values. So what are the core values on which all of us (or at least most of us) can agree? What are the core minimums that should be adhered to in all workplaces?

Please be assured that I am not trying to reduce standards for any worker. Any state that has significantly higher standards could and should keep them. Consequently, there will never be one standard code, but it would be helpful if there could be a uniform labor code that could be-come the working minimum that most in the society would agree reflect our core values.

Could the uniform code cover payday periods? Thirty states have requirements that people be paid either biweekly or semimonthly. It seems that it wouldn't be that difficult to get agreement on these require-ments, or that controversial to get them approved nationwide.

Meal breaks and rest periods? Twenty-eight states have laws requir-ing meal breaks or rest periods (the FLSA does not require breaks but governs when they must be paid.) Some states require a meal break if the employee works 5 consecutive hours, and other states after 6 or 7 hours. Would it really be so hard to pick one standard to apply nationwide?

Other examples include differing state laws on days of rest, reporting periods, working split shifts, and working on Sundays and holidays.

There are several ways standardization can happen. The standards can become part of a revised FLSA, they can become a new national bill, or they can be adopted state by state. As complicated as this state-by-state approach sounds, similar approaches have occurred on other issues.

The National Association of Insurance Commissioners drafted model laws for the insurance industry, which have been adopted in part or in full in many states. The Uniform Commercial Code is a set of standardized state laws governing financial contracts. The code was drafted by the National Conference of State Law Commissioners and was adopted in the 1950s by most states and the District of Columbia.[54] Efforts are underway to create and get states to adopt a Uniform Building Code. Again, the uniform approach would not be the "maximum," but a minimum core to which all can agree, just like the minimum wage.

The Department of Labor is the most logical, and perhaps the only, agency that can convene such parties. Getting agreement might take two years, four years, or even eight years. Whatever time frame is required, it will only be achieved if we start now. A task force can be developed that includes some national business leaders, some national union leaders, civil and immigrant rights leaders, religious leaders, and both federal and state labor agency people.

Expand core standards reflecting our values. As we have matured as a nation, so too have our workplace standards developed and matured. For decades, children worked in sweatshops and mines. The first bill to limit child labor, forbidding employment of minors under 14 for more than 10 hours per day, was passed in 1842. Although this standard seems low to us today, the law faced bitter opposition from employers when it first passed.[55] It would take decades before most adult workers got "only" a 10-hour day.

When the FLSA was passed in 1938, society agreed that basic laborers who work more than 40 hours per week should get a premium on their pay, both to boost workers' incomes and to encourage businesses to share work with more workers, although at the time, opponents called the FLSA a "tyrannical industrial dictatorship" that would destroy businesses.[56]

Standards change over time as the society and working conditions develop. If we want to remain a great nation, we must continue to set minimum standards that reflect our core values. What are the other minimum standards to which we should encourage the nation's workplaces to strive? The Department of Labor should play a role in convening representatives of business, labor, and religious communities to discuss what core standards reflect our values in the twenty-first century.

What about paid sick days? Most middle-income workers take paid sick days for granted. But fifty-seven million workers have no paid sick days. And one hundred million workers have no paid sick days that can be used to care for a sick child or ill parent. If a worker's child gets sick, the worker must decide whether to lose a day's income and risk losing a job, or work sick or leave a sick child home alone. These are not good choices. Can we agree on paid sick days? San Francisco, Milwaukee, and Washington, D.C., have passed bills mandating sick days. Such bills have been introduced in more than a dozen states and in Congress. Doesn't this seem like an appropriate minimum standard for the twenty-first century?[57]

How about limits on mandatory overtime? Workers in highly productive and highly profitable industries are often forced to work incredible amounts of overtime. So too are nurses and other workers where there are shortages in the industry and demands for workers 24 hours a day. The workers may be paid well for doing so, but their abilities to do their jobs well decline (there are many stories about the decline of patient care), they can't see their families, and they cannot attend worship services or help with homework. And excessive overtime is dangerous to workers' health and safety.[58]

Although employers need some flexibility in managing workforces, workers also need the ability to manage their lives. Surely some national standards can be developed that would allow some flexibility for employers, while safeguarding workers' lives.

Should there be a minimum number of vacation days? Most European companies have national standards for paid vacation days that are very generous. The United States does not require paid vacation days. Is there some minimum number of paid vacation days that wouldn't be too onerous for businesses to grant?

I do not know what we can collectively agree on as a nation, but we must collectively debate what minimum standards we believe are acceptable in the workplace. I do know that the real measure of a society is how it treats its poor and most vulnerable. And the Department of Labor is the appropriate agency for convening people to talk about the future of work and workers. The prophet Isaiah in chapter 58 (verses 6–12) reminds us to focus on the priorities of caring for the oppressed and fighting injustice. The key passages read:

> Is this not the fast which I choose, To loosen the bonds of wickedness, To undo the bands of the yoke, And to let the oppressed go free And break every yoke?
>
> Is it not to divide your bread with the hungry And bring the homeless poor into the house; When you see the naked, to cover him; And not to hide yourself from your own flesh?
>
> Then your light will break out like the dawn, And your recovery will speedily spring forth; And your righteousness will go before you; The glory of the LORD will be your rear guard.
>
> Then you will call, and the LORD will answer; You will cry, and He will say, Here I am. If you remove the yoke from your midst, The pointing of the finger and speaking wickedness,
>
> And if you give yourself to the hungry And satisfy the desire of the afflicted, Then your light will rise in darkness And your gloom will become like midday.
>
> And the LORD will continually guide you, And satisfy your desire in scorched places, And give strength to your bones; And you will be like a watered garden, And like a spring of water whose waters do not fail.
>
> Those from among you will rebuild the ancient ruins; You will raise up the age-old foundations; And you will be called the repairer of the breach, The restorer of the streets in which to dwell.

The Department of Labor's mission resonates with this vision of Isaiah. We all must help the Department of Labor reclaim its mission and refocus its work on stopping wage theft and lifting the employment standards for the nation. Some of the changes needed by the Department of Labor can be implemented immediately. Others will require leadership to get the staffing resources and policies in place to strengthen wage theft enforcement. But while we are revamping the policies and building the institutional capacity to stop wage theft, we must begin building the national consensus on how to more effectively deter wage theft and put in place a floor for protecting the nation's workers. These long-term conversations will equip the nation and its workforce to expand and grow.

Wage theft is a "breach" in the land. We can repair this breach. We can restore the full and fair payment of wages for workers. We can rebuild the Department of Labor so that it is a protector of workers and a leader in setting workplace standards for all the nation's workers. Doing so is not only the right thing to do for workers; it is good for America.

11

Strengthening State Enforcement

Do not exploit the poor because they are poor and do not crush the needy in court, for the Lord will take up their case and will exact life for life.

—Proverbs 22:22–23 (TNIV)

The Messenger of Allah said, "Help thy brother whether he is the doer of wrong or wrong is done to him." His companions said, "O Messenger! We can help a man to whom wrong is done, but how could we help him when he is the doer of wrong? He said: "Take hold of his hand from doing wrong."

—Manual of Hadith

In the United States, some state wage protection laws are often stronger than federal laws. In addition, state laws, initiatives, and partnerships often become models for the nation. For example, states created factory commissions and child labor commissions around the turn of the twentieth century, long before federal workplace protection laws existed. The state campaigns, driven in large part by women's organizations and led by the National Consumers League, eventually resulted in passage of the FLSA in 1938. Even though this law seems flawed today, it was a breathtaking reform at the time.

Similar to one hundred years ago, those concerned about wage theft are figuring out how to strengthen state wage protection laws and state enforcement. Although there have long been modest improvements made to state labor codes, thanks to the heroic work of legal services attorneys, in the last few years community organizing groups, unions, and workers' centers have added their voices and persistent advocacy to the mix, resulting in some significant improvements in laws and enforcement.

The states' laws and commitment to enforcing those laws vary widely. For more background on the state approaches and staff assigned to enforcement, see *Enforcement of State Wage and Hour Laws: A Survey of State Regulators*, which is the most comprehensive assessment of state staff assigned to fighting wage theft.[1] Two smaller surveys, *Enforcement of State Minimum Wage and Overtime Laws: Resources, Procedures, and Outcomes*[2] by Irene Lurie and a report from Policy Matters Ohio, entitled *Investigating Wage Theft: A Survey of the States*,[3] are also helpful background.

This chapter will review a few of the state efforts to enact general wage theft bills and payroll fraud bills, and one law expanding coverage of labor law protection. These state campaigns suggest approaches for advocates to develop their own state and local campaigns.

General Wage Theft Bills

New Mexico's Wage Theft Bill

Somos un Pueblo Unido is a statewide membership-based immigrant rights organization located in Santa Fe, New Mexico. Founded in 1995, the organization initially worked primarily on immigration-related and civil rights issues. In 2003, Somos played a leadership role in the Santa Fe Living Wage Network, which passed one of the nation's highest citywide minimum wages. As important as raising the minimum wage was, Somos staff members and leaders found themselves routinely helping members address wage theft problems. In the process, they realized how weak and ineffectual the state laws were in either protecting workers who complained or punishing employers who intentionally stole wages for workers.

Somos leaders and some attorney allies met and reviewed what others states had done to stop and deter wage theft. They discussed about twenty different proposals and settled on four ideas they thought might help. One of the attorney allies agreed to draft the bill.

Before the bill was introduced, the Somos leaders met with leaders at the New Mexico Department of Workforce Solutions, Wage and Hour Division, to talk with them about what enforcement would help and what would not.

Somos had a long history of working on immigration issues in the state legislature, and so the organization had many relationships with state legislators. Although the organization had only once before worked on a labor issue (the work on the Living Wage bill), its members were really upset about the problem of wage theft and really thought they could move an issue that would help immigrants and nonimmigrants alike. Somos saw an opportunity in the fall of 2008 to move a piece of legislation in the 2009 session, and so it quickly identified priorities and drafted a bill. Given its history of relationships, Somos was able to recruit House and Senate sponsors for the bill. Somos leaders gave presentations to groups all over the state. Its members meet with state representatives and senators about the bill. Members who had been victims of wage theft presented testimony in hearings. The bill ended up having bipartisan support and passed with a good majority. On March 6, 2009, New Mexico's governor, Bill Richardson, signed House Bill 489 into law. The bill:

- Made it illegal for employers to discharge or discriminate against any person in retaliation for asserting their right to unpaid wages, for assisting any other person in doing so, or for informing any person about their rights.
- Extended the statute of limitation for wage claims from one year to three years to file a claim and gave workers the ability to recuperate all wages stolen from them.
- Penalized employers and deterred them from stealing wages from their workers by making them liable for treble (triple) damages plus interest for unpaid or underpaid wages.
- Allowed the courts to order injunctive relief including requiring an employer to post a notice describing wage violations so other employees will know they have the right to claim unpaid wages.

Somos has used passage of the bill as an opportunity to educate more workers and employers about the issue of wage theft. Both Somos and the New Mexico Department of Workforce Solutions Wage and Hour Division have had a dramatic increase in calls about wage theft since passage of the bill. Workers who were afraid to come forward are now speaking out about wage theft in their workplaces.

Unfortunately, there are still challenges with enforcements. Because the penalties are so much greater, employers are fighting the judgments more vigorously. There aren't enough lawyers to handle all the cases, especially the smaller ones. And with the change in governors, the organization needs to rebuild relationships with staff at the Department of Workforce Solutions. Somos has put together a state wage theft task force and is working to expand outreach to workers as well as improve enforcement of the law.

Marcela Diaz, executive director of Somos un Pueblo Unido, attributes their victory to the following:

Very active workers' committees. Somos has worker committees in twenty different workplaces that help address workplace problems. These committees helped design and lead the campaign. Now they are reaching out to workers about the new bill.

A deep base in the immigrant communities. Somos is known throughout the state for its work on immigrant issues. It has deep and broad relationships within the immigrant communities that were mobilized for this campaign.

Strong ties with the religious and labor communities. Somos has solid relationships with both organized labor and the faith community that were helpful in passing the bill.

A good relationship with the Department of Workforce Solutions. Somos worked collaboratively with the staff at the agency to figure out what would work effectively in the state.

Bipartisan support. The bill was introduced and supported by both Republicans and Democrats, although much education was needed about the issues. By and large, legislators were shocked to learn about the existence of wage theft.[4]

New York State's Wage Theft Bill

New York State has long had one of the strongest state wage payment laws. Nonetheless, Make the Road New York (MRNY) found that the law didn't do enough to protect workers against retaliation, recover unpaid wages quickly, and penalize unscrupulous employers.

MRNY was created in 2007 as a merger of two grassroots organizations—Make the Road by Walking, originally formed in 1997 in Brooklyn, and the Latin American Integration Center, originally formed in 1992 in Queens and with a base in Staten Island. Both organizations educated and organized immigrants to fight for economic opportunity and civic participation, combining legal advocacy with community organizing in powerful ways.

For more than a dozen years MRNY has successfully built worker committees that help workers recover unpaid wages through direct actions and litigation, partner with unions to target specific industries, attack wage theft practices, and organize for collective bargaining, wage and benefits above and beyond what is required by law, and monitor and build strategic partnerships with agencies like the New York State Department of Labor and the Office of the Attorney General. All this was good, but MRNY members wanted to be more effective and to build a greater statewide legislative presence. Through these efforts, MRNY members, organizers, and attorneys had also become all too aware of the inconsequential penalties for wage theft and the legal loopholes that allowed employers to evade wage theft penalties.

At the end of 2009, MRNY members, many of whom had experienced wage theft or been involved in local wage theft campaigns, decided to design their own to address the problems they had experienced.

Early in 2010, MRNY attorneys, with important assistance from the National Employment Law Project, the Urban Justice Center, Outten and Golden LLP, and many others drafted legislation that reflected the members' priorities. The bill was introduced in March 2010, passed in November 2010, and on December 13, 2010, New York Governor David Paterson signed the Wage Theft Prevention Act into law. The law:

- Increased the liquidated damages penalty from 25 to 100 percent. This means if a worker had $100 stolen, the worker could be repaid $200, thus creating a meaningful penalty to employers who steal wages. The Statute of Limitation in New York is a full six years, which combined with these new "double damages" may make New York the most aggressive of the fifty states in terms of the maximum liquidated damages that can be collected in a wage theft case.
- Made it illegal for employers to threaten workers who stand up for their rights. Smart wage thieves know that a well-timed threat to fire workers or call immigration is often all that's needed to silence dissent.

- Prohibited everyone from retaliating against employees who blow the whistle on wage theft. Previously, labor law only protected workers against retaliation by those individuals who met the technical definition of an employer, leaving the boss's cousin, wife, or manager free to retaliate against workers with impunity.
- Gave the Department of Labor the power to reinstate fired workers, which the courts had but the Department of Labor lacked.
- Established a new category of damages for workers who suffer retaliation. The courts and the Department of Labor can now order payment of up to $10,000 for any act of retaliation against workers complaining of wage theft.
- Provided for an automatic increase of 15 percent in the total amount of a judgment if the employer fails to pay within ninety days; and gave the Department of Labor a range of new collection powers to use during its administrative process, such as collecting employers' asset information and ordering employers to post bonds to cover past-due wages.
- Increased the information that must be included on the "rate of pay" notice that New York employers are required to provide at the time of hire, and provided a penalty and the ability to file a lawsuit if an employer does not give a newly hired worker the notice. The basic notice requirement was in the law previously, but there were no consequences for an employer not abiding by the law.
- Required that the pre-hire notice be provided to each new hire both in English and the language identified by the worker as his or her primary language.
- Expanded requirements for information that employers must include in pay stubs in order to make it harder to disguise wage theft.

Jackson Lewis, an employer-side legal firm (known in labor circles for its antiunion efforts), advised its clients soon after the bill passed, "The Wage Theft Prevention Act significantly increases the penalties for New York State Labor Law violations. To avoid these penalties, employers should review all aspects of their compliance with the New York Labor law."[5] Passing a law that encourages employers to review their compliance is good.

Passing a bill this significant in a one-year time frame is quite remarkable. MRNY attributes the organization's success to the following:

Strong sponsor leadership. Senator Diane Savino and Representative Carl Heastie were perfect champions for the bill. Senator Savino was an experienced senior leader in the Senate. Representative Heastie was the Bronx leader who made the bill his top priority. At a decisive moment, he insisted that the Assembly pass the version of the bill that the Senate had already passed, even threatening to walk out and take the entire Bronx delegation with him, making it impossible for the Assembly to vote on key priorities in the final days of the 2010 session. Having such strong leadership in the legislature was essential to the bill's passage.

Committed and engaged membership. MRNY members not only set the priorities for the bill, but they regularly met with legislators in New York City. At a critical point in the legislative process, a bus full of members went to Albany and buttonholed legislators throughout the Capitol.

Constant focus on the issues. Throughout 2010, MRNY used every local action against wage theft, every lawsuit filed, and regular press outreach to project the need for state legislation to address the problem of wage theft.

Deep knowledge of the issues. When negotiations ensued between MRNY staff and business leaders, MRNY staff were much more knowledgeable of the concerns than was the opposition. In addition, the staff understood and had taken into consideration the concerns of state Department of Labor leadership who would have to enforce the new law.

Good messaging. MRNY recognized that often small businesses are pitted against workplace protections. The organization led with a pro-business message—"We're trying to level the playing field for small businesses." The legislation would help ethical businesses and punish the bad actors. When the organization described its membership, it would emphasize that it represented 8200 families *and six hundred small businesses.*

Key allies. United Food and Commercial Workers (UFCW) union local 1500 and the Retail, Wholesale and Department Store Union (RWDSU) made this legislation their top priority in Albany. The two unions provided the "juice" that was invaluable in moving the legislation. In addition to these two deeply committed allies, the organization had a wide swath of organizations that supported the legislation, including the AFL-CIO, other unions, legal service groups, National Employment Law Project, Drum Major Institute, Working Families Party, New York Communities for Change, Domestic Workers United, the New York State Religion Labor Coalition, and others.

Leveraged city relationships. MRNY was much stronger in New York City than it was around the state. The organization engaged its public official allies, such as the speaker of the New York City Council, in reaching out to state legislators in support of the bill.

Washington State's Wage Theft Bills

Columbia Legal Services was the driving force in 2010 in passing improvements to the state's Wage Payment Act. Columbia Legal Services is a statewide legal organization that serves low-income families. The primary ally for the campaign was Casa Latina, a Seattle-based immigrant rights organization that educates, empowers, and serves recent immigrants.

Columbia Legal Services had a long history of involvement in trying to improve the state's wage collection system. When the Washington State Department of Labor & Industries (L&I) brought agency-requested legislation forward to the state legislature in 2005 after it realized that Washington lagged behind other states in agency wage theft enforcement, legislators asked Columbia Legal Services and the Washington State Labor Council to negotiate compromise language with business representatives. Bruce Neas, the legislative coordinator for Columbia Legal Services, spent almost two years on this effort.

The Wage Payment Act passed in 2006:

- Mandated that the L&I investigate and resolve individual wage complaints, and created an administrative framework to do so.
- Gave L&I the ability to assess penalties and interest in unpaid wage cases.
- Created incentives for employers to pay workers quickly by allowing the penalties to be waived.

- Created a collections process by which unpaid citations would be collected by L&I on workers' behalf.

Despite passage of the 2006 Wage Payment Act, Columbia Legal Services and Casa Latina continued to see workers who were victims of wage theft and were struggling to recover their wages under the law.

Consequently, advocates began to put together wish lists of what they thought would improve wage recovery and deter wage theft for workers in the state. Columbia Legal Services staff met with the staff at L&I to learn about how the administrative process worked, step-by-step, and to ask L&I staff how the law could be improved. In 2010, the budget was a major concern, so the only wish-list items selected for the proposed legislation were those that could be accomplished without costing the state money. Meanwhile, the advocates contacted state senators and representatives to begin discussing the problem of wage theft. With an initial bill drafted, a supportive state legislator convened worker advocates and business leaders to create a bill that both sides would support. The negotiations were quickly completed, and the bill was brought to the sponsoring legislators. Casa Latina provided workers with compelling testimonies to speak at hearings about the bill. The bill was passed almost unanimously in both the House and Senate and was signed into law by the governor on March 12, 2010.

The improvements to the bill that were passed in 2010 were as follows:

- Stopped the clock on damages and tolled the civil statute of limitations when a worker filed a case with L&I. (Formerly, damages could expire as L&I investigated the case, and if a case wasn't resolved within three years of the last illegal act, the statute of limitations would run out and the worker would lose all of his or her rights to the wages. Now the worker's right to a full and fair process remains as long as the worker files the case within three years.)
- Increased the minimum civil penalty for a willful violation from $500 to $1000 and created another mandatory penalty for repeat violators.

- Made waiving the civil penalties for repeat violators who pay wages and interest within ten days discretionary instead of mandatory.

- Established a wage bond that L&I may require from companies if it receives a complaint and is concerned that the employer is telling workers they will be paid, but they are not being paid.

- Improved the collections rules to make it easier for L&I to collect wages and penalties from successor businesses.

Columbia Legal Services and Casa Latina attribute the 2010 bill's passage to the following:

Solid homework on the issues. Both organizations really knew the wage theft issues and the state processes well. They spent about a year and a half learning about the Wage Payment Act before moving forward with the 2010 amendments. They were well positioned to make suggested improvements.

Collaborative relationships with L&I. Over the years, both organizations had gotten to know investigators and the leadership at L&I. They appreciated the challenges facing L&I staff members and sought to work collaboratively with them.

Engagement of the business community. It was important to engage the business community in figuring out how to address the problems. Two legislators sat through negotiations between advocates and business leaders seeking solutions to which all could agree. The business community suggested the idea of the wage bond. Because the 2010 bill was mutually agreed upon before the first committee voted on it, the bill flew through the House and Senate with remarkable speed and little opposition.

Strong legislative leadership. The leaders in both the House and Senate were strong and well respected. The original 2006 House sponsor was also the sponsor in 2010.

Focused on revenue-neutral items. Given the state fiscal concerns in 2010, the advocates realized that they had to focus on ideas that would not cost the state more money.

Support of labor. Even though Casa Latina was the primary community-based organization engaged in the campaign, the bill had the strong support of the labor movement, whose leadership met weekly with the chair of the labor committee. The bill couldn't have passed without labor's support.

Despite passage of the Wage Payment Act in 2006 and the strong amendments enacted in 2010, wage theft continues to be a serious problem in the state. Although the bills have helped, L&I only manages to collect the wages and penalties from fewer than half its citations—meaning many workers aren't getting their money back. The Department is woefully understaffed and reluctant to use its scant resources on aggressive action against recalcitrant businesses.

Consequently, a broader coalition in the state has been formed to educate more Washingtonians of the crisis of wage theft, advocate stronger enforcement and varied enforcement mechanism, and build the base for even more meaningful state reforms. Given the challenges to strengthening state enforcement without significantly more staff resources for L&I, the coalition is encouraging city ordinances to criminalize wage theft and strengthen enforcement. In March 2011, Seattle City Council member Tim Burgess announced his intention to introduce a city ordinance that would criminalize wage theft and take away business licenses from businesses that engage in systematic wage theft. The announcement sparked interest in the press and is raising the profile of wage theft in the state.

Illinois's Wage Theft Bill

In the fall of 2009, tired of the ineffective and inefficient enforcement of Illinois's wage theft law (the Wage Payment and Collection Act), the members and leaders of the Chicago Workers' Collaborative, the Latino Union, and the CTUL joined together to form the Just Pay for All Coalition to tackle the state's systematic barriers to recovering stolen wages. Coalition members and leaders, along with legal assistance from the Working Hands Legal Clinic, figured out their concerns and priorities and then met with the Illinois Department of Labor's and the attorney general's offices to analyze the state's approach to wage theft enforcement. These meetings, convened by the coalition, evolved into a task force of community and government agencies concerned about wage theft. Consistent with complaints from advocates around the country, Illinois's theft enforcement mechanisms were designed for traditional employment relationships, but were not appropriate for the new economy with so many workers working in nontraditional employment relationships.

In just a few months, the Just Pay for All Coalition drafted legislation that the task force agreed upon, found House and Senate sponsorship, and organized its organizations' members to speak out and lobby in favor of the bill. The bill, SB3568, passed virtually without opposition in both the state Senate and the House. Governor Pat Quinn signed the bill into law in the summer of 2010.

The amendments to the Illinois Wage Payment bill, which passed in 2010:

- Created an administrative process for handling cases involving $3000 or less (three-fourths of the cases), thus making it easier to file and resolve cases. Previously, the only option had been to refer claims to the attorney general for enforcement, forcing the state to expend thousands of dollars and go through a burdensome legal process to try to recover wage claims often in the hundreds. As a result, the vast majority of small wage claims went unrecovered.
- Allowed workers to seek unpaid wages from individual owners and not just companies. This is particularly important when companies file for bankruptcy (sometimes in order to avoid paying workers).
- Allowed employees to recover legal fees when they take their cases to court. Without this ability, most attorneys would not take smaller cases.
- Increased criminal and civil penalties to deter future wage theft.
- Allowed civil penalties to be reinvested into a Wage Theft Enforcement Fund at the Illinois Department of Labor to help fund enforcement of the law.

The Just Pay for All coalition attributes the bill's passage to a number of factors:

Dedicated legislative sponsors. Just Pay for All found a tireless sponsor in state Senator William Delgado and state Representative Lisa Hernandez. In addition, Representative Marlow Colvin played a key support role, as did numerous other state senators and representatives.

Active involvement of workers. The coalition involved low-wage workers and victims of wage theft in all major decisions and meetings about the campaign. Workers testified at hearings, spoke to the media, and met with legislators in Springfield and in districts. The final bill-signing ceremony was held in the Logan Square neighborhood of Chicago, surrounded by dozens of workers who had experienced wage theft.

Thoughtful work with the government agencies. The coalition wanted to pass a bill that would really make the enforcement systems work more effectively, which meant it was critical to take the time to understand how the government agencies really functioned and what legislative reforms could really improve wage enforcement.

Eloquent spokespeople. Each of the member organizations had an eloquent spokesperson who presented the issues in compelling ways.

Kim Cambra, a member of the Chicago Workers' Collaborative and a victim of wage theft, said, "If I steal a piece of candy from a convenience store, I can be put in jail. When my employer steals hundreds of thousands of dollars from me and my coworkers, he can use various legal methods to escape punishment."

"We needed to figure out a way to improve our chances of recovering stolen wages more quickly," said Miguel Trujillo, a member of the Latino Union and also a victim of wage theft. "That's why we decided to focus on improving the Wage Payment & Collection Act, to make the penalties for abusive employers more severe and create a process that the workers can use if they can't get an attorney."

"About 2½ years ago, we went to the IDOL [Illinois Department of Labor] to file our case. Recently IDOL found the employer liable for unpaid wages, but was unable to collect the money owed under the previous laws. As a result, my father and I lost our home last year," said Efren Sanchez, a member of CTUL. "Although we still hope our case can be resolved by the AG's [attorney general's] office under the old law, this new law should help other workers get final judgments much more quickly."

Broad array of allies. Unions, lawyers, academics, workers' rights groups, and community organizations all supported the bill.

Payroll Fraud Bills and Task Forces

Given the widespread payroll fraud across the nation, and the resulting loss of public revenues, many states have established misclassification task forces or developed strong payroll fraud bills. Because payroll fraud is such a problem in the construction trades, many of the state bills were spearheaded by the construction unions. Others were driven by state legislators eager to find new sources of public revenues. The task forces are at least as important as the bills in addressing the problems because most state agencies, and even departments within agencies, operate in their own silos. Task forces allow for sharing of information, selecting egregious cases for criminal prosecutions, and ongoing coordination that makes enforcement more effective. Given the state fiscal crises, and the fact that cracking down on payroll fraud is a source of new revenue, addressing the issue is likely a winnable one in the coming years.

But those who commit payroll fraud are devious, and so just when a state thinks it has a clear system for cracking down on payroll fraud, unethical employers find new ways to skirt the laws.

For a comprehensive listing of studies documenting payroll fraud and information about new initiatives to crack down on it, visit a website maintained by the Carpenters International Union, www.payrollfraud.net. Below is information about a few of the state-based campaigns to crack down on payroll fraud.

Delaware's Payroll Fraud Bill

The building trades unions were concerned about Delaware employers who were lying about having employees. Some were calling workers independent contractors. Others paid workers completely off the books. Union leaders in Delaware had watched Maryland pass a strong bill, so they decided to try one in Delaware. Delaware's Workplace Fraud Act addressed concerns raised by union leaders. The bill was introduced and passed in 2009.

The Workplace Fraud Act covers a broad range of construction service workers, including landscape workers. It creates significant penalties by providing that each violation, which is a single person misclassified, subjects the employer to a civil penalty of not less than $1000 and not more than $5000. Thus if the employer had multiple employees, the fines could add up. If an employer fails to provide its books to the state Department of Labor within thirty days, the employer can be subject to a stop-work order. Even higher penalties are assessed for retaliating against complainants and violating the law more than once during a two-year period. Repeat violators can also be debarred from state contracts.

The law also stipulates that the various state divisions dealing with labor, unemployment, workers' compensation, insurance, and taxation will share information and cooperate with one another. Workers who are underpaid by virtue of being misclassified can receive treble damages (meaning they can get three times what they were originally owed.) If an employer is going to pay an individual as an independent contractor, the employer must keep records about how much the person worked and was paid, and must give the individual information in English and Spanish.

The bill passed without a huge struggle for the following reasons:

Strong union presence. The unions in Delaware had worked for years to develop strong relationships with House members and the leadership in the Senate. Union leaders could get meetings with elected leaders and their staff members and were able to explain what a problem payroll fraud was for ethical businesses in the state.

Contractors were divided. Nonunion contractors opposed the bill, but union contractors spoke in favor of it. The Chamber of Commerce stayed out of the issue.

Tax revenue argument. State legislators were very interested in figuring out how the state could generate more revenue. Pointing out how businesses were shirking their responsibilities to contribute to the public coffers was a powerful argument for the bill.

Department of Labor support. The union leaders who drafted the bill worked with the Department of Labor staff members to make sure the proposals were those that would make sense from their points of view.

Although the bill hasn't completely stopped the practice of payroll fraud, the combination of increased penalties and the expanded collaboration between agencies has greatly improved the effectiveness of enforcement efforts throughout the state.[6]

Massachusetts's Misclassification Task Force

Massachusetts passed its first version of its misclassification law in 1990. It was then amended several times, including a significant broadening of the law in 2004. The law has a clear three-prong test to determine who is and is not an independent contractor. It also authorizes the attorney general to impose substantial civil and criminal penalties and to debar serious violators from public contractors.

But enforcement really got underway in 2008 when the governor established the Joint Enforcement Task Force on the Underground Economy and Employee Misclassification. Initially involving nine member agencies, it grew to seventeen different agencies involved, including various agencies within the Office of Labor and Workforce Development, the Department of Revenue, the Office for Refugees and Immigrants, the Division of Professional Licensure, the Alcoholic Beverages Control Commission (if you misclassify workers you can immediately lose your liquor license, which is quite an incentive to comply), and others. The task force set up a toll-free referral line and aggressively pursued companies and individuals that misclassify workers in ways that have gotten workers paid and collected extra revenue for the state. Involving the various licensing agencies has ensured quick compliance from violators.

Workers' center leaders, such as Lydia Lowe, director of the Chinese Progressive Association, and Marcy Goldstein-Gelb of MassCOSH, speak highly of the work of the task force. They attribute the task force's success to its commitment to working in collaboration with community groups, the fact that all the key enforcement agencies are at the table, and the task force's commitment to investigate and punish unethical employers and *not* to target immigrant workers. There was some concern initially from workers and advocates that perhaps the task force members might report workers to the Immigration and Customs Enforcement (ICE), but that has not been the case. The task force wisely realized that it couldn't do its job without community partners and the partners wouldn't participate without a commitment to protecting workers.

Worker center leaders meet regularly with the task force. The centers refer some, but not all, of their cases to the task force for investigation, depending on how workers want their cases to proceed. Advocates have been impressed with both the dedication and the sensitivity of task force members.[7]

Illinois's Payroll Fraud Bill

Passed in 2007 and implemented in 2008, the Illinois Employee Classification Act is one of the nation's strongest misclassification bills. The idea for the bill emerged from the construction trades unions. It is focused on construction workers. Originally, advocates had wanted the bill to cover other industries, but the business community insisted that payroll fraud was not nearly as big of a problem in other sectors.

The bill applies broadly to construction work, both residential and commercial buildings, road and other infrastructure work, moving of construction-related materials, maintenance, painting, and landscaping. Contractors who hire people who are *not* paid as employees must post a note about the bill in English, Spanish, and Polish (Illinois has both Spanish-speaking and Polish-speaking immigrants in construction). The bill has very clear criteria for who is and is not an independent contractor.

The bill has especially strong deterrents. A contractor who violates the Act is subject to civil penalties up to $1500 for each violation found in the first audit and $2500 for each repeat violation. And violations are counted per person and per day. So, the penalties can add up quickly. For a second violation within a five-year period, a contractor is debarred from state contracts for four years. Willful violations or obstructing enforcement efforts can result in double penalties.

Workers can file a private lawsuit instead of just going to the state Department of Labor. When private suits are filed, workers can recover the wages and benefits they would have gotten if they had been employees instead of independent contractors, plus liquidated damage—which is a fancy way to say that the worker receives twice as much as originally owed. If the worker is retaliated against (usually fired), the worker can recover double the owed wages and benefits plus attorney's fees.[8]

The combination of clear criteria, strong penalties, and multiple ways to seek compensation makes the bill a strong one for protecting workers, but the building trades are not convinced that enough enforcement is happening around the bill. Thus they are now advocating the creation of a multiagency task force, similar to that in Massachusetts, which can assist in actual enforcement of the bill.

According to Mark Poulos, executive director of the Indiana–Illinois–Iowa Fair Contracting Foundation, the keys to the victory were:

Strong legislative leadership. Harry Osterman was a strong champion for the bill.

Good research and documentation. The Illinois building trades had commissioned studies on the impact of payroll fraud on the Illinois unemployment insurance program and the Illinois workers' compensation program. The studies provided strong economic reasons for passing the bill. The results from the studies were the basis for developing fact sheets for educating legislators about the issue.

Labor's strength. Labor in Illinois continues to have strong relationships in the state legislature.

Lengthy negotiations with the business community. The bill's advocates worked long and hard to address concerns of the business community.

State Department of Labor (DOL) cooperation. The state DOL was helpful in figuring out what improvements to the law would strengthen the bill.

Despite the passage of a strong bill, union leaders in Illinois do believe the implementation of the bill is as strong as it should be. Thus, in 2011 union leaders are pushing for the establishment of a statewide task force, similar to Massachusetts's, that can help with implementation of the bill.

Minnesota's Payroll Fraud Bill

In 2007, the Minnesota legislature passed a bill that seemed like a simple solution to address the rampant misclassification of workers. The law, which covers workers' building construction or improvement services, makes the assumption that all workers are employees unless they are certified by the state as independent contractors. Anyone paid as an independent contractor has to file a form with the state demonstrating that he or she is indeed an independent contractor.

Unfortunately, by the time the law went into effect on January 2009, contractors seeking to avoid paying workers as employees found a loophole to undermine the purpose of the law. Those working in the construction industry, many of whom were illegally paid as independent contractors when they should have been paid as employees, were told to set themselves up as limited liability companies (LLCs) in order to be hired by the contractors. Then, the contractors could not be fined for illegally hiring independent contractors. According to a report in the *Star Tribune*, "Minnesota LLCs are being created at double the pace of a year ago. Nearly seven thousand LLCs formed in the past five months have names indicating they are construction-related, and the total number probably is far higher because many firms have names that don't indicate the type of business."[9]

Soon after the bill went into effect, a task force began meeting to close the loophole. It included the state agencies, union representatives, and contractor association representatives. In March 2011, a new amendment was introduced to close the LLC loophole by clearly defining construction contractors and requiring construction contractors only to hire employees or other registered construction contractors.

New York's Payroll Fraud Bill

In 2010, New York passed the New York State Construction Industry Fair Play Act. The bill assumes that workers are employees unless they meet specific and clear criteria (the criteria were originally suggested by a small business advisory council). Contractors who violate the law are subject to significant penalties, up to $2500 per misclassified employee for first violations and double that for subsequent violations. In addition, willful violators can be charged with a criminal offense with significant fines and even possible jail time.

The law requires that contractors have to post information about the laws in relevant languages. Contractors can be fined for not posting the information. They can also be fined and charged criminally for retaliating against workers.

Expanding Coverage for Workers

Because not all workers are covered by labor law protections, advocates must not only advocate stronger laws, but broader coverage.

New York Domestic Workers' Bill of Rights

Perhaps the most important worker victory in 2010 was passage of the New York State Domestic Workers' Bill of Rights.

As explained in Chapter 5, historically, domestic workers have been excluded from labor protections, both nationally (through the FLSA) and in states. This exclusion is part of the nation's legacy of slavery/racism and sexism—the undervaluing of work done by people of color and women. Domestic Workers United (DWU) challenged the exclusionary policy and sought to expand labor protections for more than two hundred thousand domestic workers in the state.

DWU was formed through the joint organizing of two community-based organizations in New York City that had fought to protect immigrant domestic workers and recover unpaid wages. Despite heroic work in filing lawsuits, educating workers, and challenging unjust employers, the case-by-case approach didn't address the industrywide practices, nor did it serve to protect all domestic workers.

In 2002, DWU began exploring legislative fixes and in 2003 won a citywide law requiring domestic worker employment agencies to educate workers and employers about basic labor rights. Soon thereafter, DWU and its sister organizations in the Domestic Worker Justice Coalition, which organize domestic workers in the diverse communities of New York, planned a citywide convention of domestic workers. The convention outlined priorities that became the core planks in the Domestic Workers Bill of Rights, including overtime pay, one day of rest in seven, health care, living wages, paid holidays, and leave and protections from discrimination.

The first advocacy day in Albany was in 2004.

Even with strong collaborations, the handful of organizations serving domestic workers didn't have the power to win such an aggressive bill on their own. The leadership of the organizations decided they needed to expand their own base of domestic workers and simultaneously expand their outreach to other sectors.

DWU leaders began by reaching out to key allies by speaking at their meetings, engaging them in letter-writing campaigns, and recruiting them for Albany visits. By year three of the campaign, DWU decided to create a campaign-organizing committee that involved coalition partners and supporters, so they could have a role in planning the campaign. Particularly important allies were Service Employees International Union (SEIU) Local 32BJ, the New York State Labor Religion Coalition, Jews for Racial and Economic Justice, who reached out to domestic employers, and Jobs with Justice.

The next few years saw the coalition expand its base and build its power and presence. As DWU Executive Director Ai-jen Poo says,

"We swapped our vans for buses." More than one thousand DWU members and supporters made forty day-long trips to Albany to meet with legislators. In addition, the growing coalition organized rallies, press events, hearings, marches, cultural events, and days of action. More than seven thousand postcards were signed and delivered to legislators.

In year five of the campaign, DWU leaders finally met directly with the Speaker of the Assembly. That meeting helped with passage of the Assembly bill. The Senate passed the Bill of Rights in the next legislative session.[10]

According to Ai-jen Poo, the coalition won because of the following:

Strong and active domestic worker leaders. The coalition focused initially on building its own base of leaders. These leaders developed a shared vision and commitment for moving forward. Over the years, people developed strong public speaking and advocacy skills.

Realistic assessments of time, place, and conditions. The coalition continually assessed the power it had and the power it needed to win.

Clear demand. DWU had a very clear demand that was easy to explain to workers, allies, and legislators. DWU could explain the problems and why the bill would help address them.

Creative tactics. DWU used creative tactics within its overall strategy. Leaders had fun planning and leading them.

Broad coalition. The coalition built a strong and broad coalition of allies. The decision to create a forum for engaging them in planning was important in building ownership and expanding the approaches for winning.

Bridge-building with employers. The coalition worked hard to build bridges with those who employed domestic workers. This often involved patience and education.[11]

States play an important role in stopping and deterring wage theft and in helping workers recover unpaid wages. In the coming years, states will be developing models for education, outreach, and enforcement. Each state campaign that groups win to crack down on wage theft, improve outreach and education to workers, apprehend those who commit payroll fraud, and expand labor law coverage to additional groups of workers makes it easier to win the next campaign. And as states model stronger enforcement and outreach efforts, they will influence national approaches as well.

We all owe a debt of gratitude to the courageous workers, organizers, lawyers, union leaders, and business leaders who have helped push forward and improve state enforcement.

12

Strengthening Local Enforcement

Give justice to the weak and the orphan; maintain the rights of the lowly and the destitute. Rescue the weak and needy; deliver them from the hand of the wicked.

—Psalm 82:3–4 (NRSV)

O you who believe! Stand out firmly for justice, as witnesses to Allah, even as against yourselves, or your parents, or your kin, and whether it be (against) rich or poor.

—Holy Qur'an 4:135[1]

Wage theft can be stopped and deterred at multiple levels. In addition to strengthening federal and state enforcement, local communities are creating new enforcement structures and exploring new ways to help workers recover unpaid wages and deter unethical employers from stealing wages.

Local Wage Theft Bills

Multiple cities and counties around the nation are working on introducing and passing local wage theft bills. Most of the bills create new agencies to which workers can appeal for help, link various city licenses with wage compliance (for example, a business can lose a city license if it doesn't pay its workers fairly), increase penalties for not paying workers, and/or provide clear information to workers and employers. Some bills create a "theft of services" law so that local police officers can be engaged in the struggle. For detailed information about the kinds of issues that can be addressed in local bills, download a copy of *Winning Wage Justice: An Advocate's Guide to State and City Policies to Fight Wage Theft* at www.nelp.org.[2] For an up-to-date list of current campaigns, visit www.wagetheft.org.

Miami-Dade County Wage Theft Ordinance

The Miami-Dade County Wage Theft Ordinance was passed by the Board of County Commissioners on February 18, 2010, by a vote of 10–0. The law prohibits wage theft and gives the county legal authority to intervene and help workers recover unpaid wages.

The campaign to pass the ordinance grew out of the work of many organizations concerned about wage theft. In 2007, these organizations, which included faith-based groups, legal advocates, immigrations rights groups, unions, and university researchers, came together to form a loose coalition called the Florida Wage Theft Task Force. The initial organizations helping drive the work of the coalition were the Florida Immigrant Coalition, Florida Legal Services, WeCount!, American Friends Service Committee, South Florida Interfaith Worker Justice, Florida Immigrant Advocacy Center, Service Employees International Union, UNITE HERE, and the Research Institute on Social and Economic Policy.

The task force explored a variety of options for addressing the crisis. By 2009, the task force decided that it should draft and advocate passage of a local ordinance to address wage theft in the county. Initially, task force members thought it should expand the jurisdiction of the Equal Opportunities Board (EOB), the county's civil rights commission, so quite a bit of work was done meeting with EOB board members and testifying in front of the EOB. After extensive conversations with county officials regarding budgetary concerns, task force members decided to lodge enforcement of the ordinance with the County Department of Small Business Development.

Florida Legal Services staff, who are active members of the coalition, drafted the ordinance, although the entire task force worked on its language. The group met with multiple county commissioners to figure out who would support the bill and who would need more targeted encouragement in order to do so. In choosing a champion, the task force considered more than just who would support the ordinance, but also how the commissioners' support would be perceived in order to ensure success. Past voting records, district and county demographics, and potential allies were all part of the equation. Ultimately, the task force settled on County Commissioner Natacha Seijas as the sponsor of the bill. Commissioner Seijas joined the task force on November 19, 2009, a national day of action against wage theft called by IWJ, to announce that an ordinance against wage theft would be forthcoming. The bill was officially introduced on December 3, 2009.

The task force intentionally reached out to a wide variety of community partners seeking public support for the bill. Ethical businesses that were harmed by wage theft committed by their competitors were approached to provide individual letters of support. Task force groups approached their members and others to sign postcards of support. Also, while SEIU and Unite HERE had been at the task force table since the beginning, other labor unions had not, so targeted meetings were held with the South Florida AFL-CIO and its member unions to gain more support for the ordinance. This particular support proved crucial in garnering the political clout needed to move the ordinance forward. In addition, the task force approached two Miami-Dade County entities—the Community Relations Board and the Commission for Women—both of which announced public support for the ordinance.

In order to get the commissioners' support for the ordinance, the task force members had meetings with each of the thirteen commissioners. Each meeting had three to six task force members present, and the task force also shared an organizational sign-on letter with over sixty signatures from congregations, unions, and other community-based organizations. Throughout the process of committee meetings and first and second readings before the Board of County Commissioners, the task force continued to show a presence.

When the ordinance finally came up for a vote, one hundred supporters packed the room. The vote was 10–0—every commissioner present supported the bill.

The ordinance, which officially went into effect on February 28, 2010, established a process for addressing wage theft problems through the Department of Small Business Development (SBD). When a worker complains, the SBD notifies the employer of the complaint and asks both the worker and the employer to provide supporting documents. The burden of proof is on the employer. If an agreement can't be worked out between the worker and the employer, the case is set with the hearing examiner. Cases are heard one day a month. If the employer is found guilty, the employer will have to pay the worker the back wages plus damages of an additional two times the wages owed. In addition, the employer must cover the cost of the hearing examiner. The threshold for filing a claim is $60, and there is no cost to the worker. Within a few months, the SBD process was up and functioning. Wage claims were logged and processed, with many claims being settled during the conciliation process. Some complaints went to the hearing examiner, and workers' wages were ordered to be paid. Others were referred to the federal Wage and Hour Division of the Department of Labor located in Miami. The task force has met monthly with the SBD to ensure smooth functioning of the process and to develop outreach programs for informing workers and employers of their rights and responsibilities.

Jeanette Smith, director of South Florida Interfaith Worker Justice, attributes the successful campaign to the following:

Strong knowledge of the issues. The task force members really understood the problems of wage theft and thus crafted a bill that would address it in a meaningful way.

Cooperative partners on the task force. Task force members worked well together and contributed their various strengths. Florida Legal Services drafted the bill. The Florida Immigrant Coalition engaged their member groups, which in turn engaged immigrant workers. South Florida Interfaith Worker Justice engaged the religious community. The Research Institute for Social and Economic Policy provided data. Every member of the task force was crucial to the process, and the task force was also not shy about reaching out for support from groups such as the National Employment Law Project and IWJ.

Clear and engaging materials. The task force developed excellent educational resources.

Strong messaging. As the task force moved through the process, it became more adept at framing the message for its various audiences. Messages ranged from a moral call of "thou shalt not steal" to protection of small businesses.

Individual meetings with commissioners. The task force met with all commissioners and tried to address any questions and concerns that were raised.

Seattle's Wage Theft Ordinance

On April 25, 2011, the Seattle City Council unanimously approved a new wage theft ordinance that strengthens penalties against wage theft and makes it a gross misdemeanor to knowingly underpay workers. If an employer is convicted of wage theft, the city can refuse a new business license or revoke an existing one. Threatening to report a worker's immigration status in retaliation for seeking unpaid wages or failing to respond to questions about unpaid wages are deemed indicators that help prove an employer is committing wage theft.

The work to create and pass the ordinance was led by Casa Latina, a community immigrant-rights organization that has been working on wage theft issues for more than ten years. Each year, Casa Latina receives about 250 calls from workers who have been victims of wage theft and the organization's Workers' Defense Committee helps workers recover unpaid wages.

Casa Latina had worked on expanding and improving the state wage theft bills, but became convinced that the city of Seattle had a stronger role to play in stopping and deterring wage theft. Casa Latina leaders were particularly upset that they kept seeing repeat offenders and realized that some unscrupulous employers were using wage theft as a business model.

The case that crystallized the problems was Joel Coronado's complaint against SMI Building Services, a janitorial company that had repeatedly stolen from workers, although sometimes under different corporate names. The company, led by Frank Christin, had a unique scheme for stealing from workers. He kept workers' first month of pay (and sometimes their second or third months' pay) as a "payroll deposit." When workers left, which many did given no pay, he would keep their "deposits," owing workers thousands of dollars. When Joel Coronado went to report him to the Washington State Labor & Industries and the Federal Department of Labor, he found that Mr. Christin had previous claims against him in both agencies for nonpayment of wages and payroll tax fraud, but he had not cooperated with the agencies.

SMI Building Services had cleaning contracts with very well-known Seattle area businesses such as The Cheesecake Factory, Legal Cinemas, and Pyramid Ale House.

Casa Latina leaders talked with Seattle City Council members about the problems of wage theft and used the case to demonstrate the need for stronger enforcement action. Council member Tim Burgess, chair of the Public Safety Committee, took a particular interest in the issue and became its champion. He invited Casa Latina leaders to educate the committee about the problem. He asked business leaders, including the Seattle Restaurant Association, to review the proposed bill ahead of time. He shepherded the bill through both the Committee and the full City Council.

Tim Burgess issued a press release to publicize the need for the ordinance and generate extensive media coverage about this horrible case of wage theft that was not being adequately addressed through existing mechanisms. Casa Latina mobilized members of the Washington State Stop Wage Theft Coalition and other community allies to testify in front of City Council. SMI Building Services became the poster child for wage theft.

Hilary Stern, executive director of Casa Latina, attributes the ordinance's quick passage to the following:

Strong City Council leadership. Council member Tim Burgess was an articulate spokesperson and a careful legislator who made sure that his fellow council members were well educated about the issues and that key stakeholders, such as the Restaurant Association, got a chance to weigh in on the proposed ordinance.

Informed worker leadership. Casa Latina leaders had a ten-year history with the issue of wage theft. The Workers' Defense Committee reviewed the proposed ordinance and suggested ways to strengthen it. Workers educated City Council members on the problems of wage theft, testified at the Public Safety Committee hearing on the ordinance, and attended the City Council on the actual day of the vote.

Deep alliances. Casa Latina has a long history of working with organized labor, immigrant rights organizations, and religious groups around multiple issues and was active in several broad alliances. Through these relationships, Casa Latina organizers were able to quickly mobilize a broad base of supporters who testified in support of the ordinance at City

Council meetings, including white middle-class church members who had experienced wage theft in their families, thus demonstrating the broad impact wage theft has on the community. *Extensive media coverage with a good story.* The ordinance generated extensive television and print media interest. Casa Latina had identified a clear case of systemic wage theft with a brave and articulate worker who could tell his story. Having such a "great" story demonstrating wage theft and the failure of the current systems helped garner media attention. *Strong relationships with city agencies.* Casa Latina has strong relationships with the Seattle police chief and the city attorney, both of whom supported the ordinance and pledged to prioritize prosecuting cases under the law.[3]

The Miami-Dade County Wage Theft Ordinance and the Seattle Wage Theft Ordinance have inspired other communities to consider similar campaigns. By May 2011, more than a dozen communities were developing or working on local wage theft bills. For an up-to-date list of campaigns, visit www.wagetheft.org.

Advocating Better Enforcement

In many communities, the laws on the books are decent, but the actual enforcement is lackluster. Consequently, advocates have focused on getting more efficient, focused, and strategic enforcement.

MADISON DISTRICT ATTORNEY CAMPAIGN: If a worker is the victim of wage theft in Wisconsin, the worker can file a complaint with the Department of Workforce Development (DWD). The DWD assigns an investigator to look into the complaint and makes a determination whether or not the worker is owed money. If the DWD determines the worker is owed money but the employer continues to refuse to pay, the DWD refers it to the county district attorney for prosecution.

The Madison Workers' Rights Center first identified a problem in Dane County in 2003, when it received word from the DWD that the district attorney (DA), Brian Blanchard, had decided that his office would no longer pursue wage complaints because of budget and staff shortages. The Center quickly mobilized a community coalition to encourage the

DA to continue this important part of his office's work. Unfortunately, it wasn't until the South Central Federation of Labor withheld its endorsement for his reelection because of his position on this issue that he agreed to modify his position. His office agreed to prosecute the most egregious cases and the repeat offenders. This worked well for a number of years, but over time the DA's office again drifted away from prosecuting wage theft cases.

By 2010, the DWD was once again no longer referring cases to the DA's office because no one was prosecuting wage theft as directed by statute. "Steal a $2 candy bar and the DA is going after you," said Patrick Hickey, executive director of the Workers' Rights Center. "Steal $1000 from an employee's paycheck, and the DA's office is too busy to bother with it." A new DA had been appointed that year, so steps were taken to reach out to him. The Workers' Rights Center and the Interfaith Committee for Worker Justice called on the new DA, Ismael Ozanne, to recommit the Dane County DA's office to fighting wage theft and standing with workers who had been robbed by their employers. Advocates argued that Dane County should be a leader in Wisconsin and set an example for counties across the state for strong and effective wage theft enforcement.

On November 18, 2010, as part of IWJ's National Day of Action against Wage Theft, thirty workers and their supporters gathered in front of the Dane County Courthouse to rally against wage theft and call for vigorous prosecution of wage thieves in their community. The new DA, Ismael Ozanne, spoke at the rally and affirmed his support for prosecuting wage theft. The Workers' Rights Center and Interfaith Committee for Worker Justice coordinated several meetings over the next few months to solidify the commitment and enhance coordination between the DA's office and the Department of Workforce Development Labor Standards Division. Monitoring of the commitments and protocols will be an ongoing process.

Keys to this campaign were:

Experience with the issues. The center had repeatedly assisted workers who were still owed money because the DA had not recovered their funds.

Connection with organized labor. Clearly, the connection with labor really mattered to an elected DA.

Persistence. The meetings with the DA and the Department of Workforce Development did not involve large numbers of people, but it was clear that the group was persistent and would continue pressing. The importuning widow approach[4] is often effective.

D.C. POLICE ENFORCEMENT CAMPAIGN: Washington, D.C., is one of many communities with a Theft of Services law. If an employer doesn't pay a worker, it is a theft of services. As with other thefts, people can call the police.

When workers in Washington were stiffed of wages, some would call the police. The response was varied. Some police officers would go with workers and ask employers to pay them. Other officers would claim they couldn't do anything.

When police officers did go with workers to meet with employers who had cheated them of wages, it was effective. Workers felt empowered having the police on their side. Police officers are usually skilled at mediating conflicts and quickly ask the question, "Can't we settle this now?" When employers know they have cheated workers, they are intimidated by the police involvement and pay workers quickly, often immediately.

In 2010, DC Jobs with Justice/Interfaith Worker Justice decided to seek a standard police department policy for assisting workers with wage theft. The organization began talking with friendly officers about how to approach the department. It met with domestic violence groups that had worked extensively on educating the police department on how to handle domestic violence cases.

The group initially met with the department's Latino liaison. A meeting has been requested with the chief of police. DC Jobs with Justice/Interfaith Worker Justice plans to ask him to educate police officers about how the Theft of Services law applies to wage theft and how pervasive the problem is, create a protocol for responding to workers' requests for help recovering unpaid wages, and issue a memo outlining the protocol and distribute it to all officers and community organizations.

SAN FRANCISCO HEALTH DEPARTMENT CAMPAIGN: On September 17, 2010, San Francisco-based Chinese Progressive Association (CPA) and key research partners released a study exposing sweatshop conditions for restaurant workers in the popular tourist district, Chinatown. This groundbreaking report examined health and working conditions in Chinatown restaurants, with more than four hundred workers interviewed by their peers, and found that 50 percent of workers were paid below minimum wage. Over the years, the CPA has organized many groups of low-wage immigrant workers to recover wages lost due to wage theft. Part of the strategy included filing complaints with the city and state wage enforcement agencies. Unfortunately, investigations from these agencies were slow.

Understanding that wage theft could not be solved one case at a time, CPA began to work with the city and other workers' centers to explore ideas around strategic enforcement, utilizing the enforcement power of other city agencies to revoke licenses and permits from employers violating labor laws. For example, the Department of Public Health (DPH) has the power to suspend or revoke a restaurant's health department permit if it violated city laws, such as the San Francisco Minimum Wage Ordinance. In its first experiment to utilize this power, the city was able to finally recover unpaid back wages in a Chinatown restaurant case that has stagnated in legal appeals for over two years and to revoke a food permit from another company that had repeatedly reneged on an agreed-upon wage payment plan. This exciting precedent, a result of pressure from CPA and other workers' centers organizing around wage theft, paves the way for greater interagency collaboration to protect workers' rights.[5]

Creating Task Forces

Many elected leaders do not realize what a serious problem wage theft is for workers and the community. Several communities have created task forces to study the problem and suggest solutions. Even the process of advocating a task force becomes an educational process for the community. The research and deliberations over the scope of the problem and needed remedies engages key community leaders in the problem. Then, the release of the task force results creates additional educational opportunities and helps move the next steps of a broader enforcement agenda.

FAYETTEVILLE, ARKANSAS, MAYORAL TASK FORCE: In 2010, the Northwest Arkansas Workers' Rights Center formed a communitywide wage theft task force to explore how to address the problems in the community. The task force decided to organize a public forum to educate community members about the crisis of wage theft. Center staff member Fernando Garcia asked Mayor Lioneld Jordan to issue a proclamation at the beginning of the forum declaring that date "Ending Wage Theft Day." And of course, Fernando offered to assist the mayor's staff in drafting the statement. On the evening of the forum, the mayor opened the forum issuing the proclamation. Then workers told their stories, and experts talked about the extent of wage theft. At the end of the forum, the mayor stood up and admitted that he hadn't previously appreciated the extent of the problem and offered to set up a mayoral task force to investigate it. The informal wage theft task force became the Mayor's Task Force. The mayor promised to assign police officers to investigate cases. Since the forum, police officers have been active members on the task force working with community leaders to figure out how they can play a role in stopping and deterring wage theft.

GRAND RAPIDS, MICHIGAN, MAYORAL TASK FORCE: In the summer of 2010, Reverend Vern Hoffman, a retired seminary professor from Western Theological Seminary in Holland, Michigan, and the volunteer organizer at the Micah Center in Grand Rapids, ordered one hundred copies of the first edition of *Wage Theft in America* and organized book study groups in the early fall to read it. In October, I was invited to speak at a monthly program organized by the Micah Center.

Frankly, I didn't know quite what to expect, but the room was packed, and many participants brought their books with them. They'd either read it or were trying to get through it. During the presentation, I talked about Fayetteville's task force.

Soon thereafter, Vern followed up with me. People wanted to do more to combat wage theft in Grand Rapids. The Micah Center decided to make wage theft one of its four priorities and thus created a Micah Center Task Force on wage theft. Vern thought that perhaps they might be able to get a Mayor's Task Force in Grand Rapids. Vern said, "I know the mayor. He's a great guy. I taught him in seminary."

The Micah Center organized twenty-five people to meet with the mayor. His response was, "Wage theft had not been on my radar, but this makes sense. Workers should get paid their wages and the employers should be paying taxes. We need those tax revenues." On November 18,

2010, as part of Interfaith Worker Justice's Wage Theft Day of Action, the Micah Center and the mayor's office announced the creation of a mayoral task force to investigate wage theft and recommend what could be done to help stop wage theft.

Ten people were appointed to the Mayor's Task Force, including Jordan Bruxvoort, a lead organizer with the Michigan Organizing Project.

Between the Mayor's Task Force and the Micah Center Task Force, community leaders are collecting stories of workers who have had their wages stolen, are working to develop an ordinance to address the problems, and are exploring ways to build a workers' center in Grand Rapids. The task force hopes to present the city council with a video of workers who are owed money.

Creating local approaches to addressing the issue of wage theft is growing in popularity. As the second edition of *Wage Theft in America* goes to print, local enforcement campaigns are underway in at least seven other communities. These campaigns will strengthen enforcement, help workers recoup wages, honor ethical businesses, put unethical businesses on notice, and educate the broader community about the issues. For information on the status of local wage theft campaigns, visit www.wagetheft.org. Local campaigns are useful and effective and will build the base for future state and national work.

Part IV

What You Can Do to Stop Wage Theft

13

Stopping Wage Theft Is Good
for America

What you are doing is not right. Shouldn't you walk in the fear of our God to avoid the reproach of our Gentile enemies? ... Give back to them immediately their fields, vineyards, olive groves and houses, and also the usury you are charging them.

—Nehemiah 5:9,11 (TNIV)

My favorite book in the Hebrew Scriptures is Nehemiah. Every time I read Nehemiah I am struck by how relevant the prophet's message is for today's economic challenges, particularly for our national crisis of wage theft. (If you haven't read Nehemiah recently, keep in mind that it has only thirteen chapters—a quick read.)

The book of Nehemiah begins with the prophet weeping over the disrepair of the walls of Jerusalem. Whenever I hear workers' stories of being cheated of their wages, I feel like weeping that we could allow such injustice in our land. Most of us wept when the winds of Katrina exposed the poverty and racism in New Orleans, but the tears kept flowing in the months and now years later when well-connected contractors have received multibillion dollar contracts and have refused to put in place mechanisms to ensure that workers will be paid.[1]

The book describes Nehemiah's four-step process for rebuilding the walls. Perhaps we can use his basic approach to stop wage theft and rebuild the foundations of the nation.

First, Nehemiah made a *comprehensive assessment* of the situation (Nehemiah 2:13–16). He went undercover and rode around checking out what needed to be done. He did not just take the word of officials; he studied the situation for himself. So, too, we must check out the situation for workers in the nation and must make a comprehensive assessment of how to stop wage theft.

Second, Nehemiah and his colleagues organized the rebuilding process in such a way that everyone had a *share in the rebuilding* (Nehemiah 3:1–32). If you read the text, you'll even find examples of some affirmative action—women were used to help rebuild the wall. Rebuilding the fabric of ethical workplaces will require all of us to be involved. We need active business leadership, strong government enforcement agencies, strengthened unions, and faith communities that care as much about what happens in the workplace as what happens in the bedroom.

Third, Nehemiah challenged those who stole workers' livelihoods, the fields and vineyards from which the Israelites made a living, to *distribute wealth and resources fairly*. Nehemiah was in the faces of the nobles and officials, accusing them of wrongdoing (Nehemiah 5:7). If he were alive today, he would be in unethical employers' faces about stealing wages. Stealing fields and vineyards was wrong then. Stealing wages is wrong today.

And last, Nehemiah encouraged the people to *have faith in rebuilding*. Skeptics told Nehemiah the city couldn't be rebuilt. He said it could (Nehemiah 4:1–5). Skeptics will say we can't stop wage theft, but we can. Nehemiah says, "The people worked with all their heart" (Nehemiah 4:6). The American public is up to the challenge. We've seen the religious communities work with all their hearts to house and feed poor people. Now we must call the American people to work with all their hearts to rebuild the fabric of work in the nation, combating the scourge of wage theft and moving workers from poverty to dignity. Stopping wage theft is good for all of us.

Good for Our Faith

In recent years, many congregations have drifted away from prophetic messages like Nehemiah's that condemn those who plunder the poor and have instead embraced a prosperity message. These "prosperity gospel" preachers suggest that God's blessing is shown through the provision of material wealth—if I'm wealthy, I must have been good and God blessed me. Challenging the scourge of wage theft cuts to the heart of this prophetic versus prosperity debate. Although the debate about "prosperity being a blessing from God" is most clearly seen in the Christian community, the same struggle echoes within other U.S. religious traditions that grapple with great wealth within faith communities in the midst of great disparity in the society at large.

The U.S. religious community is united in its support of soup kitchens and shelters for the economically disadvantaged, but many within this community extend their support without challenging the economic disparity and unequal opportunities that underlie the problems of the poor. One can accept a prosperity message, ignore the prophetic tradition, and donate to a soup kitchen. For many years I served on my congregation's soup kitchen board and found that the soup kitchen often has too many people who want to serve. Adults and young people will drive in from wealthy suburbs, don a hairnet and apron, and serve food for an evening. When I first suggested to fellow board members that we should encourage people to talk with the patrons and understand their economic struggles, my colleagues were not sure volunteers would be willing or comfortable having such conversations. Serving food without conversations about why people need food allows volunteers to ignore structural injustice. Wage theft puts issues of structural injustice front and center. Although most of those who actually run soup kitchens and shelters understand the deep economic problems that are at the source of the need for such social services, the unity surrounding support for these services doesn't challenge the prosperity message. To their credit, the board members decided to revamp how serving food occurs and to build in opportunities for patrons and servers to talk with one another.

The other barrier to greater involvement by faith communities is the desire to be nonpolitical and noncontroversial. Although congregations should steer clear of partisan politics, it is not right for them to avoid broader public (e.g., "political") debates of the day. The public arena is where broader questions of justice and equity are debated and enacted— or not. Nehemiah was intimately involved in politics. He pushed the political leaders of his times to enact land redistribution. Jesus spoke out in the streets and on the hilltops, and he spoke about caring for the poor— political issues of that day as well as ours. He didn't restrict himself to praying in the synagogues. Avoiding partisan politics is appropriate. But avoiding conversations about the priorities of the nation, small "p" politics, limits God and God's power to only the congregation's walls or only the issues of the family. Our faith values have a lot to say about the direction of the nation's priorities.

Although being involved in public (political) debate is not necessarily controversial, it often becomes so. Most struggles for economic and social justice were initially considered controversial. Those who fought against slavery were controversial. Those who fought to limit the hours children worked in factories were controversial. Those who advocated a federal minimum wage were controversial. It is hard not to be considered controversial if one is pushing the society in "bending the arc towards justice."[2]

Challenging wage theft requires the faith community to stand in the center of the prophetic tradition, engage in political issues, and remain firm amidst controversy. Wage theft is not just about a few people having a hard time making ends meet. It is the intentional stealing of people's livelihoods by unethical employers in order to enrich themselves. Wage theft requires justice, not just charity. It demands a structural look at how the economy operates and the kinds of incentives and disincentives playing out in the economic arena. Wage theft forces the religious community to take a position on the side of justice, the side of the prophetic tradition, even if it might be political and controversial. Consequently, curbing wage theft is good for our faith. Wage theft makes us uncomfortable. It requires us to take a position. Wage theft refines and fortifies our principles.

Good for Ethical Employers

Stopping wage theft is good for law-abiding ethical employers who are placed at a competitive disadvantage by employers who steal wages from workers. It levels the playing field.

Chapter 8 told the story of ethical employers who pay their workers legally despite operating in sectors that are rife with wage theft. Although it is possible to do this, it is very difficult to compete when unscrupulous employers thwart the law and steal from workers and public treasuries. Ethical employers need and want a level playing field. If Americans want an environment in which businesses can flourish, we must support businesses by creating level playing fields around wage and tax payments. Allowing tens of thousands of employers to steal wages and commit payroll fraud creates an unhealthy and unsustainable business environment. Let me explain.

Illegal unethical Employer A hires a group of janitors to clean buildings. Employer A pays the workers $10 per hour but commits payroll fraud by lying and calling them all independent contractors. Legal and ethical Employer B hires the janitors at the same wage rate of $10 per hour but pays all the payroll taxes and insurances that employers are required to pay for workers (approximately $3 per hour), and in addition the employer voluntarily provides some sick days, vacation days, and a partial contribution to health care ($2 per hour), making Employer B's total compensation cost $15 per hour, 50 percent higher than Employer A. Ethical Employer B has a hard time competing with unethical Employer A. If people prefer to hire the firm with the lowest bid, Employer B will go out of business, resulting in the society losing good jobs, replacing them with poor ones, and losing tax revenues. This is bad for workers, bad for ethical businesses, and bad for taxpayers.

As a society, if we don't do everything possible to stop wage theft, we undermine all the good, hardworking businessmen and women who play by the rules and treat their employees fairly. As the Department of Labor said in its 1996 budget justifications to Congress, labor law enforcement "helps foster a level competitive playing field for employers who seek to comply with the law."[3]

In Los Angeles, forty janitorial firms, which have signed union contracts ensuring that workers are paid decent wages, are jointly funding an initiative called the Maintenance Cooperation Trust Fund. This organization supports investigators who expose wage theft among unethical employers. Since 1999, this Trust Fund has helped five thousand janitors recover $26 million in back pay and helped level the playing field between unethical and ethical employers in the Los Angeles area.[4] Some of these janitorial firms pay $3 per hour, dramatically undercutting the union janitorial wages of $11.98 per hour.[5]

Labor leaders and ethical construction firms have formed fair contracting associations in thirty communities around the country. According to the National Alliance for Fair Contracting, "These organizations promote a level playing field through compliance with all applicable laws in public construction. When responsible contractors bid and perform public construction projects, the taxpayer gets a high-quality project performed by contractors who comply with the laws of the land."[6]

Other than the fair contracting groups in construction and the Maintenance Cooperation Trust Fund, there are few worker–management collaborations fighting wage theft. There are courageous business leaders (see Chapter 8) who are beginning to condemn wage theft and advocate better corporate behavior and stronger enforcement of wage standards. More associations, individual business leaders, business ethics groups, and business schools are needed in the fight against wage theft. Stopping wage theft is the only way to level the playing field for ethical employers.

Good for Public Revenues

Those who steal wages from employees almost always steal revenues from public treasuries. Employers who don't pay minimum wage usually operate in the "underground" economy; this means that true labor costs don't get reported to the government and no payroll taxes are paid.

Employers who fail to pay workers overtime underpay workers their employer share of taxes and anything else based on a percentage of the total wage. Employers who illegally pay people as "exempt" employees, who should be "nonexempt," are usually doing so to avoid paying overtime and taxes.

Committing payroll fraud by lying about having employees is the big robber of dollars from the public coffers. As discussed in Chapter 3, if a worker is paid as an employee, the employer deducts the worker's share of social security and Medicare taxes and then matches it with the employer share. When workers are paid as independent contractors, usually nothing is deducted and the employer does not pay his or her share of the taxes. For workers, calculating the "independent contractor" share of taxes is complicated and often doesn't happen at all or accurately. The IRS estimated in 1984 that it was losing $1.6 billion (or $3.3 billion in 2008 dollars) from just the misclassification of workers.[7] The Government Accounting Office estimated that $4.7 billion in federal income tax revenues are lost due to employers misclassifying workers as independent contractors instead of employees.[8] A 1994 study by Coopers and Lybrand estimated that proper classification of employees would increase tax receipts by $34.7 billion over the period 1996–2004.[9]

In December 2007, the IRS slapped the FedEx Corporation with $319 million in taxes and penalties for misclassifying its fourteen thousand drivers as independent contractors instead of employees. This back tax and penalty figure is just for the misclassification found in year 2002. Analysts expect that eventually, FedEx could owe nearly $1.5 billion in taxes and expenses when all the audits are finished.[10]

The Fiscal Policy Institute, looking only at the construction industry in New York City, found that the public was being cheated of $489 million in 2005 and an estimated $557 million in 2008 by using just three categories of costs: "$272 million in unpaid legally mandates payroll taxes for social security and Medicare, and social insurance premiums covering workers' compensation, unemployment insurance, and disability insurance; $148 million in health care costs shifted onto the workers themselves, taxpayers, and other employers that provide employee health insurance; $70 million in lost personal income taxes because there is no withholding for underground economy workers and/or they are paid off the books."[11]

Especially in this time of state and federal budget deficits, it is critical that every dollar owed the state and federal governments be collected. These public dollars support our fire and police protection, social services, social security, health care, schools, and other core government programs. The tax cuts and overall decline in public dollars have been used to justify the cutbacks at the state and federal departments of labor. But investments in state and federal departments of labor investigators to challenge wage theft, combined with stronger referral systems to revenue-collecting agencies, make sense as a means of strengthening the overall budgets. Stopping wage theft is good for increasing public revenues.

Good for Communities

Making sure that workers are paid all their wages is obviously good for the workers and their families. It is also a tremendous economic boost for low- and moderate-income communities.

In 2008, the federal government wanted to "stimulate" the economy, so it gave a tax rebate to taxpayers. In 2011, it reduced the employee share of social security taxes from 6.4 percent to 4.2 percent, again to "stimulate" the economy. Economists claim that the most effective rebates, those that got spent the fastest in the community, are those given to low- and moderate-income families. Workers whose wages are rightfully paid to them will spend those wages on food, clothes, down payments for homes, and other spending that benefit local communities. The Congressional Budget Office explained that the best economic stimulus rebate is "generally likely to be more effective the more it is focused on people who are likely to spend it."[12]

Unlike the tax rebates, making sure that employers pay workers all the wages they are owed does not increase the nation's deficit. Although there certainly are some costs associated with increasing the federal government's enforcement staff capacity, they are modest compared with the potential benefits of employers paying workers wages and the economic stimulus this would provide.

Good for Fighting Criminals

Drug dealers operate in the underground economy, as do other criminals and would-be terrorists. The underground economy is where people operate in cash, avoiding banks and avoiding government rules. The worst exploitation of workers, the human-trafficking cases, all operate in the underground economy.

Although some *workers* may operate in the underground economy because they need jobs and are fearful of deportation, most *employers* who operate in the underground economy do so to steal wages, steal government revenues, and sometimes worse.

Bruno Caballero Cruz first encountered Gabriel Francois's Twin Cities' firm in September 2007 when Bruno and a few other immigrant workers were hired by Integrity Construction Service to do miscellaneous jobs on construction work sites (No, I did not make up this firm's name). The workers were promised $12 an hour. Bruno was excited because with this wage he thought he could send money home to his wife and six kids in Mexico.

Bruno was paid for the first two weeks. Then the third week, Francois didn't pay the workers and refused to return their calls. The workers turned to the Minneapolis–St. Paul-based Centro de Trabajadores Unidos en Lucha (CTUL) workers' center for help. As the staff and volunteers began looking into Integrity Construction Service and Gabriel Francois, they learned of his long history of criminal activity. Francois has operated more than sixteen businesses and has been the subject of approximately 186 lawsuits in Hennepin County, Minnesota, alone. In 1999, he was convicted of bankruptcy fraud. He has sold phony vending machines, cleaning contracts, and property.[13] In 2004, he was sentenced to thirty-seven months in state prison after pleading guilty to two counts of theft by swindle.[14] Throughout his notorious career, he has routinely stolen wages from workers.

After Francois got out of jail, he started stealing from workers once again. He would pay for the first few weeks but then stop paying workers. He would bounce checks. He would shortchange workers on their hours. With the help of the workers' center, Bruno and four other workers filed lawsuits against Francois. Bruno was awarded $2527 in back wages and damages, and two other friends got awards as well. Unfortunately, they'll probably never see the funds despite Francois and his wife continuing to live in a $457,400 home in Bloomington. Francois has at least forty-two judgments against him and owes almost a million dollars to people.[15]

"Few of these judgments are for wage theft, but Francois has stolen wages throughout his criminal career," insists Brian Payne, an organizer with CTUL. "Low-wage workers have neither the time nor the resources to pursue stolen wages through the legal system." Brian knows another ten workers who claim they are owed more than $40,000 in back wages from Francois, but Brian believes that figure is just a small portion of the wages he owes workers. In March 2008, CTUL passed out leaflets at places where Francois recruits workers warning other immigrants of Francois's practice of stealing wages.

Anyone who willfully and repeatedly steals wages from workers is a criminal. Had Francois been stopped years ago, he might not have swindled the entire community.

Good for Nonimmigrants and Immigrants

Stopping wage theft will enable us to have a more rational conversation as a nation about immigration reform, although it won't address the global economic disparities that are fueling the migration of workers across borders.

Although many citizens and legal residents have their wages stolen, immigrants who are here in the country without authorization to work are the most vulnerable to wage theft because they are fearful about being deported and so many are afraid to complain. Unethical employers, recognizing how vulnerable these workers are, exploit them cruelly. They threaten to have workers and their families deported if they complain about working conditions. Immigration and Customs Enforcement (ICE) unwittingly becomes a tool that unscrupulous employers use against workers.

Immigrants, both legal and undocumented, are joining together around the nation to fight against wage theft. They are helping pass laws and implement new policies that protect all workers from wage theft. In the process, they are reaching out and building ties with other groups hurt by and fighting back against wage theft.

Together, as workers find ways to better protect all workers, including immigrant workers, in such a way that unethical employers cannot drive down wages by hiring immigrants and exploiting them, then we take away a point of tension between immigrant and U.S. citizen workers, thus creating opportunities for conversations about creating a rational immigration system.

Ending wage theft must become a priority, regardless of workers' immigration status. ICE should stop all workplace raids until the nation develops a rational immigration policy. Too often, unethical employers call ICE when workers are organizing a union or complaining to government agencies about working conditions, but they had no problem hiring immigrant workers when they thought the immigrant workers would be silent and compliant. Labor enforcement agencies, including the U.S. Department of Labor, must publicize (and keep) an "iron wall" between their work and the work of ICE. If workers feel secure, they will stand up for their rights. Workers who stand up for themselves can play a role in improving workplaces, and not just drive down standards as sometimes happens when workers feel they have to work for whatever an employer offers. If all workers have opportunities to improve conditions, they will all be more inclined to join together to work for their collective betterment. When immigrant and citizen workers are not pitted against one another by unethical employers, it will be easier to have civil conversations about immigration reform.

Good for Democracy

Stopping wage theft is good for our nation's democracy. Workers who have wages stolen and who are exploited by their employers do not believe their government works for them. Those who feel they are out of society's mainstream do not participate in the democracy. Our democracy will only work well if the majority of its citizens participate.

In a speech given in April 1886, Frederick Douglass said, "Where justice is denied, where poverty is enforced, where ignorance prevails, and where any one class is made to feel that society is an organized conspiracy to oppress, rob and degrade them, neither persons nor property will be safe."

We recognize that when young people don't get an education and thus can't get jobs, they are much more likely to end up on the streets and in jail. Those who stand on our cities' corners or rot in our nation's jails don't participate in the nation's democracy. Some aren't allowed to vote, but those who can often don't. Young, disenfranchised workers don't feel they are a part of the society and are skeptical about the democratic process.

Although there are always some courageous leaders who will fight against employer exploitation by organizing a union or initiating a class-action lawsuit, too many victims of wage theft feel that both their employers and their government have abandoned them. Frustrated and discouraged, they join the millions of low-income citizens who don't vote and don't participate in the democratic process. The United States has very low voter participation rates compared to most industrialized nations, and even compared to many developing countries. Voter participation, one powerful indicator of people's engagement in the democratic process, is particularly low among low-income and young workers.

To rebuild this nation and our democracy, workers must feel they have a stake in the society. It is hard to get this feeling, however, if employers steal wages from them, and their government does nothing about it. If workers can be paid fairly, and if those who steal wages are punished, we have a better chance to more fully engage all the nation's citizens. The democracy of our nation is a precious gift to be preserved, nurtured, and expanded. Stopping wage theft will help preserve and expand our democracy by giving opportunity and hope to millions of hardworking Americans.

Our nation is at a crossroads. Like the city of Jerusalem, the key foundational walls of our society are in disrepair. What could be more foundational for the society than seeing to it that workers are paid for their work? We can choose to ignore the crisis of wage theft, but only at our peril.

Instead, like the prophet Nehemiah, we must first conduct a comprehensive assessment of what's going on. How are employers stealing wages, and how can they most effectively be stopped?

Second, we must involve the broad community in our rebuilding efforts. We must engage workers, unions, religious leaders, and business groups in creating meaningful and appropriate ways to curb wage theft and ensure that workers get paid everything they are due.

Next, we must look at the long-term changes we need in our society to ensure that workers receive their fair share of the wealth and resources of this society. Nehemiah pushed Jerusalem's leaders to redistribute the fields and vineyards. What are the modern-day equivalents of fields and vineyards that enable workers to share more fully in the wealth and bounty generated by the society?

And lastly, we must have faith that together we can help rebuild the nation. As terrible as wage theft and payroll fraud are, unlike many of the nation's problems, these are clearly solvable. We can encourage ethical businesses in challenging unjust employers. We can rebuild the enforcement staffs so that workers have effective places to turn. We can support unions and workers' centers as alternatives for helping workers. We can and must do this. We can end wage theft and payroll fraud. But we need all of us—working together.

14

You Can Make a Difference

What good is it, my brothers and sisters, if you say you have faith but do not have works? Can faith save you? If your brother or sister is without clothes and lacks daily food and one of you says to them, "Go in peace; keep warm and eat your fill," but you do not supply their bodily needs, what is the good of that? So faith by itself, if it has not works is dead.

—James 2:14–17 (NRSV)

None of you has faith unless you love for your brother what you love for yourself.

—Prophet Muhammad

These prophetic words challenge people of faith to consider how faith impacts what we do. The problems of wage theft described throughout the book aren't someone else's problems. They are yours and my problems. It is not sufficient for us to express regret or even anger about it. We've got to do lots more.

Will we continue to allow unethical employers to steal wages from workers, deprive the public coffers of revenues, and undercut law-abiding businesses, or will we collectively challenge unjust employers and build the political will in our communities and nation to end this scourge of evil-doing?

The coming years are a time to turn the nation around, setting new standards for ethical behavior and punishment of wrongdoing. In our nation's history, we have seen waves of reform, which often follow very bleak periods. For example, workplace reform at the end of the nineteenth century resulted in the early state laws limiting hours of work and setting minimum standards for particular sectors of workers. Later, the Great Depression reforms resulted in passage of the FLSA and the NLRA. The 1960s marked yet another period of reform and expansion of workplace laws and protections. The next few years could well be another period of great workplace advances. At no time in the last thirty years has there been a greater disparity of incomes, more discouragement about families' economic prospects, or such an epidemic of employers stealing wages. We must all help address the challenges facing working families.

Each of us has a role to play in stopping wage theft and putting in place mechanisms for reform. We can do many positive things as individual consumers, as employers, as members of congregations, as educators, as public officials, as lawyers, as judges, and as citizens in communities. Some things are small. Some are large. All are important!

Stopping Wage Theft as Individual Consumers

The United States is a consumer economy in which all of us participate. By virtue of our purchases of good and services, we have the power to influence companies. Although we hardly know how workers are treated (and paid) by all the companies whose products we purchase or consume, there are some simple things we can and should do as individuals to help stop wage theft:

Give tips to restaurant wait staff in cash. Given how many restaurants steal wages and tips from workers, don't put your tip on your credit card and don't just leave it on the table. Give the cash tip directly to the person who serves you. Tips that are put on credit cards sometimes are not actually given to the wait staff.

Support ethical employers and avoid those who steal wages. Unfortunately, it is not all that easy to know which employers are ethical and which ones steal wages. A few good resources for you, though none is foolproof, include:

ResponsibleShopper.org: This website, compiled by Coop America, provides information about the labor and environmental policies of hundreds of name-brand companies. This website does a better job helping you eliminate rather than locate places to shop.

ShopUnionMade.org: One way you can be confident that workers are being paid all their wages is to shop for products made by workers represented by unions. As discussed in Chapter 5, unions ensure that workers are paid all their wages, as well as help workers gain good wages, benefits, and working conditions. This website connects you with many, though certainly not all, union-made products.

FairTradeFederation.org: This is a clearinghouse for products that are made in fair trade workplaces in the United States and in other countries. Generally speaking, these workplaces are cooperatives or community-sponsored projects that seek to pay workers fair wages. Most of these stores sell fair trade food products (like coffee, tea, and chocolate), arts and crafts-type gifts, clothes, and jewelry. Unfortunately, these stores do not sell many products that families regularly use.

San Francisco's Dining with Justice: A Guide to Guilt-Free Eating: This guide prepared by Young Workers United can help you choose restaurants in San Francisco. Visit www.young workersunited.org for the list. Hopefully, there will be similar guides for other cities in the near future.

HotelWorkersRising.org/HotelGuide. This Union Hotel Guide lists union hotels around the nation. It also tells which hotels are having labor disputes so you can avoid them.

Pay well those who work around your home. If you hire any individual to help clean your house, care for your kids, mow your grass, or remove debris from gutters, pay them well, promptly, and fairly. Remember household workers who earn $1700 or more in cash or equivalent forms of compensation must have social security and Medicare taxes paid on their behalf. (See IRS Document 15-A for more information.)

Ask questions of contracted businesses before hiring them. If you hire a firm, even a small one, for work in your home, your congregation, or your organization, you should check out how the workers are paid and be sure that the company provides insurance for its work and workers' compensation for its employees. Here are the key questions to ask:

1. Are all your workers paid as employees? If not, why not?
2. How much are your workers paid? (You can ask for a range for the various workers if the employer is uncomfortable with the question.)
3. What benefits do you provide for your workers? (Key benefits are health care, pension, paid sick days, and paid vacation. None of these benefits are required in most states, but workers and families need them.)
4. Are all your workers covered by workers' compensation? May I see a copy of your workers' compensation insurance coverage? (In some terribly abusive industries, such as landscaping, you may need to verify the coverage with the state workers' compensation board.)
5. Are your workers in a union? Given the declining percentage of unionized workplaces, most workers will not be represented by a union. If the workers are in a union, the employer is probably paying people legally and fairly. If the workers are not in a union, you will need to be more careful in verifying answers to the previous questions.

Ask workers in your community how they are paid. If you have the opportunity, talk with people about local working conditions. Be careful not to ask workers about their working conditions in front of their employers. You might not get the same response as you would in another setting. Young people may often have information about local employers because they may have worked temporarily in neighborhood stores, restaurants, or nursing homes. If you consistently hear about problems in one business, organize a small delegation of concerned community residents to talk with the business owner. You can also raise the concerns with the local Chamber of Commerce and urge the Chamber to talk with that business owner.

Make sure your children and family members get paid. Complain if an employer steals wages, either intentionally and unintentionally, from a family member who is working. Seek to get the money back and make sure the employer changes the policies to ensure that other workers get paid. Assist your family member in filing a complaint with either the state labor agency or the federal Wage and Hour Division. If your child or a family member receives a 1099 instead of a W-2, investigate whether the employer has committed payroll fraud. It may be tempting to ignore problems, but if an employer steals from one person, the employer is likely to steal from another.

Stopping Wage Theft as Employers

Employers have legal and ethical responsibilities to pay their employees fairly. They also have a responsibility to ensure that the firms with which they contract and do business pay their workers.

Make sure that your workers are paid fairly. Could you be underpaying your workers, either illegally or unethically? Most of the laws, such as minimum wage, are pretty clear. Understanding who is covered by overtime and who is not is not quite as clear. If you are unclear about this issue after reading the Department of Labor website, ask the Wage and Hour Division to audit your records and review who is considered exempt and nonexempt. If you have not paid someone properly, you will owe them back wages, but if you ask for help from the Department of Labor, you will not likely be assessed any penalties unless you have previously been told what to do and ignored it. Ethical questions about what is fair to pay workers are harder and more subjective, but perhaps even more important to consider.

Train your managers and line staff about paying workers fairly. Make sure that those implementing your company's policies understand the law and your values relating to fair pay. Never assume that people understand either the laws or your policies. As many large companies with good labor polices have discovered, if your managers and line staff don't understand how wrong you consider wage theft, they may not obey the labor laws and your policies. You must "inspect" what you "expect."

Build in incentives to pay people fairly. If your internal systems require your managers to keep expenses down at all costs (and they are rewarded for such), you will likely be inadvertently building in incentives for managers to steal wages from workers. As described in Chapter 4 companies need incentives for managers to follow all labor laws. If you have incentives for keeping staffing costs low without such incentives for paying people fairly, you may experience wage theft problems. For more details on how this happens, read chapter 8 of Steven Greenhouse's *The Big Squeeze: Tough Times for American Workers*. Consider rewarding your managers for keeping staff turnover low or not having any FLSA violations in two years, or receiving high employee satisfaction ratings.

Create and monitor contractor guidelines. Many companies have contractor or subcontracting guidelines in place. Even more important than the guidelines are the regular inspecting and monitoring of those companies' employment and payment practices. Developing guidelines without figuring out how to monitor them is a cosmetic gesture, not a meaningful way to ensure workers get paid.

Include treatment of workers in your questions asked contractors. Of course, you will ask prospective contractors what quality of work they will do at what price and over what time period. Those are all appropriate questions. You should also ask how the contractor will pay workers. If you don't include questions about treatment of workers, you will inadvertently send a message that the only things you value are quality of work, price, and timeliness. Use the same questions you should use if you hire someone to work in your home:

1. Are all your workers paid as employees? If not, why not? Do you provide them with W-2s rather than 1099s?
2. How much are your workers paid? (You can ask for a range for the various workers if the employer is uncomfortable with the question.)
3. What benefits do you provide for your workers? (Key benefits are health care, pension, paid sick days, and paid vacation. None of these benefits are required in most states, but workers and families need them.)
4. Are all your workers covered by workers' compensation? May I see a copy of your workers' compensation insurance coverage? (In some terribly abusive industries, such as landscaping, you may need to verify the coverage with the state workers' compensation board.)
5. Do your workers believe that they have the right to join a union and engage in collective bargaining?

Stopping Wage Theft in Our Congregations and Religious Institutions

Congregations are respected community institutions. Approximately 40 percent of the American public claim they attend religious services at least once a week (although polls show actual attendance is a bit lower). Unlike many institutions, congregations support people across racial, ethnic, and economic lines. Although any particular congregation may be somewhat segregated by race or class, congregations collectively reach and serve people across all sectors of American society.

Congregations provide education and training for people on a host of personal and social issues. For example, congregations organize classes and programs on family issues, such as parenting skills and marriage counseling. They also offer health programs, such as dieting classes and exercise programs. In addition, they help people with financial matters by offering retirement planning classes, tax preparation clinics, and home ownership workshops.

Congregations also help their members grapple with critical social issues. Many congregations have social concerns or peace and justice committees that educate and engage their members in social issues. Others organize youth and adult education programs to study current social issues.

Concern about poverty and other issues facing the poor is important for most congregations, as is demonstrated by the vast majority of congregations contributing to soup kitchens, food banks, or shelters. In the June 2008 Pew Forum on Religion and Public Life survey, nearly two-thirds of churchgoers supported more government assistance for poor people even if it meant the United States would go further into debt.[1]

Congregations care about poverty and poor people, which is why they are such natural allies in educating workers (and employers) and fighting wage theft. Figuring out how to train workers about their rights in the workplace, as well as give them tools for challenging injustice and for obtaining a vision of broader societal change, makes sense. Congregations can:

Conduct worker rights training sessions aimed at stopping wage theft. If your congregation includes many low-wage workers, it is especially important to offer worker rights education programs. But even if your congregation is more affluent, you might be surprised to learn how often young people get taken advantage of in the workplace because they don't understand the basic labor laws. Invite a workers' center leader, a federal Wage and Hour investigator, or a local labor attorney to lead the session.

Young workers are often taken advantage of in the workplace, and 70 to 80 percent of teens work for pay during their high school years.[2] Make sure the teens (and their parents) are offered worker rights training sessions.

Distribute worker rights bulletin inserts. IWJ has prepared simple worker rights bulletin inserts to educate workers about their core rights.

Provide worker rights materials. Congregations usually have educational flyers and materials available in the vestibule or a library. General "know your rights" materials should be made available. Get state-specific information from workers' centers or legal clinics in your area. See Appendix D for contact information.

Talk with youth groups about work issues. Given the frequency of problems young workers experience, youth group leaders should prepare to talk with young people about how to handle problems they experience in the workplace.

Counsel and refer workers. Clergy should develop a basic understanding of worker issues so that they are equipped to counsel workers and refer them to appropriate agencies for additional help with problems. Increasingly, seminaries and rabbinic schools are offering courses on worker justice,[3] and clergy can learn about community resources through IWJ coalitions.

Preach a new vision. Wage theft is not inevitable. It can be stopped. Religious leaders can use their preaching to express a new vision and a new hope for what our nation can be. Religious leaders can offer hope to workers that they can change working conditions and challenge employers to set higher standards for ethical treatment in the workplace. Preaching is faith-based education providing hope and vision.

Make sure your congregation is paying most workers as employees. Congregations are known to misclassify workers and pay workers as independent contractors, which shifts the responsibility for payroll taxes from the employer to the employee and may deny the worker unemployment insurance, workers' compensation, and overtime pay.

Within the first month after Reverend Dr. George Abrams became the new senior pastor of Cheney United Methodist Church (UMC) in Cheney, Washington, he learned that all twelve staff members at the church were being paid as independent contractors. Knowing this was wrong, he immediately got the church leadership to pass an employment standards resolution and started paying people as employees instead of independent contractors. Here's an abridged version of the standard:

> We are called by God to be good stewards of all that God has given us including our financial resources. We are also called to do justice, love, mercy, and walk humbly with our God. Thus, as a Godly people we affirm work that enhances human life and shun work that destroys human life.
>
> To take unfair financial advantage of an employee is to create a major injustice. Accordingly, it shall be the policy of Cheney UMC to provide all employees with a fair and equitable wage, and with a safe, healthy, and wholesome working environment.
>
> 1. All attempts shall be made to pay each and every employee a living wage, taking into consideration the prevailing rate in the community and the employee's knowledge, skills, and abilities.
> 2. No employee shall be asked to volunteer to perform work that they are being paid to do.
> 3. All employees shall be entitled to a safe, healthy and wholesome work environment.
> 4. Employees shall be paid a pension when they become eligible for a pension under the Book of Discipline.
> 5. Employees shall be provided health benefits when they become eligible for such benefits under the Book of Discipline.

Carefully monitor overtime rules. Clergy members are not subject to overtime rules, but other employees may be, depending on what they do. Don't assume that overtime rules don't apply to your congregation. *Determine how janitors and yard service people are paid.* If your congregation contracts out its janitorial or yard service work, find out how those workers are paid. Nonunion janitorial and yard service firms are notorious for stealing wages from workers.

Explore thoroughly those who would provide repairs or new construction work for your congregation. Use the "Ethical Questions to Ask Building Contractors," which can be downloaded for free from www.iwj.org to ensure that you have thoroughly checked out how workers are paid by construction contractors. Nonunion and most residential construction is notorious for its wage theft.

Lift up workers and employers during services. Both workers and employers need the prayers and encouragement of religious communities. Organize "Labor in the Pulpits/Bimah/Minbar" programs that focus on worker issues over Labor Day weekend. Include worker justice inserts in your bulletins. Pray regularly in services for both workers and employers.

Organize adult educational forums on the crisis of wage theft and the challenges facing workers in low-wage jobs. Use this book or another book such as Steven Greenhouse's *The Big Squeeze* (2008) as the basis for an adult educational forum. A congregational study guide for this book is in Appendix G. A congregational study guide for *The Big Squeeze* is available at www.stevengreenhouse.com.

Invite a Wage and Hour investigator to talk with congregants about problems in the community. If you are unsure about whether wage theft exists in your community, invite an investigator to talk with you about what he or she has found. Also, ask how you might work together to combat wage theft and payroll fraud.

Create a business leaders' discussion group to allow them to examine their leadership roles in light of Scripture. Help business leaders consider how they can help promote ethical practices within the business community. Perhaps these leaders can meet privately with employers known to steal wages and urge them to reconsider and change their actions.

Stopping Wage Theft through Educational Institutions and Libraries

Educational institutions and libraries reach large numbers of young people and those seeking jobs. They can play critical roles in reaching workers who might not be reached in other forums.

Organize educational programs on worker rights. A few years ago I participated in DePaul University's orientation for first-year students. I was asked to explain IWJ and the work we do. I decided to begin by asking the twenty-five students in the group if any of them had ever experienced any problems in the workplace. I expected to hear one or two stories that I could work from in my presentation. Nineteen of the students told me about their experiences of wage theft. Employers had worked them off the clock, not paid overtime, not given them their last paychecks, and closed businesses without telling them. By and large, these were 18-year-old college students from middle-class backgrounds. If almost four-fifths of the students had experienced wage theft, imagine the problems that first-generation immigrants or young people from poor families experience.

Organize courses on worker rights for high school students. High schools should offer two or three sessions on worker rights for junior and senior high school students right before classes adjourn for the summer. Labor lawyers, ethical business leaders, worker center advocates, DOL staff, or union leaders can help lead the sessions. Perhaps the National Educational Association or the American Federation of Teachers can develop and distribute curriculum for this training.

Establish worker rights satellite programs at community colleges. Community colleges serve students who are usually working at least part-time, many full-time, and often at low-wage jobs that are known to cheat workers of pay. Community colleges have been a key partner with the Department of Labor in efforts to prepare workers for jobs. Community college placement centers can function as worker rights centers by helping students learn about their rights and challenge wrongdoing they experience. Community colleges can offer monthly worker rights forums in conjunction with workers' centers, labor education centers, or government agencies, distribute worker rights materials at the career counseling offices, and provide links to worker rights information on their websites.

Train librarians to assist workers in finding resources. Most public and school libraries, especially if they have free computers with Internet access, are hopping places where workers search for jobs, young people do homework and research colleges they want to enter, and community organizations hold meetings. Libraries and librarians should be a major resource to help fight wage theft. One might envision any number of activities, all of them consonant with the mission of librarianship that might be added to the regular agenda of a local library.

Distribute worker rights flyers. Most libraries and college placement offices have racks for free literature. State and federal worker fact sheets can be distributed. If the Department of Labor had "do it yourself kits" for filing wage claims, these could be available here too.

Host worker rights educational meetings. Federal and state labor agencies can be invited to conduct worker rights programs at the main libraries or on college campuses on a regular basis. Labor attorneys, labor law professors, union leaders, and workers' center leaders might volunteer to lead workshops as well.

Direct workers to helpful worker rights websites. The librarians who assist patrons with computers should be familiar with the websites that help workers in their communities, such as www.canmybossdothat.org.

Establish worker rights resource sections. Most libraries have a travel section, a job resource section, and a college research section that are conveniently located. Libraries can create a worker rights section that would make it easy for workers to research their problems and find solutions.

Stopping Wage Theft in Our Communities

Support workers' centers. Workers' centers are on the front lines of fighting wage theft. They do awesome and heroic work. Most operate on $50,000 to $150,000 budgets, some on even less. All the workers' centers are largely volunteer run and operated. Workers' centers are worthy of broader public and private support. Your help is needed. Contact information for workers' centers is available in Appendix D. You can:

Give money. Donations large and small are accepted. Most of the workers' centers either have a 501(c)3 tax designation or are affiliated with an organization that has one, so donors can receive a tax deduction for gifts as allowed by the IRS.

Give stuff. Most workers' centers need furniture, computers, and fax machines. They can also use donated office or meeting space, donated cars, or even the occasional use of an apartment (remember from Chapter 2 the phone book delivery workers who showed up at the workers' center with suitcases in hand).

Volunteer. All workers' centers need volunteers. They are most eager for people who are willing to make a long-term commitment (e.g., someone who'll come one day a week for the next year). Because so many immigrants need help, people with knowledge of foreign languages are highly prized. Those with specialized skills, such as retired Labor Department staff, attorneys, bookkeepers, or people with web development skills are also highly valued.

Invite leaders to speak. Invite workers' center staff and leaders to speak at your congregation, community organization, union, or other association. This will acquaint others with the work.

Support public campaigns. Workers' centers often engage the community in public rallies, demonstrations, and prayer vigils to urge employers to pay workers their wages. Get on the e-mail list or mailing list to learn about those events and participate.

Create a workers' center in your community. If no workers' center exists, consider working with allies to create one. Workers' centers are valuable tools in a community's fight against wage theft. IWJ can assist you in putting a plan together to build a workers' center.

Support workers' rights to organize unions. If janitors, hotel workers, security guards, construction workers, or any other groups of workers are trying to organize a union and get a first contract, you can assume they will have a struggle to do so. Call the union leadership and ask how you can help. (They might initially not be sure who you are or what you want, but persevere in doing good.)

Explore ways you might partner with the Department of Labor Wage and Hour Division. The Department of Labor is eager to partner with community organizations. Call them and ask to meet. Begin by getting to know the leadership of your local Wage and Hour office. Explore what connections the office already has in the community and share how you might help. Explore the possibility of convening a community task force to educate and reach out to workers about wage theft.

Urge business associations to lead the way in stopping wage theft. Meet with your local Chamber of Commerce or industry association. Ask what it might do to challenge the crisis of wage theft. Offer to partner in outreach to workers.

Arrange worker rights sessions at shelters and soup kitchens. Increasingly, soup kitchens and shelters serve people who are employed but don't make enough to make ends meet. Many of the soup kitchen and shelter patrons are probably having their wages stolen. Make sure the patrons are familiar with the opportunities to reclaim their unpaid wages.

Partner with tax preparation volunteers. Volunteers who help low-income families prepare their tax returns see evidences of wage theft and probably don't recognize it. By asking a few simple questions, the tax preparers can spot wage theft and refer workers to a workers' center for help in recovering unpaid wages. For workers with W-2s, ask: Do you ever work more than 40 hours per week? If so, are you paid time-and-a-half for hours worked over 40? For workers with 1099s, ask: Who decided you were an independent contractor? You or your employer?

Strengthen wage enforcement in your community. Review Chapter 12 and the ways other communities are working to strengthen local enforcement. Can you work with your city leaders to strengthen wage enforcement locally?

Stopping Wage Theft in Your State

Support a state campaign to stop wage theft. There are many state efforts to address wage theft and payroll fraud. Visit IWJ's wage theft website (www.wagetheft.org) to connect with the latest campaigns.

Convene or join a cross-agency task force. Many states have created or are discussing creating a cross-agency task force to crack down on payroll fraud and wage theft. Some of these task forces are open to community and religious organizations participating.

Engage statewide faith organizations in the issue. State ecumenical and interfaith organizations often have annual meetings at which you might organize a workshop on wage theft. State judicatory organizations, such as the United Methodist Conference, may also have statewide meetings at which wage theft and state wage enforcement issues can be addressed.

Stopping Wage Theft in the Nation

As citizens, we can all help make stopping wage theft a priority for the nation. We can:

Write to our congressional representative and two U.S. senators. Write a letter to your elected leaders urging them to address the crisis of wage theft in the nation. Their addresses are:

Your Representative	Your Senator
U.S. House of Representatives	U.S. Senate
Washington, DC 20515	Washington, DC 20510

Arrange to meet with your congressional representative and/or senators. In most states with larger populations, it is possible to meet with your representative and a bit more difficult to meet with your senators, but you can always meet with elected representatives' staff members. The best way to get a meeting is to recruit a group of constituents and jointly ask for a meeting during an upcoming congressional recess. Our federally elected leaders usually have breaks in January, springtime (around Easter and Passover), Memorial Day, July 4, August, and December. Check out www.senate.gov and www.house.gov to get their current calendars of recesses (the Senate and the House have slightly different recess dates).

Organize a community forum on wage theft. One way to bring issues to the attention of elected leaders is to organize forums about the issues in their congressional districts. Invite workers who have had their wages stolen to tell their stories. Ask a professor who studies these issues to give a presentation documenting the extent of the problem in your community. Invite your elected leader to listen to the other speakers and to respond about what he or she can do in Congress to stop wage theft. Be sure to get the media to cover your forum.

Submit op-eds or letters-to-the-editor about wage theft. Politicians read their constituents' op-eds and letters-to-the-editor. They provide an indication of the concerns of constituents. Help lift up these concerns by writing to the local papers and calling in on radio talk shows.

Follow and support legislative initiatives to stop wage theft. The best way to follow and support legislative initiatives to stop wage theft is to join the e-mail advocacy and mailing network of IWJ. Join by visiting www.iwj.org.

If none of the ideas suggested here appeal to you, find something else you can do. Talk with friends, pray for workers, draw a picture depicting wage theft. Almost every time I attend a party or a social gathering, the issue of wage theft comes up (I wonder why?). Almost without fail, people know someone who has experienced wage theft, but they thought it was an isolated problem. Most people are shocked to learn that we have a national crisis of wage theft. So if you can't do anything else, talk about the problem. It will help. The national epidemic of wage theft is not inevitable. A hundred and fifty years ago, we weren't sure we could end slavery. We did. A hundred years ago, few thought we could stop child labor in industries. We did. A hundred years ago women could not vote. Now they can. Seventy years ago, people questioned whether we could pass a minimum wage. We did. Ending wage theft and payroll fraud will not be easy, but together we can put a stop to illegal acts and rebuild protections and standards for workers. Ending wage theft and payroll fraud is essential for workers, important for ethical businesses, and critical for America.

APPENDICES
Additional Resources

Appendix A

Department of Labor Wage and Hour Settlements

Ways Wages Are Stolen	Date on DOL Press Release	Company	Suit or Settlement	Back Wages Owed (or estimated)	Number of Workers Owed $
not paying prevailing wage rate, not paying overtime	3/17/2011	Pythagoras General Contracting Corp.	Settlement	$792,396	79
withholding benefits	3/16/2011	Parkland Hotel Investors LP	Suit	$1,350,000	96
not paying employees	3/9/2011	Coin Builders LLC	Suit	$1.3 million	n/a
not paying overtime	3/9/2011	Beck Disaster Recovery Inc.	Settlement	$754,578	89
not paying back wages	2/28/2011			$700,000	151
not paying back wages	2/28/2011	Quinco Electrical Inc.	Settlement	$68,778	14
not paying overtime	2/28/2011	VIP Hotel Services	Settlement	$242,000	541
misclassifying workers	2/28/2011	P.K. Management	Settlement	$64,733	37
misclassifying workers	2/28/2011	All American Air and Electric Inc.	Settlement	$55,499	61
not paying back wages	2/28/2011	Los Matadores Inc.	Court order	$200,000	62
not paying back wages	2/28/2011	GeoPharma Inc.	Settlement	136,700	82
misclassifying workers	2/7/2011	UnitedHealthcare	Settlement	$934,000	479
misclassifying workers, not paying wages	2/3/2011	Green Bay Dressed Beef LLC	Settlement	$1.65 million	970
depriving workers of minimum wage and overtime pay	2/3/2011	The Mandarin House restaurant	Settlement	$85,290	9
depriving workers of minimum wage and overtime pay	1/13/2011	Angel's Finishing Inc.	Settlement	$158,952	110
not paying overtime	1/13/2011	Total Enterprise Inc.	Suit	$1.3 million	140

Violation	Date	Employer	Resolution	Amount	Workers
not paying overtime	1/6/2011	CEMEX Inc.	Settlement	$1,514,449	1705
misclassifying workers, not paying overtime and poor recordkeeping	2/9/2011	Treviicos-Soletanche JV	Settlement	$104,159.86	24
misclassifying workers and not paying wages for all hours worked	2/17/2011	RDL Logistics LLC	Settlement	$50,258	8
not paying overtime	2/17/2011	Los Avina Mexican Restaurants	Settlement	$60,000	5
not paying minimum wage or overtime	2/24/2011	Bini Bakery Corp.	Settlement	$42,244	7
charging employees for uniforms, not paying minimum wage or overtime and poor recordkeeping	2/17/2011	Subway eateries operated by Scripture Only Inc.	Settlement	$8558	159
misclassifying workers, not paying overtime and poor recordkeeping	2/9/2011	Aaron Auto Glass Inc.	Settlement	$199,464	30
misclassifying workers, not paying overtime and poor recordkeeping	2/9/2011	Miguel Castro	Settlement	$397,703	129
not paying overtime	1/26/2011	Genesis Group Homes Inc.	Settlement	$67,140	17
not paying overtime	1/9/2011	Sanford Regional Hospital	Settlement	$77,000	21

(continued)

Appendix A (continued)

Ways Wages Are Stolen	Date on DOL Press Release	Company	Suit or Settlement	Back Wages Owed (or estimated)	Number of Workers Owed $
failing to provide contractually obligated pay for medical leave	1/11/2011	Welch Foods Inc.	Settlement	$14,110	1
misclassifying workers and not paying overtime	3/9/2011	MESA Products Inc.	Settlement	$190,000	57
not paying workers minimum wage or for time worked or for overtime, misleading investigators	2/24/2011	Hong Kong Market	Settlement	$2 million	400
not paying overtime	12/16/2010	Westminster, CA	Settlement	$887,554	115
not paying overtime	12/9/2010	Sant-Tec Electric Inc.	Settlement	$339,000	27
misclassifying workers, not paying overtime	12/9/2010	Enwisen Inc.	Settlement	$209,176	29
not paying wages	12/9/2010	Peri Software Solutions Inc.	Suit	$638,449	67
not paying wages	11/4/2010	Aspen Nursing Services	Suit	$512,000	22
not paying overtime	10/14/2010	NYC Dollar Store Chain	Suit	$485,000	120
unauthorized use of pension funds	9/29/2010	Journey Electrical Technologies Inc.	Suit	$920,000	264
not paying minimum wages or overtime	9/28/2010	Xero-Fax Inc.	Suit	$107,500	34
not paying overtime	8/26/2010	Prairie River Home Care Inc.	Suit	$150,000	144
not paying wages	8/26/2010	Naval Station Mayport	Settlement	$166,667	105

Violation	Date	Company	Type	Amount	Number
not paying overtime, forcing employees to work off the clock	8/26/2010	Walt Disney Parks and Resorts U.S.	Settlement	$433,819	69
not paying overtime or minimum wage	7/26/2010	Liberty Fruits & Produce Corp.	Settlement	$840,000	42
not paying overtime	7/13/2010	Bill Taylor, president of B&D Taylor Inc.	Settlement	$20,502.05	5
not paying overtime	7/12/2010	Sterling Caterers & Restaurant LLC	Settlement	$93,110	14
not paying wages or overtime	7/8/2010	Evergreen Produce	Suit	$119,886	18
not paying wages	11/18/2010	J&R Baker Farms LLC	Suit	$1.3 million	244
not paying wages	4/11/2010	Aspen Nursing Services	Suit	$256,292.13	22
not paying minimum wage	4/23/2010	Bravo Supermarket and C-Town Supermarket	Settlement	$288,000	38
not paying overtime	2/4/2010	Health Services Group Inc.	Settlement	$265,451	1971
not paying minimum wage or overtime	1/26/2010	King's Garden 1 Chinese Restaurant Inc.	Settlement	$30,795.61	7
not paying wages	1/21/2010	Shawn Malik Inc.	Settlement	$38,609	34
not paying minimum wage	1/14/2010	MT Transportation & Logistics Services Inc.	Settlement	$1.8 million	500
not paying overtime and poor recordkeeping	12/16/2010	Nanak Oil Inc, Paul Mart Inc., Metro Petro Inc., and Route 28 Inc.	Settlement	$57,389.48	32

(continued)

Appendix A (*continued*)

Ways Wages Are Stolen	Date on DOL Press Release	Company	Suit or Settlement	Back Wages Owed (or estimated)	Number of Workers Owed $
not paying overtime	8/11/2010	CenturyLink	Settlement	$144,593	1434
not paying minimum wage and poor recordkeeping	8/11/2010	Central Florida Investments	Settlement	$868,443	1065
not paying minimum wage or overtime	3/25/2010	Tom Johnson Camping Center	Settlement	$144,984	54
not paying overtime	3/5/2010	Peachtree Maintenance Inc.	Settlement	$449,436	81
not paying minimum wage or overtime	8/11/2010	APC Workforce Solutions	Settlement	$61,191	81
not paying prevailing wage	8/17/2010	Smartsoft International Inc.	Settlement	$1 million	135
not paying wages	8/24/2010	L-3 Communications Vertex Aerospace LLC	Settlement	$166,667	105
not paying overtime or for work-related travel expenses	8/30/2010	Lee Electrical Construction Inc.	Settlement	$213,533.94	54
not paying wages	9/9/2010	Belcorp of America, Electrolytic Technologies Corp.	Suit	$173,807	53
not paying overtime	11/3/2010	Las Margaritas Inc.	Settlement	$140,711	66
not paying overtime	12/20/2010	Kevin Misch Trucking and Excavating Inc.	Court order	$50,952	31
not paying wages	11/18/2010	Illinois Machining Group Inc. and IMG Products Co.	Court order	$103,912	35
not paying minimum wage or overtime	11/4/2010	Aspen Nursing Services	Suit	$512,000	22

Violation	Date	Company	Resolution	Amount	Number
not paying minimum wage or overtime and poor recordkeeping	10/4/2010	Barlen Contracting Inc. and Barlen PG Inc.	Court order	$173,000	16
not paying over time	9/25/2010	Prairie River Home Care Inc.	Settlement	$150,043	44
not paying overtime	9/3/2010	Warsaw Wireless	Settlement	$29,445	25
not paying overtime	3/3/2010	Husky Energy Corp.	Settlement	$969,182	173
not paying minimum wage or overtime and poor recordkeeping	2/23/2010	New Liberty Hospital in Liberty	Settlement	$282,166	1032
not paying minimum wage or overtime and poor recordkeeping	2/3/2010	Custom Electric Inc.	Settlement	$39,466	21
not paying for all hours worked or for overtime and poor recordkeeping	8/17/2010	Eastok Inc.	Settlement	$232,773	110
misclassifying workers and not paying overtime or for all hours worked	4/10/2010	Williams Brothers Construction, Cimolai USA, and Cosme	Settlement	$136,679	140
not paying overtime and poor recordkeeping	7/29/2010	Morgan Well Service Inc.	Settlement	$69,728	76
not paying minimum wage or overtime and poor recordkeeping	6/27/2010	BCI Technologies	Settlement	$248,192	126
not paying overtime and poor recordkeeping	6/12/2010	Castillo Ready Mix Inc.	Settlement	$147,568	87

(continued)

Appendix A (*continued*)

Ways Wages Are Stolen	Date on DOL Press Release	Company	Suit or Settlement	Back Wages Owed (or estimated)	Number of Workers Owed $
not paying minimum wage or overtime	6/3/2010	Texas De Brazil Corp.	Settlement	$177,502	715
not paying overtime	5/19/2010	Teleperformance USA	Settlement	$2 million	15,862
not paying overtime	5/5/2010	J.A.B. Inc.	Settlement	$106,709	37
not paying minimum wage or overtime	4/28/2010	UFE Inc.	Settlement	$285,000	200
not paying wages	4/23/2010	Advaitaa Technologies Inc.	Settlement	$22,989	24
not paying overtime	3/5/2010	Cobra Stone Inc.	Settlement	$364,403	169
requiring employees to pay for work equipment, not paying minimum wage and not paying overtime, and poor recordkeeping	2/22/2010	Moss Landscaping Inc.	Settlement	$89,819	283
not paying overtime	2/10/2010	Universal Project Management Inc. and Fluor Enterprises Inc.	Settlement	$1 million	54
not paying overtime	2/8/2010	Dawson Geophysical Co.	Settlement	$100,356	24
not paying minimum wage or overtime	2/8/2010	Pine Bluff-based Davis Life Care Center Inc.	Settlement	$61,962	21
not paying for all hours worked or for overtime	12/8/2010	Kwong Yet Lung Co. Inc.	Settlement	$63,470	119

Violation	Date	Company	Type	Amount	Workers
not paying for all hours worked and not paying overtime	6/14/2010	Umatilla Chemical Depot	Settlement	$4.2 million	603
not paying for all hours worked and not paying overtime	6/1/2010	Maricopa County Board of Supervisors and Maricopa County Sheriff's Office	Settlement	$2 million	1690
extreme violation of labor laws: forcing employees to work in sweatshop-like conditions, not paying minimum wage and for overtime	5/13/2010	Thuy Thi Le	Suit	$172,832	47
not paying for all hours worked	1/25/2010	FoodPro International	Court order	$47,800	n/a
not paying wages and benefits	12/15/2009	VMT Long Term Care Management Inc.	Settlement	$1.7 million	483
not paying wages and poor recordkeeping	12/10/2009	EcomNets Inc.	Suit	$92,032.06	13
not paying minimum wages or overtime	11/24/2009	Grand China Buffet and Grill	Settlement	$29,054	35
misclassifying workers and not paying wages	10/8/2009	Computer Sciences Corp.	Settlement	$1.4 million	237
misclassifying workers	9/31/2009	SI International SEIT Inc.	Settlement	$1.5 million	272

(continued)

Appendix A (*continued*)

Ways Wages Are Stolen	Date on DOL Press Release	Company	Suit or Settlement	Back Wages Owed (or estimated)	Number of Workers Owed $
not paying wages or providing benefits	9/4/2009	J.O. Jett Trucking and Jeffrey O. Jett	Suit	$59,458	21
not paying minimum wage and poor recordkeeping	8/26/2009	Martino's Pizzeria Inc.	Suit	n/a	24
not paying overtime and poor recordkeeping	8/4/2009	Tri-County Staffing Corp.	Settlement	$28,446	61
not paying minimum wage or overtime	7/23/2009	Partners HealthCare Systems Inc.	Settlement	$2.7 million	700
not paying minimum wage and providing benefits	7/20/2009	Robert Elevator Co. Inc. and Morgan Vertical Consultants Inc.	Settlement	$215,000	25
not paying wages	6/30/2009	Atlantic Auto Care Center Inc., First Avenue Corp., Michael's Car Wash Inc., and Howard Beach Car Wash Corp.	Settlement	$3.4 million	1187
not paying overtime and poor recordkeeping	6/29/2009	S. Cooper Brothers Trucking Inc.	Settlement	$140,883	105
not paying for all hours worked, overtime, and poor recordkeeping	5/20/2009	Sprint	Settlement	$259,429	1013
not paying overtime and poor recordkeeping	5/12/2009	Innovate Inc.	Settlement	$20,525	24

Violation	Date	Company	Type	Amount	Number
not paying overtime	4/20/2009	Exclusive Detailing Inc.	Settlement	$57,936	8
not paying overtime and poor recordkeeping	4/16/2009	Advanced Professional Marketing Inc.	Settlement	$211,120	247
not paying overtime and poor recordkeeping	4/15/2009	The Trevin McGregor Group Inc.	Settlement	$179,349	54
not paying correct wages and poor recordkeeping	3/30/2009	Cognizant Technology Solutions	Settlement	$509,607	67
not paying overtime	3/24/2009	Merrill Lynch & Co.	Settlement	$516,924	60
not paying overtime	1/29/2009	Phenomena Wash LTD	Settlement	$219,985	58
not paying overtime	1/28/2009	Jorge Morales, Astoria Queens	Settlement	$55,360	7
not paying wages	1/27/2009	MTP Operating Corp.	Settlement	$191,895	68
not paying overtime and poor recordkeeping	1/22/2009	Cascarino's Brick Oven Pizzeria & Ristorante	Settlement	$190,000	106
not paying overtime	8/9/2009	Kyojin Japanese Buffet, New Century China Buffet, China Buffet, Shinju Japanese Buffet in Miami, Shinju Japanese Buffet in Coral Springs, and China Buffet in Stuart	Settlement	$356,770	102
not paying wages	8/14/2009	Hoover Industries	Settlement	$44,485	49
not paying minimum wages or overtime	8/12/2009	Next Level Financial LLC and its president, Christopher Pilo	Settlement	$63,500	25

(continued)

Appendix A (continued)

Ways Wages Are Stolen	Date on DOL Press Release	Company	Suit or Settlement	Back Wages Owed (or estimated)	Number of Workers Owed $
not paying overtime	8/12/2009	MW Therapeutic	Settlement	$318,246	105
not paying overtime	3/6/2009	Harris Farms Inc.	Settlement	$374,184	417
not paying minimum wage, overtime, and poor recordkeeping	1/7/2009	New China Buffet, Dragon Gourmet Buffet, and Kamado's Japanese Seafood Buffet	Settlement	$233,234	55
not paying overtime and poor recordkeeping	1/6/2009	Meat & Produce Corp.	Settlement	$78,272	102
not paying overtime	12/11/2009	Family Buffet Inc.	Settlement	$42,330	14
not paying minimum wage or overtime, poor record-keeping, and failing to provide adequate break time to employees	12/8/2009	SSM Health Care	Suit	$1.7 million	40,000
not paying minimum wage or overtime and poor recordkeeping	12/1/2009	Marc's	Settlement	$426,504	50
not paying minimum wage or overtime and poor recordkeeping	11/12/2009	Oriental Forest	Court order	$2 million	129
not paying minimum wage or overtime and poor recordkeeping	8/23/2009	Schlumberger Technology Corp.	Settlement	$280,605	236

Violation	Date	Company	Action	Amount	Number
not paying minimum wage	8/2/2009	Flying Dove Inc.	Settlement	$64,000	35
not providing breaks for employees	5/14/2009	Linhart Construction Inc.	Settlement	$65,772	50
not paying minimum wage or overtime	3/2/2009	Big Ridge Inc.	Court order	$510,000	500
not paying minimum wage or overtime and poor recordkeeping	2/4/2009	G-2 Commercial Cleaning	Settlement	$28,249	41
not paying overtime	1/29/2009	Hong-Fa Corp.	Settlement	$24,360	7
not reimbursing travel expenses or paying overtime and poor recordkeeping	12/17/2009	Rife Industrial Marine	Settlement	$401,355	567
not paying wages agreed upon in contract	12/15/2009	A&B Mail Transporting Service	Suit	$530,000	29
not paying minimum wage or overtime and poor recordkeeping	12/4/2009	Bodard Bistro, Café 101, Tan Tan Restaurant, and Arirang Korean Restaurant	Settlement	$334,146	154
not paying minimum wage or overtime and poor recordkeeping	11/25/2009	General Structors Contractors Inc.	Settlement	$126,745	254
not paying minimum wage or overtime	11/18/2009	RBG USA Inc.	Settlement	$400,000	482
not paying prevailing wage	11/12/2009	Computer Careers and Consulting Inc.	Settlement	$17,831	8

(continued)

Appendix A (*continued*)

Ways Wages Are Stolen	Date on DOL Press Release	Company	Suit or Settlement	Back Wages Owed (or estimated)	Number of Workers Owed $
not paying minimum wage or overtime and poor recordkeeping	10/8/2009	Stone and Webster Construction Inc.	Settlement	$562,901	1411
not paying for all hours worked or for overtime	8/29/2009	Mana & Associates LLC	Settlement	$119,501	101
not paying minimum wage or overtime	8/28/2009	O'Connor Packaging and Distribution Inc.	Suit	$85,000	95
not paying wages for all hours worked	8/20/2009	Mesa Mail Service LLC	Settlement	$27,957	4
not paying overtime	8/20/2009	Glencalo Inc.	Settlement	$21,380	49
not paying minimum wage or overtime	8/5/2009	MT Supermarket	Settlement	$186,624	34
not paying overtime	7/6/2009	Drywall Companies	Settlement	$535,145	752
not paying minimum wage or overtime and poor recordkeeping	7/27/2009	QuikTrip Corp.	Settlement	$747,729	3819
not paying overtime	7/23/2009	Schlumberger Technology Corp.	Settlement	$280,605	246
not paying wages for all hours worked	4/29/2009	Plains Builders Inc.	Suit	$101,050	90
not paying overtime	4/23/2009	Butch's Waterproofing LP	Settlement	$127,468	55
not paying overtime	4/9/2009	America's Car Mart Inc.	Settlement	$117,023	103

Violation	Date	Company	Action	Amount	Workers
not paying overtime and poor recordkeeping	4/7/2009	IFCO Systems North America Inc.	Settlement	$1.6 million	1751
continuing to disregard FLSA, not paying for hours worked or overtime and poor recordkeeping	2/18/2009	El Torero Inc. and Pres. Ken Andover	Court order	$600,000	19
not paying for all hours worked and not paying overtime	1/15/2009	Wynne Police Department	Settlement	$69,366	22
not paying overtime	1/9/2009	Sandia Corp.	Settlement	$2 million	2657
not paying for all hours worked and misclassifying workers	12/15/2009	HWA Inc.	Settlement	$1 million	206
not paying minimum wage or overtime and poor recordkeeping	6/16/2009	New United Motors Manufacturing Inc.	Settlement	$862, 285	3672
not paying overtime	5/12/2009	O&K Inc.	Court order	$55,152	88
not paying minimum wage or overtime	5/5/2009	Akal Security Inc.	Settlement	$115,056	7
not paying for all hours worked	4/16/2009	Gardena	Suit	$3.5 million	385
not paying for all hours worked	4/2/2009	Lozano Inc.	Settlement	$268,501	270
not paying for all hours worked	1/15/2009	Nestle Prepared Foods Co.	Settlement	$5.1 million	6000

(continued)

Appendix A (*continued*)

Ways Wages Are Stolen	Date on DOL Press Release	Company	Suit or Settlement	Back Wages Owed (or estimated)	Number of Workers Owed $
not paying overtime	11/17/2008	Miles Properties Inc.	Settlement	$217,050	291
not paying minimum wage and overtime	6/5/2008	El Atlacatl Restaurant	Settlement	$50,717	39
not paying prevailing or minimum wage, not paying overtime, and failing to compensate for federally required paid days off	3/7/2008	T.L. Wallace Construction Inc.	Settlement	$168,220	27
not paying overtime	2/25/2008	Miami grocer JYMD Food Corp.	Settlement	$76,595	104
not paying overtime and poor recordkeeping	2/4/2008	Woodman Insulation of Cummings	Settlement	$187,500	309
not paying overtime	1/28/2008	Heaven and Earth Landscaping	Suit	$52,240	187
not paying overtime and incorrectly granting comp time	1/11/2008	Florida Agricultural & Mechanical University	Settlement	$272,988	352
not paying wages	1/9/2008	Gannaway Builders	Settlement	$127,000	33
not paying minimum wage, failing to provide adequate breaks and, in some instances, not paying overtime	1/3/2008	Star America	Settlement	$23,664	137

Violation	Date	Company	Type	Amount	Number
not paying overtime	1/3/2008	Senior Care Group Inc.	Settlement	$95,511	57
not paying overtime	1/3/2008	Boulton Enterprises	Settlement	$146,926	94
not paying overtime or for all hours worked	1/3/2008	ECo Consultants	Settlement	$167,454	44
not paying minimum wage or overtime	12/4/2008	Hudson, NH, construction companies	Settlement	$491,100	99
not paying overtime	12/4/2008	Masouleh Corp.	Settlement	$200,731	28
not paying wages	12/3/2008	Reconstruction Home and Health Care Center Inc.	Settlement	$71,010	94
misclassifying workers and not paying overtime	12/2/2008	888 Consulting Group Inc.	Suit	$1.8 million	973
not paying overtime and poor recordkeeping	11/24/2008	Thomas Caterers Inc.	Suit	$20,669	3
not paying minimum wage and overtime	11/6/2008	Construction & Contracting Zone Inc. and TWA Mechanical LLC	Settlement	$475,000	70
not paying minimum wage	11/3/2008	HCL Systems Inc.	Settlement	$92,644	7
not paying wages and requiring workers to pay unnecessary training fees	10/30/2008	GlobalCynex Inc.	Settlement	$1.7 million	343
not paying wages	10/24/2008	Global Tek Inc.	Settlement	$270,822	24

(continued)

Appendix A (continued)

Ways Wages Are Stolen	Date on DOL Press Release	Company	Suit or Settlement	Back Wages Owed (or estimated)	Number of Workers Owed $
not paying minimum wage or overtime and poor recordkeeping	9/9/2008	Pollos Ala Brassa Pio Pio Inc., Pio Pio Restaurant Inc., Pio Pio Express Inc, Pio Pio NYC Inc., Pio Pio 85 Inc., Sipan Restaurant of New York Inc, and owner Augusto Yallico	Settlement	$282,713.47	62
not paying overtime and poor recordkeeping	7/23/2008	S.M.E. Holding Corp.	Suit	$60,987	11
not paying minimum wage and overtime	7/14/2008	Marjan Corp.	Settlement	$23,207	59
not paying minimum wage or overtime	5/21/2008	Hachi-Hachi Corp.	Settlement	$593,222	66
not paying minimum wage or overtime	5/20/2008	Paperific	Suit	$93,897	28
not paying wages	4/30/2008	Ortega General Contracting Inc. (Ortega) and its subcontractors, AB Contracting Inc., AMSCO Air Conditioning and Heating Corp, and Rose Electrical Contractors Inc.	Settlement	$200,000	20

Violation	Date	Company	Action	Amount	Number
misclassifying workers	4/28/2008	Quest Diagnostics Inc.	Settlement	$688,772	238
not paying overtime and poor recordkeeping	4/15/2008	A&E Development	Settlement	$55,535	35
not paying minimum wage and overtime	4/7/2008	AHN Corp.	Suit	$55,000	16
not paying minimum wage or overtime and poor recordkeeping	4/3/2008	Esteemed Patrol Inc.	Settlement	$149,231	186
not paying required wages, filing lawsuits against employees, and poor recordkeeping	3/25/2008	Advanced Professional Marketing Inc.	Suit	$3 million	156
not paying required wage	3/19/2008	PR Consultants Inc.	Settlement	$121,133	25
not paying overtime	3/19/2008	Singh Brothers Petroleum	Settlement	$29,458	6
not paying minimum wage and overtime	3/19/2008	Adler Industrial Services Inc.	Settlement	$174,771	57
not paying minimum wage or overtime	3/10/2008	B&M Cosmetics	Settlement	$90,301	8
not paying minimum wage or overtime	3/6/2008	Forest Hills Physical Therapy P.C.	Suit	$74,541	22
not paying minimum wage or overtime	3/4/2008	Hong Kong Supermarket	Suit	$340,400	57
not paying minimum wage or overtime	2/28/2008	Stout Inc.	Suit	$70,697	70

(continued)

Appendix A (*continued*)

Ways Wages Are Stolen	Date on DOL Press Release	Company	Suit or Settlement	Back Wages Owed (or estimated)	Number of Workers Owed $
not paying minimum wage or overtime and poor recordkeeping	2/26/2008	Party Linen USA Inc. and Schlaeffen Laundry Corp.	Settlement	$41,255	16
not paying minimum wage or overtime and poor recordkeeping	2/14/2008	Cable Line LLC	Suit	$60,000	80
not paying overtime and illegally docking pay	2/12/2008	Moon Site Management Inc.	Settlement	$59,935	17
not paying minimum wage or overtime and poor recordkeeping	2/4/2008	717 Fifth Avenue Gourmet Corp.	Suit	$72,000	31
not paying minimum wage or overtime and poor recordkeeping	1/17/2008	Tremont Car Wash Inc. and Webster Car Wash Inc.	Suit	$707,298	237
not paying minimum wage or overtime	12/29/2008	U.S. Bank	Settlement	$140,787	464
not paying overtime	12/17/2008	22 day care centers in Indiana	Settlement	$16,869	82
not paying minimum wage or overtime and misclassifying workers	11/29/2008	Quicksilver Express Courier Inc.	Settlement	$590,039	950
not paying minimum wage or overtime	10/18/2008	Los Tres Caminos	Settlement	$45,697	13

not paying minimum wage or overtime	10/17/2008	Las Limas Mexican Restaurant	Settlement	$40,665	20
not paying minimum wage or overtime	10/17/2008	El Arriero Mexican Restaurant	Settlement	$66,922	16
not paying overtime	8/20/2008	Super Clean Inc.	Settlement	$50,000	58
not paying wages or overtime	3/4/2008	Hennepin Healthcare System Inc.	Settlement	$127,935	974
not paying overtime	1/24/2008	Barbeque Ventures, BBQ Ventures of Nebraska, and Old Market Ventures LLC	Court order	$92,516	25
not paying overtime	12/23/2008	Thai Delice LLC	Settlement	$94,033	39
not paying overtime	12/3/2008	JVA Insulation Inc.	Settlement	$203,640	53
misclassifying workers and not paying overtime	12/3/2008	Fire Safe Protection Services Ltd.	Settlement	$173,288	25
not paying overtime	11/20/2008	Phillips & Jordan Inc.	Settlement	$600,190	1467
not paying minimum wage and poor recordkeeping	11/12/2008	Dong HWA International Inc.	Settlement	$10,519	n/a
not paying minimum wage or overtime and poor recordkeeping	10/30/2008	Tepanyaki Japanese Steakhouse	Settlement	$200,000	230
not paying overtime	10/25/2008	CEMEX Inc.	Suit	$5 million	2000
not paying for all hours worked and not paying minimum wage	10/17/2008	Earl's Restaurants Limited	Settlement	$499,566	234

(continued)

Appendix A (*continued*)

Ways Wages Are Stolen	Date on DOL Press Release	Company	Suit or Settlement	Back Wages Owed (or estimated)	Number of Workers Owed $
not paying overtime	10/16/2008	Coma Bien Inc.	Settlement	$47,359	15
not paying minimum wage or overtime	8/26/2008	De Maiz Tortilleria LLC	Settlement	$401,314	13
not paying overtime	8/7/2008	Optimum Personal Care Inc.	Settlement	$115,303	86
not paying overtime	7/28/2008	Artiaga Solutions LLC	Settlement	$118,183	288
not paying for all hours worked	7/10/2008	Dean Baldwin Painting	Settlement	$227,353	255
not paying minimum wage or overtime	6/27/2008	Service King Manufacturing Inc.	Settlement	$393,497	239
not paying overtime	6/6/2008	Universal Project Management Inc. and Fluor Enterprises Inc.	Suit	$1.8 million	154
not paying prevailing wage or legally required health insurance and vacation and holiday time	5/19/2008	ARS Enterprises LLC	Settlement	$155,288	20
not paying overtime and misclassifying workers	5/7/2008	Cotton ginners in eastern Arkansas	Settlement	$97,278	270
not paying for all hours worked and not paying overtime	4/30/2008	Martobill Inc. and Martobill 2 Inc.	Settlement	$166,171	36
not paying for all hours worked	4/28/2008	Arkansas Health Center	Settlement	$149,786	123

Violation	Date	Company	Action	Amount	Number
not paying for overtime	4/28/2008	Polaris Engineering Inc.	Settlement	$292,393	38
not paying minimum wage and poor recordkeeping	4/25/2008	Regency Nursing and Rehabilitation Centers Inc., Harlingen Nursing and Rehabilitation Center Inc., Kingsville Nursing and Rehabilitation Center Inc., and Donald Kivowitz and Heber Lacerd	Suit	$151,325	114
not paying minimum wage or overtime and poor recordkeeping	4/23/2008	Robco Oilfield Service Inc.	Settlement	$115,082	12
not paying minimum wage or overtime and poor recordkeeping	4/23/2008	Control Services Inc.	Settlement	$116,035	71
not paying for all hours worked or overtime and poor recordkeeping	4/21/2008	Aggregate Industries, WRE Inc, a subsidiary of Bardon US Corp.	Settlement	$1 million	302
not paying for all hours worked	4/11/2008	LJC Defense Contracting Inc.	Settlement	$202,508	828
not paying minimum wage or overtime and poor recordkeeping	4/11/2008	Rufino's Painting & Construction	Settlement	$278,639	328
not paying minimum wage or overtime	4/10/2008	Addison-based Razzoo's Inc.	Settlement	$98,046	666

(continued)

Appendix A (continued)

Ways Wages Are Stolen	Date on DOL Press Release	Company	Suit or Settlement	Back Wages Owed (or estimated)	Number of Workers Owed $
not paying for all time worked or for overtime	4/4/2008	Golden Restaurants Inc.	Settlement	$82,177	77
not paying for all time worked or for overtime	3/25/2008	Quick Clinic LLC	Settlement	$41,071	97
not paying for all time worked or for overtime, forcing employees to pay for job-related equipment	10/21/2008	Alan Berman Trucking	Settlement	$825,000	80
not paying minimum wage or overtime and poor recordkeeping	11/24/2008	Sheep Café Chinese	Settlement	$175,000	161
not paying minimum wage or overtime and poor recordkeeping	8/13/2008	La Villita Imports	Settlement	$73,194	12
not paying overtime	6/30/2008	Circle Foods	Settlement	$76,317	32
not paying for all hours worked	4/23/2008	To Me Collections	Settlement	$202,400	142
not paying for all hours worked or overtime and poor recordkeeping	3/13/2008	Salazar Construction and Technician Construction	Settlement	$495,809	261

Appendix B

Private Wage and Hour Lawsuits

Company	ALLEGED Violation	Employees Affected	Settlement Amount	Year Settled
New Horizons Worldwide, Inc.	unpaid overtime	not specified	$1.7 million	2004
Big Lots	misclassification of employees and unpaid overtime	1451 managers and assistant managers	$10 million	2004
Longs Drug	misclassified workers, unpaid overtime, meal breaks	1000 employees	$11 million	2004
Group Voyagers, Inc.	unpaid overtime and did not include some employees in retirement plan	200 tour escorts	$14 million	2004
Automobile Club of Southern California	unpaid overtime, required workers to pay for "gifts" to promote sales	1300 sales agents	$19.5 million	2004
Phoenix University	unpaid overtime, time for meals and rest periods	admissions counselors	$2.7 million	2004
Farmers Insurance Exchange	unpaid overtime	2402 claims adjusters	$200 million	2004
Safeway, Vons, Albertsons, and Ralph's	unpaid overtime	2000 janitors	$22.4 million	2004
City of Houston, TX	unpaid overtime	600 paramedics	$72 million	2004
Humana Inc.	unpaid overtime	2510 call center workers	$1 million	2005
Gap, Inc.	asked to pay for clothes		$1.8 million in vouchers	2005
Allstate Corp.	unpaid overtime	3000 California-based adjusters	$120 million	2005

State Farm Group	unpaid overtime	2600 California claims adjusters	$135 million	2005
Electronic Art	unpaid overtime	unspecified number of graphic artists	$15.6 million	2005
Honda Manufacturing Inc.	did not pay for prep time	1200 employees	$2 million	2005
Computer Sciences Corp.	unpaid overtime	30,000 technical support workers	$24 million	2005
Office Depot	misclassified workers, unpaid overtime (Colorado)	100 assistant managers	$3.3 million	2005
24 Hour Fitness	unpaid overtime	50,000 employees at California locations	$38 million	2005
Cheesecake Factory	denying breaks, forcing employees to work off the clock	California employees	$4.5 million	2005
Cingular Wireless	misclassified workers		$5.1 million	2005
Chinese Daily News	unpaid overtime	200 workers	$5.19 million	2005
Bank of America	unpaid overtime	mortgage and personal loan consultants in California	$9 million	2005
Cablevision	unpaid overtime	1000 Cablevision call center employees	undisclosed amount	2005
Wells Fargo & Co.	misclassified workers	4500 employees	$12.8 million	2006
Pacific Maritime Association	unpaid hours—not paying for travel time	12,000 California dockworkers	$12.9 million	2006

(continued)

Appendix B (*continued*)

Company	ALLEGED Violation	Employees Affected	Settlement Amount	Year Settled
Electronic Art	unpaid overtime	unspecified number of programmers	$14.9 million	2006
Abercrombie & Fitch	misclassified workers	250 managers in California	$2 million	2006
Merrill Lynch	unpaid overtime	3250 stockbrokers	$37 million	2006
Service Corp.	unpaid overtime	600 employees	$4.45 million	2006
Rent-A-Center, Inc.	unpaid overtime	6000 employees	$4.95 million	2006
Morgan Stanley & Co.	unpaid overtime	5000 financial advisers	$42.5 million	2006
Dollar Financial Corp.	misclassified workers, unpaid overtime		$5.8 million	2006
Farmers Insurance Exchange	unpaid overtime	2600 claims adjusters	$52 million	2006
Carnival Corp.	unpaid overtime	not specified	$6.25 million	2006
AnnTaylor Stores Corp.	misclassified workers	800 managers and assistant managers	$6.5 million	2006
IBM	unpaid overtime, misclassified workers	32,000 tech workers	$65 million	2006
UBS Financial Services	unpaid overtime	13,000 brokers	$89 million	2006
Citigroup Global Markets (Smith Barney)	unpaid overtime	20,000 brokers	$98 million	2006
Cargill Meat Solutions Corp.	workers not paid for required pre- and postshift work	6400 employees	$1.1 million	2007
Foster Farms	unpaid overtime, meal and break periods	50 long-haul drivers	$1.5 million	2007

Company	Violation	Affected	Amount	Year
Group Health	unpaid overtime	1000 employees	$1.6 million	2007
E-Loan Inc.	unpaid overtime and meal breaks	500 mortgage loan consultants in California	$13.6 million	2007
Total Health Home Care Corp.	unpaid overtime	3000 employees	$2.2 million	2007
Rochester Institute	unpaid overtime	170 employees	$2.5 million	2007
Siebel Systems	unpaid overtime	800 engineers	$27 million	2007
Zale Corp.	unpaid overtime	not specified	$3.8 million	2007
Staples, Inc.	misclassified assistant managers, unpaid overtime	1700 assistant managers	$38 million	2007
Albertsons LLC	unpaid overtime	7000 employees	$53.3 million	2007
Rubio's Restaurant	unpaid overtime	not specified	$7.5 million	2007
Sony Computer Entertainment America, Inc.	unpaid overtime	not specified	$8.5 million	2007
RadioShack Corp.	misclassified workers, unpaid overtime	not specified	$8.8 million	2007
UPS	unpaid overtime, meal and rest period pay, and pay stub penalties	20,000 drivers	$87 million	2007
MasTec	unpaid overtime (no pay for obligatory meetings)	not specified	up to $12.6 million, with $4.6 million minimum	2007
Sigma Capital, Inc. and AC Electrical Systems	violated prevailing wage law	–	$50,000	2008

(continued)

Appendix B (*continued*)

Company	ALLEGED Violation	Employees Affected	Settlement Amount	Year Settled
Texas Instruments, Inc.	unpaid overtime		$355,000	2008
Quest Diagnostic	misclassification of employees and unpaid overtime	238 employees	$688,772	2008
New York Mortgage Trust, Inc.	unpaid overtime	not specified	$1 million	2008
Yellow Rat Bastard	unpaid overtime	1000 employees	$1.4 million	2008
Hutchinson Technology, Inc.	not paid for prep time	5600 current and former employees	$2.5 million	2008
Caribou Coffee Co.	misclassified managers	not specified	$2.7 million	2008
Darden Restaurants (parent company of Olive Garden and Red Lobster)	not paying minimum wage	undisclosed	$4 million	2008
Colorado Springs Police Department	unpaid overtime, unpaid off-the-clock work	700 officers	$5.25 million	2008
Lafayette Consolidated Government	deducted $300 per month from paychecks when a state supplemental pay raise was initiated	police officers, firefighters, city marshal's office employees	$7.5 million	2008
networks and producers of the reality shows *Trading Spouses* and *The Bachelor*	did not pay overtime	400 workers	$4 million	2009
Wal-Mart	various violations	undisclosed	$49 million	2009

Company	Violation	Number	Amount	Year
Wal-Mart	forced its employees to work off the clock, prevented employees from taking breaks, and changed employee time cards	178,000	$90 million	2009
Michael Bianco Inc.	denied overtime pay or docked wages	750	$850,000	2009
NCR	forced employees to work through rest periods and meal times	undisclosed	$12 million	2009
Northeast Health, Albany Medical Center, St. Peter's Health Care Services, Ellis Hospital, Seton Health, and St. Mary's Hospital	reducing wages illegally	2500	$1.2 million	2009
Masco Contractor Services	did not pay for all time worked	3100	$8.5 million	2009
Tenet Healthcare	did not pay overtime	23,000	$85 million	2009
Excell Cleaning and Building Services Inc.	misclassified workers, did not pay employment taxes, and did not pay overtime	300 janitorial workers	$13 million	2009
Aerotek	took away accrued leave time	1300	$1.2 million	2009
Casey's General Stores Inc.	undisclosed	78,000	$11.7 million	2009
Wachovia Corp.	did not pay overtime	10,000	$39 million	2009
Zumiez	did not pay overtime	1	$1.3 million	2009

(continued)

Appendix B (*continued*)

Company	ALLEGED Violation	Employees Affected	Settlement Amount	Year Settled
Wal-Mart	did not pay for rest breaks or overtime and occasionally locked employees in stores and forced them to work off the clock	88,000	$35 million	2009
Cintas	did not pay overtime	100s+	$22.75 million	2009
Lowes	forced employees to work off the clock	1000s+	$29.5 million	2009
Kelly Girl	shorted employees on vacation pay	96,000	$11 million	2009
BJ's	misclassifying workers and not paying overtime	1500	$9.3 million	2009
Staples	misclassification of its assistant store managers concerning overtime pay	5500	$42 million	2010
Hann & Hann Construction Services	did not pay overtime	200	$600,000	2010
Mohawk Industries	depressed wages	undisclosed	$18 million	2010
Wal-Mart	did not pay overtime or holiday pay	232,000	$86 million	2010

Company	Violation	Workers	Settlement	Year
Polo Ralph Lauren	did not pay overtime, denied rest breaks, and reduced potential commission earnings	6700	$4 million	2010
Charter Communications	did not pay overtime	8000	$18 million	2010
Coca Cola Bottling Company	did not pay overtime	undisclosed	$1.1 million	2010
Waste Management of Massachusetts, Inc.	did not pay prevailing wages	526	$7 million	2010
Spherion Pacific Workforce	did not pay employees for time worked or provide rest breaks	undisclosed	$13 million	2010
Madison Square Garden	did not pay overtime	300	$1.3 million	2011
Roberts Hawaii	did not pay overtime	undisclosed	$330,000	2011
Dick's Sporting Goods	did not pay overtime	undisclosed	$15 million	2011
Premera Blue Cross	misclassified workers in order to avoid paying overtime	133	$1.45 million	2011

Appendix C

Catholic Labor Schools

This is a list of Catholic labor schools that operated for various lengths of time between the 1930s and the 1960s. The list was developed by reviewing correspondence and reports located in Box 40, Collection 10, of the American Catholic History Research Center and University Archives, located at Catholic University of America in Washington, D.C. This list demonstrates the strong historic commitment of Catholic dioceses, parishes, and colleges to assisting workers in understanding and exercising their rights in the workplace.

Locations

Albany, NY	Sienna College
Baltimore, MD	Social Action Committee (held labor schools in seven parishes including St. John's Church, St. Martin's Church)
Boston, MA	St. John's Seminary
	Boston College
Buffalo, NY	Labor College—Diocese of Buffalo
Burlington, VT	St. Michael's College
Camden, NJ	The Catholic Institute of Industrial Relations
Chicago, IL	Catholic Labor Alliance
	Sheil School of Social Studies
	Department of Sociology, Loyola University
	Hubbard Woods (Hillebrand)
	Epiphany Church
	St. Gabriel's Labor School
	Holy Name Cathedral Labor School
	Catholic Teachers' Lecture Course
Cincinnati, OH	Mt. St. Mary of the West Seminary
	Xavier University

Cleveland, OH	Institute of Social Education, St. John's College, John Carroll University
Columbus, OH	Social Action Institute, St. Charles College
Davenport, IA	Labor School, St. Ambrose College
Detroit, MI	Archdiocesan Social Action Institute (34 parishes ran "labor schools") Association of Catholic Trade Unionists Duns Scotus Labor School, Duns Scotus College Workers' Educational Program, University of Detroit
East St. Louis, IL	Institute of Industrial Relations, Belleville Diocese
Erie, PA	Gannon College Sacred Heart Parish
Evansville, IN	Institute on Labor-Management Problems
Fort Wayne, IN	ACTU Labor School
Grand Rapids, MI	*No institution listed*
Hartford, CT	Diocesan Labor Institute
Indianapolis, IN	Labor Relations School, Diocesan program
Joliet, IL	Joliet Labor School, St. Mary's Hall
Kansas City, MO	Kansas City School of Christian Workmen, Rockhurst College
Kenosha, WI	Catholic Social Action School
Lansing, MI	Cathedral Labor School
Los Angeles, CA	Catholic Labor Institute of Los Angeles Leo XIII School of Social Action, sponsored by Knights of Columbus Institute of Industrial Relations, Loyola University
Lynn, MA	St. Mary's Church
Manchester, NH	Diocesan Industrial Institute (St. Ann's Parish)
Menlo Park, CA	St. Patrick's Seminary
Menominee, MI	Christian Workers Academy
Milwaukee, WI	Marquette University Labor College
Minneapolis, MN	Minneapolis Labor College
Mundelein, IL	St. Mary of the Lake Seminary
Newark, NJ	St. Peter's Institute of Industrial Relations
New Haven, CT	Diocesan Labor Institute
New Orleans, LA	Catholic Committee of the South Institute of Industrial Relations, Loyola University of the South New Rochelle, NY College of New Rochelle Labor School

New York, NY	Association of Catholic Trade Unionists (Manhattan and Bronx)
	Xavier Free Labor School (Manhattan)
	Catholic College Faculty House (Manhattan) *No institution listed*
	(Staten Island) Catholic Charities/ Social Action Department (operated Labor Schools in four Brooklyn parishes: Our Lady of Perpetual Help, St. Peter Claver's, St. Sylvester's, St. Thomas Aquinas and four Queens locations: St. Michael's, Presentation of the B.V.M. Jamaica, Council K of C Clubhouse, St. John's University School of Social Action)
	Crown Heights Labor School (Brooklyn)
	Sacred Heart Rectory
	St. Nicholas of Tolentine Church
	St. Mark the Evangelist Church (Manhattan)
	St. Ignatius Church (Manhattan)
Omaha, NE	Institute of Industrial Relations, Creighton University
Peoria, IL	*No institution listed*
Philadelphia, PA	Institute of Industrial Relations, St. Joseph's College
Pittsburgh, PA	Catholic Workers School of Pittsburgh (ACTU)
	Labor Management Institute, Duquesne University
Portland, OR	Portland Catholic Conference on Industrial Problems
Providence, RI	Providence Social Action Institute, Our Lady of Providence Seminary
Richmond, VA	Richmond Catholic Social Action League, Cathedral Parish House
Rochester, NY	Rochester Catholic Labor College
Rock Hill, SC	Rock Hill Educational Committee
Saginaw, MI	*No institution listed* (Reverend Neil O'Connor)
St. Louis, MO	St. Louis University Labor College
	Institute of Social Order
	Holy Name Labor School
St. Paul, MO	Catholic Labor Institute, St. Paul Seminary
San Antonio, TX	Labor Forum
	Catholic Forum

San Francisco, CA	Association of Catholic Trade Unionists Young Christian Workers Institute of Industrial Relations, University of San Francisco
Scranton, PA	Scranton Institute of Industrial Relations, University of Scranton
Sheyboygan, WI	Catholic Social Action School, Holy Name School
Spokane, WA	Gonzaga Labor School, Gonzaga University
Springfield, MA	Institute of Industrial Relations, Holy Cross College
Stuebenville, OH	Social Action Office
Syracuse, NY	School of Industrial Relations, LeMoyne College
Toledo, OH	Diocese
Trenton, NJ	The Cathedral Institute of Industrial Relations
Waltham, MA	*No institution listed* (Reverend John Quinlan)
Washington, DC	Catholic Social Action School (two schools: one in NW and one in SW)
Waterbury, CT	*No institution listed* (Reverend Joseph Donnelly)
Waukegan, IL	Waukegan Labor School, Mother of God Church
Wilkes-Barre, PA	School of Social Action, St. Mary's Auditorium
Winooski, VT	St. Michael's College

Appendix D

Workers' Centers and Legal Clinics

Arizona

Arizona Worker Rights Center, Phoenix
Tuscon Immigrant Workers Project, University of Arizona James E. Rogers College of Law, Tucson

Arkansas

Northwest Arkansas Workers' Justice Center, Springdale

California

Asian Immigrant Women Advocates, Oakland & San Jose
Asian Law Caucus, San Francisco
Asian Pacific American Legal Center of Southern California, Los Angeles
La Asociacion de Jornaleros de San Diego, Vista
Bet Tzedek Legal Services Employment Rights Project/La Casa de Justicia, Los Angeles
Caring Hands Workers' Association (Mujeres Unidas Y Activas), San Francisco
Central American Resource Center, Los Angeles
Centro Laboral de Graton, Graton
Centro Legal de la Raza, Oakland
Chinese Progressive Assoc. Worker Organizing Center, San Francisco
Coalition for Humane Immigrant Rights of Los Angeles, Los Angeles
Day Worker Center, Mountain View
East Bay Workers' Rights Clinic, Berkeley
ENLACE, Los Angeles
FOCUS/Filipino Community Support, San Jose

Garment Worker Center, Los Angeles
Golden Gate University School of Law Women's Employment Rights
    Clinic, San Francisco
Instituto de Educación Popular del Sur de California, Los Angeles
Instituto Laboral de la Raza, San Francisco & San Jose
Koreatown Immigrant Workers Alliance, Los Angeles
La Raza Centro Legal, San Francisco
Legal Aid Society Employment Law Center, East Bay, South Bay, San
    Francisco
Los Angeles Taxi Workers Alliance, Los Angeles
Low Income Self-Help Center, San Jose
Malibu Community Labor Exchange, Malibu
People Organized to Win Employment Rights, San Francisco
Philipino Workers' Center, Los Angeles
Pomona Economic Opportunity Center, Pomona
Public Law Center, Santa Ana
Restaurant Opportunities Center, Los Angeles
Santa Clara University Law School Katharine & George Alexander
    Community Law Center, San Jose
Stanford Community Law Clinic, East Palo Alto
United Farm Workers, Delano Greenville, Oxnard, Salinas, Santa Rosa,
    Watsonville
United Taxicab Workers, San Francisco
Watsonville Law Center, Watsonville
Young Workers United, San Francisco

Colorado

Centro San Juan Diego, Denver
El Centro Humanitario para los Trabajadores, Denver
Front Range Economic Strategy Center, Denver
Mi Casa, Denver
University of Denver Sturm College of Law, Civil Litigation and Civil
    Rights Clinics, Denver

Connecticut

ConnectiCOSH, Newington
Jerome Frank Legal Services Organization Worker and Immigrants
    Rights Advocacy Clinic, Yale Law School, New Haven
New Haven Workers Association, New Haven

District of Columbia

American University Washington College of Law, Immigrant Justice
   Clinic
D.C. Employment Justice Center
George Washington University Law School, Public Justice Advocacy
   Clinic
Philippine-American Legal Assistance and Defense Fund
Restaurant Opportunities Center
Shared Communities

Florida

Coalition of Immokalee Workers (CIW), Immokalee
Farmworker Association of Florida (FWAF), Apopka
Farmworkers Self-Help Inc., Dade City
Florida Immigrant Advocacy Center, Ft. Pierce & Miami
Miami Worker Center, Miami
Restaurant Opportunities Center, Miami
Unite for Dignity, Miami
We Count, Homestead

Georgia

Northeast Georgia and Rural Worker Center for Economic Justice,
   Athens

Illinois

Albany Park Workers' Center, Chicago
Arise Chicago Worker Center, Chicago
Centro de Trabajadores Unidos, Chicago
Centro Romero, Chicago
Chicago Area Committee for Occupational Safety Health, Chicago
Chicago Coalition for the Homeless Law Project, Chicago
Chicago Legal Clinic, Inc., Chicago
Chicago Workers Collaborative, Chicago & Rolling Meadows
Farmworker's Advocacy Project, Chicago
Latino Union of Chicago, Chicago
Loyola University Community Law Center, Chicago
Mexican American Legal Defense and Educational Fund, Chicago
Restaurant Opportunities Center, Chicago

United Taxidrivers Community Council, Chicago
University of Chicago Edwin F. Mandel Legal Aid Clinic, Employment
    Discrimination Project, Chicago
Warehouse Workers for Justice, Chicago
Women Employed, Chicago
Working Hands Legal Clinic, Chicago

Indiana

St. Joseph Valley Project Workers' Center, South Bend

Iowa

Iowa Citizens for Community Improvement, Des Moines &
    Marshalltown

Kansas

Kansas City Worker's Justice Project, Prairie Village & Kansas City
Lawrence Worker Justice Coalition, Laurence
Sunflower Community Action, Wichita

Kentucky

Kentucky Equal Justice Center, Lexington

Louisiana

Loyola Law School's Stuart H. Smith Law Clinic, New Orleans
New Orleans Worker Center for Racial Justice, New Orleans

Maine

Food AND Medicine/Worker Center of Eastern Maine, Brewer
Maine Rural Workers Coalition, Lewiston
Restaurant Opportunities Center of Maine
Southern Maine Workers' Center, Portland

Maryland

CASA de Maryland, Hyattsville, Silver Spring, Wheaton, Baltimore, &
    Rockville

Public Justice Center's Workplace Justice Project, Baltimore
United Workers Association, Baltimore
Women's Law Center of Maryland Employment Law Hotline,
    statewide
Workplace Justice Project, Baltimore

Massachusetts

Alliance to Develop Power, Springfield
Brazilian Immigrant Center, Allston
Centro Presente, Somerville
Chinese Progressive Association's Workers Center, Boston
Fair Employment Project, Boston
Harvard Law School's Wilmer Hale Legal Services Center, Employ-
    ment Discrimination Clinic, Jamaica Plain
Harvard Legal Aid Bureau Wage and Hour Project, Cambridge
MassCOSH Immigrant Worker Center, Dorchester
MetroWest Worker Center/Casa do Trabalhador, Framingham

Michigan

Lansing Worker's Center, Lansing
Michigan Organizing Project, Grand Rapids & Kalamazoo
Michigan Unemployment Insurance Project, Ann Arbor
Restaurant Opportunities Center, Detroit
Washtenaw County Workers' Center, Ann Arbor

Minnesota

Centro Campesino, Owatonna
Centro de Trabajadores Unidos en Lucha, Minneapolis
Resource Center of the Americas, Minneapolis
University of Minnesota Law School Workers' Rights Clinic, Minne-
    apolis
William Mitchell College of Law Civil Advocacy Clinic, St. Paul

Mississippi

Mississippi Immigrant Rights and Advocacy, Biloxi, Jackson, &
    Tunica
Mississippi Workers Center for Human Rights, Greenville

New Jersey

Asian American Legal Defense and Education Fund, Jersey City
Casa Freehold, Freehold
New Labor, New Brunswick
Wind of the Spirit/Viento del Espiritu, Morristown

New Mexico

Somos, Santa Fe

New York

Adhikaar, Woodside
Andolan Organizing South Asian Workers, Jackson Heights
Asian American Legal Defense and Education Fund, New York
Benjamin N. Cardozo Law School Labor and Employment Law
    Clinic, New York
Brandworkers International, Long Island City
Capital District Workers' Center, Albany
Casa Mexico, New York
Chinese Staff and Workers' Association (CSWA), New York
Committee Against Anti-Asian Violence—Women Workers Project,
    Bronx
CUNY School of Law Immigrant and Refugee Rights Clinic, Flushing
Damayan Migrant Workers Association, New York
Domestic Workers United, New York
Filipino Workers Center, New York
Haitian Women for Haitian Refugees, Brooklyn
HIRE Legal Action Center, New York
Hispanic Resource Center of Larchmont and Mamaroneck,
    Mamaroneck
Latin American Workers Project, Brooklyn
Make the Road by Walking, Brooklyn
New York Taxi Workers Alliance, New York
New York University School of Law Employment and Housing
    Discrimination Clinic, New York
Restaurant Opportunities Center of New York, New York
Tompkins County Workers' Center, Ithaca
Unemployment Action Center, New York
Workers Center of Central New York, Syracuse
Workers Defense League, New York

Workers' Rights Law Center of New York, Kingston
Workplace Project, Hempstead

North Carolina

Black Workers for Justice, Rocky Mount
Central Carolina Workers' Center, Greensboro
Eastern Carolina Immigrants' Rights Project, Raleigh
Farm Labor Organizing Committee, Dudley
North Carolina Occupational Safety and Health Project, Greensboro
Western NC Workers' Center, Morganton

North Dakota

University of North Dakota School of Law Housing and Employment
Law Clinic, Grand Forks

Ohio

Advocates for Basic Legal Equality, Dayton & Toledo
Cincinnati Interfaith Workers' Center, Cincinnati
Cleveland-Marshall College of Law Employment Law Clinic, Cleveland
Farm Labor Organizing Committee, Toldeo
Immigrant Worker Project, Canton

Oregon

Center for Intercultural Organizing, Beaverton & Portland
Centro Cultural, Cornelius
Enlace, Portland
Northwest Workers' Justice Project, Portland
Pineros y Campesinos Unidos del Noreste, Woodburn
UNETE Center for Farm Worker Advocacy, Medford
United Farm Workers, Hermiston
VOZ Workers Rights Education Project, Portland

Pennsylvania

Civil Justice Clinic (Villanova University School of Law), Villanova
Civil Practice Clinic (University of Pennsylvania), Philadelphia
Comité de Apoyo a los Trabajadores Agrícolas, Kennett Square
Employee Advocacy Project (University of Pennsylvania), Philadelphia

Farmworker Legal Aid Clinic (Villanova University School of Law),
Villanova
Philadelphia Unemployment Project, Philadelphia
PhilaPOSH, Philadelphia
Taxi-Workers Alliance of Pennsylvania, Philadelphia

Rhode Island

Dare to Win—Direct Action for Rights & Equality, Providence
Fuerza Laboral, Central Falls
Institute for Labor Studies Immigrant Workers Rights Project, Cranston
Progreso Latino, Central Falls

South Carolina

Carolina Alliance for Fair Employment, Greenville

Tennessee

Memphis Workers' Center, Memphis

Texas

Equal Justice Center's Central Texas Workers' Rights Project, Austin
Equal Justice Center's South Texas Workers' Rights Project,
San Antonio
Fuerza Unida, San Antonio
Houston Interfaith Worker Justice Center, Houston
Justice & Equality in the Workplace Program, Houston
La Mujer Obrera, El Paso
Paso del Norte Texas Civil Rights Project, El Paso
Southwest Workers' Union, San Antonio & Rio Grande Valley
Workers' Defense Project / Proyecto Defensa Laboral, Austin

Utah

Community Legal Center Project, Salt Lake City

Vermont

Vermont Law School South Royalton Legal Clinic, South Royalton
Vermont Workers' Center, Burlington

Virginia

African Community Center, Arlington
Justice4All Legal Aid Justice Center, Charlottesville & Falls Church
Tenants' and Workers' Support Committee, Alexandria & Falls
   Church

Washington

Casa Latina Workers' Defense Committee, Seattle
Northwest Women's Law Center Legal Voice, Seattle
Street Law (Center for Justice), Spokane
Unemployment Law Project, Seattle

Wisconsin

Madison Workers Rights Center, Madison
Neighborhood Law Project (University of Wisconsin Law School),
   Madison
Unemployment Compensation Appeals Clinic (University of Wiscon-
   sin Law School), Madison
Voces de la Frontera Workers' Center, Milwaukee & Racine
Wisconsin Committee on Occupational Safety and Health, Milwaukee

Appendix E

Faith Body Positions on Wages and Working Conditions

Buddhist

LIVING WAGE

Sigālovāda Sutta (Dīgha Nikāya 31)

In five ways should an employer respect workers and servants...: 1) by allocating work according to their aptitude, 2) by providing them with wages and food, 3) by looking after them when they are sick, 4) by sharing special treats with them, and 5) by giving them reasonable time off work. So respected, workers and servants reciprocate with compassion in four ways: 1) by being willing to start early and finish late when necessary, 2) by taking only what their employer gives them, 3) by doing their work well, and 4) by promoting their employer's good reputation.

More at: http://www.accesstoinsight.org/tipitaka/dn/dn.31.0.nara. html

Narada Thera, translator, "Sigalovada Sutta: The Discourse to Sigala" (DN 31), at *Access to Insight* (June 8, 2010), [quote edited by Joshua A. Eaton].

Thirteenth Dalai Lama, Thubten Gyatso

People who make religious images and print spiritual books should do so out of a pure motivation. As professionals they should make a reasonable living from their time and efforts, but their attitude should be to bring benefit to people and not merely to make a large profit. From our side we should take care that the artifacts we acquire are purchased from sincere people.

Thub-bstan-rgya-mtsho, Dalai Lama XIII, *Path of the Bodhisattva Warrior: The Life and Teachings of the Thirteenth Dalai Lama*, compiled

and translated by Glenn H. Mullin (Ithaca, NY: Snow Lion, 1988), 144.
Special thanks to Joshua A. Eaton, who conducted original research to locate Buddhist statements on worker justice-related issues.

Islam

RIGHT TO ORGANIZE AND BARGAIN COLLECTIVELY

Fatawa: Rights of Workers in Islam

Freedom to form unions. Based on all the above principles [see link below for full article], we can also infer that workers in Islam have a right to exercise the freedom of association and the right to form unions. Special trade unions and associations help workers in their work and socialization. They can also help workers to seek justice for their rights and bargaining power to receive proper compensations. However, employers and employees all must fear Allah in the exercise of their rights and duties.

More at: http://58.26.99.53/modules.php?op=modload&name=News &file=article&sid=9846

LIVING WAGE

The Qur'an and the Prophet Muhammad (PBUH)

"And O my people! Give just measure and weight, nor withhold from the people the things that are their due" (Qur'an 11:85). Prophet Muhammad, peace and blessings of God be upon him, also said, "I will be the opponent of three types of people on the Day of Judgment," and he listed one of them as "one who hires a worker, but does not pay him his right wages owed to him after fulfilling his work." (Bukhari collection, prepared by *Hussam Ayloush, executive director of the Council on American-Islamic Relations.*)

Fatawa: Rights of Workers in Islam

Proper and timely wages. Workers should be given proper and just wages. Exploitation of any person is not allowed in Islam. Allah says [To the Madyan people We sent Shu'aib, one of their own brethren. He said: "O my people, worship Allah; you have no other god but Him. Now has come unto you a Clear (Sign) from your Lord. Give just measure and weight, nor withhold from the people the things that are their due; and do no mischief on the earth after it has been set in order: that will be best for you, if you have Faith]" (Al-A'raf 7:85). Allah warns those who take full measure but give less to others: [Woe to those that deal in fraud. Those who, when they have to receive by measure from men, exact full measure. But when they have to give by measure or weight to men, give less than due. Do they not think that they will be called to account? On a Mighty Day. A Day when (all) mankind will stand before the Lord of the Worlds] (Al-Mutaffifin 83:1-6). Workers should also be paid on time. The Prophet Muhammad (peace and blessings be upon him) said, "Give to the worker his wages before his sweat dries" (Ibn Majah).

More at: http://58.26.99.53/modules.php?op=modload&name=News &file=article&sid=9846

(Al-A'raf 7:85), (Al-Mutaffifin 83:1-6) and (Ibn Majah).

FAIR WORKING CONDITIONS

The Prophet Muhammad (PBUH)

Prophet Muhammad, peace and blessings of God be upon him, said, "Your servants/workers are your brothers whom God the most High has placed under your authority. Therefore, a person who has a brother under his authority, should feed him out of that which he eats himself and should dress him with the same kind of clothes which he wears himself; he should not assign work to him which is beyond his capacity, and if you do so, then help him in his work" (Bukhari collection, prepared by *Hussam Ayloush, executive director of the Council on American-Islamic Relations.*)

Jewish

RIGHT TO ORGANIZE AND BARGAIN COLLECTIVELY

Union for Reform Judaism

The Union for Reform Judaism highlighted its concern for immigrant laborers in a 2007 Resolution on Comprehensive Immigration Reform, opposing "the exploitation of immigrants in the workplace" and encouraging "employers to maintain the highest safety standards and provide fair and just compensation for all workers.

More at: http://urj.org//about/union/governance/reso//?syspage= article&item_id=1909

(Union for Reform Judaism, Resolution on Worker Rights, Ethical Consumerism and the Kosher Food Industry, 2008)

The Union for Reform Judaism resolves to support the rights of workers to organize and bargain collectively.

More at: http://urj.org/Articles/index.cfm?id=8996

(Union for Reform Judaism, Resolution on Workers' Rights in the United States, 2005)

Central Conference of American Rabbis

For many years the CCAR has sought just working conditions for members of the American Labor force.... The CCAR, in reaffirming the right of American Labor to self-determination, protests this injustice, supports the nationwide boycott against Farah products, and, in conjunction with other religious leaders, calls on store owners to discontinue the sale of Farah slacks until the workers are allowed to be represented properly.

(Central Conference of American Rabbis, Right of the Farah Slack Workers to Organize Resolution, 1973)

LIVING WAGE

Union of American Hebrew Congregations

The Union of American Hebrew Congregations resolves to support living wage ordinances and bills to bring wages to at least the poverty line, preferably higher; encourage our congregations across North America to become involved in living wage campaigns in their local communities.

More at: http://rac.org/advocacy/issues/issuelw/issuemwres/

(Union of American Hebrew Congregations, Living Wage Resolution, 2000)

Jewish Council for Public Affairs

The JCPA has long believed that those who work at full time jobs should earn enough to support their families above poverty line.

More at: http://www.jewishpublicaffairs.org/equal/resolutions/low-income-2-28-00.html

(Jewish Council for Public Affairs, Resolution on Living Wage and Low-Income Workers, 2000)

The Union for Reform Judaism

The Union for Reform Judaism resolved to support living wage ordinances and support bills to increase wages as well as call upon congregations to examine their employment and contract practices. The resolution also calls upon communities to support a living wage and to advocate for nonprofits to support a living wage without curtailing their services. Furthermore, the resolution encourages congregations across North America to become involved in living wage campaigns in their local communities.

More at: http://urj.org/Articles/index.cfm?id=7201&pge_prg_id= 29601&pge_id=4590

(The Union for Reform Judaism, Living Wage Campaign Resolution, Adopted-Orlando, Florida, December 1999)

The Women of Reform Judaism

The Women of Reform Judaism resolved that Judaism requires that workers be fairly compensated with "adequate wages, benefits, and protections," and that this applies to our neighbors and strangers amongst us. Therefore, the WRJ called upon its affiliates to seek a living wage, health care, and other benefits for workers, to educate members about treatment of those who work in homes and to further educate about how service providers, production workers and migrant farm workers are treated, and to prevent the retraction of ethical labor practices and standards.

More at: http://www.womenofreformjudaism.org/programming/reso lutions-statements/workerjustice/

(Women of Reform Judaism, Resolution on Worker Justice)

FAIR WORKING CONDITIONS

United Synagogue of Conservative Judaism and the Rabbinical Assembly

In response to the continuing disturbing allegations of unacceptable worker conditions at the Agriprocessors plant in Postville, Iowa, the United Synagogue of Conservative Judaism and the Rabbinical Assembly are united in their request that consumers of kosher meat evaluate whether it is appropriate to buy and eat meat products produced by the Rubashkin's label.

More at: http://www.rabbinicalassembly.org/press/docs/hekhsher 2008.doc

(United Synagogue of Conservative Judaism and the Rabbinical Assembly's statement regarding Rubashkin's meat products, 2008)

The Commission on Social Action of Reform Judaism

The Commission on Social Action of Reform Judaism Resolves to: Support legislation that requires employers to provide reasonable paid sick leave to employees to attend to their own health care and the health care of their families, in a manner sensitive to potential impacts on employers; urge our congregations across North America to engage in paid sick days campaigns in their local communities; and call upon our congregations and all arms of the Reform Movement to examine their employment and contracting practices reflecting the spirit of this resolution and set an example for their communities.

More at: http://urj.org/socialaction/aboutus/reso/?syspage=article &item_id=1875

(Commission on Social Action of Reform Judaism, Resolution on Paid Sick Days, 2008)

Central Conference of American Rabbis

Jewish leaders, along with our Catholic and Protestant counterparts have always supported the labor movement and the rights of employees to form unions for the purpose of engaging in collective bargaining and attaining fairness in the workplace. We believe that permanent replacement of striking workers upsets the balance of power needed for collective bargaining, destroys the dignity of working people, and undermines the democratic values of this nation.

More at: http://data.ccarnet.org/cgi-bin/resodisp.pl?file=fairness &year=1993

(Central Conference of American Rabbis, Workplace Fairness Resolution, 1993)

Protestant

RIGHT TO ORGANIZE AND BARGAIN COLLECTIVELY

American Baptist Churches, USA

We reaffirm our position that workers have the right to organize by a free and democratic vote of the workers involved. This right of organization carries the responsibility of union leadership to protect the rights of workers, to guarantee each member an equal voice in the operation of its organization, and to produce just output labors for income received.

More at: http://www.abc-usa.org/Resources/resol/labor.htm

(American Baptist Churches Resolution on Labor, 1981)

Church of the Brethren

Laborers are always to be regarded as persons and never as a commodity. Industry was made for man, and not man for industry. Employees as well as employers have the right to organize themselves into a union for wage negotiations and collective bargaining.

(Brethren Service Commission, Church of the Brethren)

Christian Methodist Episcopal Church (CME)

Free collective bargaining has proved its values in our free society whenever the parties engaged in collective bargaining have acted in good faith to reach equitable and moral solutions of problems dealing with wages and working conditions. We do not support the opinion voiced in some quarrels that strikes should be made illegal. To declare strikes illegal would be to deprive workers of their right to collective action and, even more seriously, would place in the hands of government the power to force workers to remain on the job.

More at: http://www.c-m-e.org/core/Social_Creed.htm
(Discipline of the CME Church Social Creed, 1982)

Christian Church (Disciples of Christ)

We believe in the right of laboring men to organize for protection against unjust conditions and to secure a more adequate share of the fruits of their toil. The right to organize implies the right to hold and wield power, which in turn implies responsibility for the manner in which this power is exercised.

(Resolution on the Church and Labor, Disciples of Christ, 1938)

The Christian Church (Disciples of Christ) over the years has supported the right of all workers, including farm workers, to organize the union of their choice for the purpose of collective bargaining with employers.

More at: http://www.discipleshomemissions.org/PDF/PublicWitness/Resolutions/7555.pdf
(Resolution concerning support of farmworkers, 2007)

For more than 20 years the Christian Church (Disciples of Christ) gave active support to farm workers in their struggle for social justice by participating with the National Farm Worker Ministry (NFWM).

More at: http://www.djan.net/resolutions/farm-workers2001.pdf
(Farm Workers, Social Justice, and the Church, 2001)

The members of the Christian Church (Disciples of Christ) support national movements toward the passage of legislation that guarantees workers sufficient wages to supply adequate food, clothing, shelter, and health care for themselves and their families.

More at: http://www.djan.net/resolutions/living_wage.pdf
(Resolution concerning the living wage, 2005)

The Episcopal Church

Resolved, the House of Bishops concurring, That the 76th General Convention of the Episcopal Church urge the Congress of the United

States to pass, and the President to sign into law, labor law reform legislation designed to better protect employees seeking to engage in collective bargaining, to simplify and streamline the procedures by which employees may choose to organize, and to assist employers and employees in reaching agreement.

More at: http://gc2009.org/ViewLegislation/view_leg_detail.aspx ?id=1006&type=final

(76th General Convention of the Episcopal Church, 2009)

The 75th General Convention reaffirms the right of workers in the United States to organize and form unions as a means to securing adequate wages, benefits, and safety conditions and encourage all levels of the church to be informed about, and act accordingly, when rights of workers to associate is being jeopardized.

More at: http://gc2006.org/legislation/view_leg_detail.aspx?id= 171&type=ORIGINAL

(75th General Convention, 2006)

We reaffirm the right and desirability of workers in the United States to organize and form unions... we decry the growing wage of anti-unionism mounting in the nation today which asks people to forget the struggles that led to this form of negotiation as a just way to settle differences. We urge church people and others not to judge this issue on the basis of a particular case but rather on the basis of the fundamental principles involved.

(A pastoral message from the Urban Bishops Coalition of the Episcopal Church, Labor Day 1982)

Evangelical Lutheran Church of America (ELCA)

[The ELCA] commits itself to advocacy with corporations, businesses, congregations, and church-related institutions to protect the rights of workers, support the collective bargaining process, and protect the right to strike.

(Resolution of the ELCA Church-wide Assembly, 1991)

Presbyterian Church (U.S.A.)

Justice demands that social institutions guarantee all persons the opportunity to participate actively in economic decision-making that affects them. All workers—including undocumented, migrant, and farm workers—have the right to choose to organize for the purposes of collective bargaining.

More at: http://www.nycpresbytery.org/pdf/PSM_Process-Guide _7-1.pdf

(Principles of Vocation and Work, General Assembly Presbyterian Church [U.S.A.], 1995)
Employment for all, at a family-sustaining living wage, with equal pay for comparable work. The rights of workers to organize, and to share in workplace decisions and productivity growth. Protection from dangerous working conditions, with time and benefits to enable full family life. More at: http://www.pcusa.org/resource/selected-social-witness-poli cies-work-vocation-uni

(Presbyterian Church USA, A Social Creed for the 21st Century, 2008)

United Church of Christ

The 21st General Synod reaffirms the heritage of the United Church of Christ as an advocate for democratic, participatory, and inclusive economic policies in both public and private sectors... the responsibility of workers to organize unions for collective bargaining with employers regarding wages, benefits, and working conditions; and to participate in efforts further to democratize, reform, and expand the labor movement domestically and abroad.
More at: http://www.ucc.org/synod/resolutions/AFFIRMING-DEMO CRATIC-PRINCIPLES-IN-AN-EMERGING-GLOBAL-ECON OMY.pdf

(Resolution Affirming Democratic Principles in an Emerging Global Economy, 1997)
International workers' rights must be recognized and honored in ways that protect their basic right to organize and collectively bargain, job portability.
More   at: http://72.14.205.104/search?q=cache:LIrCObtz74QJ: www.globalministries.org/news/staff-board-news/global-ministries -statement-rega.html+united+church+of+christ+statement+worker+ rights&hl=en&ct=clnk&cd=3&gl=us

(Global Ministries statement regarding immigration issues)

LIVING WAGE

Church of the Brethren

Resolves to... Recognizing that the provision of wages and other benefits sufficient to support individuals and families in dignity is a basic necessity to prevent the exploitation of workers, and that the dignity of workers also requires adequate health care, security for old age or against disability, unemployment compensation, healthful working conditions, weekly rest, periodic holidays for recreation and leisure, and reasonable security against arbitrary dismissal.

(Church of the Brethren)

Resolves to... Work for changes in the social, economic, and political structures that deny workers their rights and seek to maintain conditions that lead to deprivation and degradation of human life. Support legislation that provides for a regular review and establishes a minimum wage that is just and equitable in relation to compensations paid in other sectors of the economy.

More at: http://www.brethren.org/site/PageServer?pagename= HungerandPoverty#annual

(Church of the Brethren, Resolution for a Just Minimum Wage, March 1988)

The Episcopal Church

That the 75th General Convention support actively the right of workers to form a union, and increase the support in our cities and states for passage of "living wage" legislation.... That the Convention commit the Church at all levels to contract solely with union hotels in its meetings, or to obtain confirmation that local prevailing "living wages" are paid by all hotels the Church uses.

More at: http://gc2006.org/legislation/view_leg_detail.aspx?id= 318&type=ORIGINAL

(75ᵗʰ General Convention, 2006)

Evangelical Lutheran Church of America (ELCA)

We believe it is God's intent that all people are provided with those things that protect human dignity and make for healthy life: adequate food and shelter, meaningful work, safe communities, healthcare and education... a living wage assures social and economic benefits for the community as well as a supportive environment for employers who try to maintain fair wages.

More at: http://www.lutheranssw.org/documents/2008all.esolutions pdf.pdf

(ELCA Resolution, 2008)

Employers have a responsibility to treat employees with dignity and respect. This should be reflected in employees' remuneration, benefits, work conditions, job security, and ongoing job training.

More at: http://archive.elca.org/socialstatements/economiclife

(Social Statement on Sufficient Sustainable Livelihood for All, 1999)

Presbyterian Church (U.S.A.)

Urge United States government agencies and authorities to increase the minimum wage toward a living wage and enforce minimum wage

laws, worker safety regulations, and rights of workers to organize and bargain collectively.
> More at: http://www.pcusa.org/oga/publications/resolution-on-just -globalization.pdf
> *(Resolution on Just Globalization, 2006)*

United Methodist Church

We support the right of public and private employees and employers to organize for collective bargaining into unions and the groups of their own choosing. Further, we support the right of both parties to protection in so doing, and their responsibility to bargain in good faith within the framework of the public interest.
> More at: http://www.umc-gbcs.org/site/apps/nlnet/content.aspx?c =frLJK2PKLqF&b=3119825&content_id=%7BE5B745CA-ECB5 -4B45-9619-E9800AC28238%7D&notoc=1
> *(United Methodist 2008 Book of Discipline, IV. The Economic Community. 2008)*

Every person has the right to a job at a living wage. Where the private sector cannot or does not provide jobs or all who seek and need them, it is the responsibility of government to provide for the creation of such jobs.
> More at: http://www.umc-gbcs.org/site/c.frLJK2PKLqF/b.3713153/k .DB35/182163_The_Economic_Community/apps/nl/newsletter.asp
> *(Social Principles of the United Methodist Church, 2004)*

We call upon all members of the global United Methodist Church to work in partnership with persons, communities, and governments everywhere around the world to bring about the creation of conditions that encompass fundamental workers' rights, fair wages, a safe and healthy workplace, reasonable hours of work, decent living standards, support for community infrastructure, and commitment to community economic development.
> More at: http://www.umc-gbcs.org/site/apps/nlnet/content3.aspx ?c=frLJK2PKLqF&b=2954227&ct=8533779&notoc=1
> *(Social Principles of the United Methodist Church, 2008)*

The United Methodist Church demands that employers treat farm workers and their families with dignity and respect; and that corporate processors, food retailers, and restaurants take responsibility in proportion to the power they possess for the treatment of the farm workers in their supply chains; calls on the General Board of Church and Society, the General Board of Global Ministries, annual conferences, and local churches to support state and federal legislation that would strengthen the laws protecting farm workers' rights and provide the funding necessary for adequate enforcement of laws protecting farm workers rights, health, and safety.

More at: http://www.umc-gbcs.org/site/apps/nlnet/content3.aspx?c
=frLJK2PKLqF&b=2954221&ct=8533953&notoc=1
(Social Principles of the United Methodist Church, 2008)

Quaker

AMERICAN FRIENDS SERVICE COMMITTEE BOARD STATEMENT
ON HUMAN RIGHTS

Quaker tradition provides good examples of profitable businesses conducted according to high levels of integrity even in the absence of laws requiring such social responsibility. Many business people already adhere to ethical business codes and believe that good labor practices, satisfied employees and sustainable production methods make for good business. To make the transition to a just global economy, we want to encourage all businesses to operate with rules that are both clear and ethical.

(American Friends Service Committee Board Statement on Human Rights)

Roman Catholic

RIGHT TO ORGANIZE AND BARGAIN COLLECTIVELY

A Statement of the U.S. Bishops

All people have the right to economic initiative, to productive work, to just wages and benefits to decent working conditions, as well as to organize and join unions or other associations.

More at: http://www.catholiclabor.org/gen-art/nccb-1.htm
(A Catholic Framework for Economic Life, A Statement of the U.S. Bishops, 1996)

National Conference of Catholic Bishops

The Church fully supports the right of workers to form unions or other associations to secure their rights to fair wages and working conditions. This is a specific application of the more general right to associate.... No one may deny the right to organize without attacking human dignity itself. Therefore we firmly oppose organized efforts, such as those regrettably seen in this country, to break existing unions or prevent workers from organizing.

More at: http://www.osjspm.org/economic_justice_for_all.aspx

(Economic Justice for All, a pastoral letter of the National Conference of Catholic Bishops, 1986)

Pope John Paul II

Their [unions] task is to defend the existential interests of workers in all sectors where their rights are concerned. The experience of history teaches that organizations of this type are an indispensable element of social life, especially in modern industrialized societies. [Unions] are indeed a mouthpiece for the struggle for social justice, for the just rights of working people in accordance with their individual professions.

More at: http://www.ewtn.com/library/ENCYC/JP2LABOR.HTM

(On Human Work, encyclical of Pope John Paul II, 1981)

The important role of union organizations must be admitted: their object is the representation of the various categories of workers, their lawful collaboration in the economic advance of society, and the development of the sense of their responsibility for the realization for the common good.

More at: http://www.osjspm.org/majordoc_octogesima_adveniens _official_text.aspx

(A Call to Action, encyclical of Pope Paul VI, 1971)

Second Vatican Council

Among the basic rights of the human person must be counted the right of freely founding labor unions. These unions should be truly able to represent the workers and to contribute to the proper arrangement of economic life. Another such right is that of taking part freely in the activity of these unions without risk of reprisal.

More at: http://www.vatican.va/archive/hist_councils/ii_vatican_ council/documents/vat-ii_cons_19651207_gaudium-et-spes_en.html

(Pastoral Constitution of the Church in the Modern World, Second Vatican Council, 1965)

Also see: Living Wage: a way to break the chains of poverty

http://www.vatican.va/archive/hist_councils/ii_vatican_council/ documents/vat-ii_cons_19651207_gaudium-et-spes_en.html

LIVING WAGE

USCCB

In Catholic teaching, the principle of a living wage is integral to our understanding of human work. Wages must be adequate for workers to provide for themselves and their families in dignity. Because the minimum wage is not a living wage, the Catholic bishops have supported increasing the minimum wage over the decades.

The minimum wage needs to be raised to help restore its purchasing power, not just for the goods and services one can buy but for the self-esteem and self-worth it affords the worker.

More at: http://www.usccb.org/sdwp/national/minwage206.shtml

(USCCB, 2006)

Sikh

JUSTICE WITHIN SOCIETY

Siri Guru Granth Sahib

There is a city called City-of-no-Sorrows. There is no suffering or anxiety there. There are no troubles or taxes on commodities there. There is no fear, blemish or downfall there. My friends, I have found myself a wonderful hometown. There is lasting peace and safety there, O Siblings of Destiny. God's Kingdom is steady, stable and eternal. There all are equal, none second or third. That city is populous and eternally famous. Those who live in it are satisfied and contented. They stroll about freely, just as they please. They know the Mansion of the Lord's Presence, and no one blocks their way. Says Ravi Daas, the emancipated shoe-maker: whoever is a citizen of this City of no Sorrows, is a friend of mine.

(From Siri Guru Granth Sahib, prepared by Dr. Tarunjit S. Butalia)

Unitarian Universalist

RIGHT TO ORGANIZE AND BARGAIN COLLECTIVELY

The Unitarian Universalists Association urges its member congregations and individual Unitarian Universalists in the United States...to work specifically in favor of mechanisms such as:...reform of labor legislation and employment standards to provide greater protection for workers, including the right to organize and bargain collectively, protection from unsafe working conditions, and protection from unjust dismissal.

More at: http://www.uua.org/socialjustice/socialjustice/statements/14246.shtml

(Working for a Just Economic Community, 1997)

FAIR WORKING CONDITIONS

Grounded in our stance for justice, equity, and compassion in human relations, we ally ourselves with the National Farm Worker Ministry and its efforts with the United Farm Workers to provide fair and respectful working conditions for the Gallo farm workers. The Unitarian Universalist Association can be among the first religious assemblies to stand with the farm workers on this issue at this immediate time. More at: http://www.uua.org/socialjustice/socialjustice/statements/13417.shtml

(Support of the United Farm Workers' Boycott of Gallo Wines, 2005)

WORKPLACE DISCRIMINATION

That the 1987 General Assembly of the Unitarian Universalist Association urges...that the UUA and its affiliates, districts and member societies act to eliminate gender-based wage discrimination in their own organizations. More at: http://www.uua.org/socialjustice/socialjustice/statements/14492.shtml

(Ending Gender-Based Wage Discrimination, 1987)

Joint Statements

REFORM JEWISH MOVEMENT, THE UNITED SYNAGOGUE OF CONSERVATIVE JUDAISM, AND THE JEWISH RECONSTRUCTIONIST FEDERATION AND PRESBYTERIAN CHURCH (U.S.A) JOINT STATEMENT ON INCREASING THE MINIMUM WAGE

As members of the religious community, morally guided by our religious texts, our shared prophetic traditions value compassion, economic justice, and cultivating strong families and communities. We take to heart the words from Deuteronomy and that command us to open our hands to the poor and moreover, to help others establish self-sufficiency. An increase in the federal minimum wage gives those in minimum wage jobs a little more help in their struggles to support themselves. While we cannot alleviate all poverty, we must do everything we can to alleviate the fact that too many full time workers are hungry, homeless, and without health care in our society. More at: http://www.uscj.org/Joint_Statement_on_I7227.html

INTERFAITH ASSOCIATION OF CENTRAL OHIO (IACO), COMPILED OF BAHAI, BUDDHIST, CHRISTIAN, HINDU, JAIN, JEWISH, MUSLIM, AND SIKH COMMUNITIES STATEMENT ON COLLECTIVE BARGAINING RIGHTS

As an association of seven Communities of Faith, the Interfaith Association of Central Ohio (IACO) cannot stand idly by and allow anti-worker legislation like SB 5 to move out of the Insurance, Commerce, and Labor Committee (ICLC) without voicing our strong objection.

Religious or sacred writings would not support undermining working families and communities. The Insurance, Commerce, and Labor Committee should not advance SB 5 as a means to address Budget deficits. Our Communities of Faith include teachers, city, county, and state workers, and professionals who would be directly harmed by SB 5. Moreover, the whole economy of Ohio could be weakened by social decay that would develop in a state that does not respect a day's work with a livable wage and sustainable retirement systems. The concerns argued by SB 5 proponents can be addressed in accordance with protocol of the Ohio Revised Code 4117, and through faith, labor, government, and business leaders seeking solutions to the current budget crisis. The Interfaith Association of Central Ohio (IACO) voices its strong opposition to SB 5 and any other legislation that does not create secure, productive, and healthy communities.

(Adopted by IACO Executive Committee, February 28, 2011 [on recommendation of the IACO Task Force on Social Justice])

Appendix F

National Organizations Fighting Wage Theft

Legal Networks

The following organizations can help workers and attorneys find legal assistance for wage theft problems:

AFL-CIO Lawyers Coordinating Committee (LCC) was founded to better the conditions of working men and women and their families by enhancing the quality of legal representation that is available to the AFL-CIO and the national, international, and local unions affiliated with the AFL-CIO. The LCC is comprised of more than eighteen hundred union-side labor lawyers in more than five hundred firms and union legal departments nationwide. For more information, visit the AFL-CIO's website.

   http://lcc.aflcio.org

Law Help helps low- and moderate-income people find free legal aid programs in their communities and answers questions about their legal rights. These programs address a range of issues but do not focus exclusively on employment issues.

   www.lawhelp.org

Low-Wage Worker Legal Network is an informal network of attorneys who help workers' centers, farm worker groups, and other low-wage workers. They are coordinated by Michael Dale of the Northwest Worker Justice Project (NWJP). Contact him via the NWJP website.

   www.nwjp.org

National Employment Law Project (NELP) was originally created thirty years ago to help legal services attorneys deal with workers' problems. Over the years, it has become the premier legal advocacy group ensuring that employment laws cover all workers; supporting worker organizing and alliance building among key constituent groups working with low-wage workers; helping workers stay connected to jobs and employment benefits; and expanding employment laws to meet the needs of workers and families in changing economic conditions. Its **National Wage and Hour Clearinghouse** contains extensive litigation materials, information on public agency wage enforcement, model legislative reforms, research, data, and practice guides, and information on different sectors and types of workers. National Wage and Hour Clearinghouse membership is free to nonprofit advocacy groups like workers' centers and has a $100 fee for private attorneys, unions, and academics. In 2007, the Brennan Center's Economic Justice Project merged with NELP, giving the organization even greater capacity to draft legislation and support workers' rights.

   www.nelp.org

National Employment Lawyers Association (NELA) is the country's largest professional organization that is exclusively comprised of lawyers who represent individual employees in cases involving employment discrimination and other employment-related matters. NELA and its sixty-eight state and local affiliates have more than three thousand members. Use its "Find a Lawyer" section, after you've agreed to all the disclaimers, of course, to locate an attorney to help with workplace problems.

   www.nela.org

National Immigration Law Center (NILC) protects and promotes the rights of low-income immigrants and their family members. NILC is a leading expert on immigration, public benefits, and employment laws affecting immigrants and refugees.

   www.nilc.org

Southern Poverty Law Center (SPLC) began in 1971 as a small civil rights law firm. Today, SPLC is a nonprofit legal advocacy center known for its tolerance education programs, legal victories against white supremacists, and tracking of hate groups. It undertakes important workers' rights cases in the South. For example, in 2007 SPLC filed important cases supporting exploited workers in post–Katrina New Orleans and migrant workers in forestry.

   www.splcenter.org

Workplace Injury Law and Advocacy Group (WILG) is a nonprofit association of plaintiffs' attorneys who support the rights of workers and the advocate for the fair and just treatment of injured workers and their families. Find one of its six hundred attorney members at its "Find an Attorney" button on its website.

   www.wilg.org

Religious and Community Allies

The following national organizations help the religious community and other community allies fight for improved working conditions and policies for U.S. workers:

American Friends Service Committee (AFSC) is a Quaker human rights organization whose major emphasis is on issues of economic justice, including the rights of immigrant workers. It has offices in twelve communities in the United States.

> **www.afsc.org**

American Rights at Work investigates workers' rights abuses and the inadequacy of U.S. labor law, stimulates public debate on workers' rights issues, promotes public policies supporting the rights of workers to organize, and publicizes success stories of profitable companies and public agencies that respect workers' rights. The organization produces excellent fact sheets and resources that are available on its website.

> **www.americanrightsatwork.org**

Enlace is a membership organization comprised of workers' centers, unions, and organizing groups in the United States and Mexico. For more information visit its website.

> **www.enlaceintl.org**

Farmworker Justice empowers migrant and seasonal farm workers to improve their living and working conditions, immigration status, health, occupational safety, and access to justice. Using a multifaceted approach, Farmworker Justice engages in litigation, administrative and legislative advocacy, training and technical assistance, coalition-building, public education, and support for union organizing.

> **www.farmworkerjustice.org**

Freelancers Union and its members are building a new support system to help the growing independent workforce thrive. A free membership gives you solidarity, benefits, community, and a political voice.

> **www.freelancersunion.org**

Interfaith Worker Justice (IWJ) is a national network of local religion–labor groups, people of faith, and workers' centers that engage people of faith in issues and campaigns to improve wages, benefits, and working conditions for workers, especially workers in low-wage jobs. Join its e-mail action list, download congregational resources, offer to volunteer with a worker center, or find a local affiliate at its website.

> **www.iwj.org.**

Jewish Labor Committee (JLC) describes itself as a Jewish voice in the labor movement and a voice for the labor movement in the Jewish community. The JLC is an independent secular organization that helps the Jewish community and the trade union movement work together on important issues of shared interest and concern. JLC has excellent resources for conducting a labor seder. It has local affiliates in thirteen communities. Visit its website for information.

    www.jewishlabor.org

Jobs with Justice (JwJ) engages workers and allies in campaigns to win justice in workplaces and in communities where working families live. JwJ, founded in 1987 with the vision of lifting up workers' rights struggles as part of a larger campaign for economic and social justice, builds and supports coalitions of labor, religious, student, and community organizations in more than forty cities in twenty-five states. Visit its website for a list of affiliated coalitions and information about current campaigns.

    www.jwj.org

Let Justice Roll (LJR) is a coalition of more than ninety faith, community, labor, and business organizations committed to raising the minimum wage. LJR is organizing actively at the federal level and in selected states to raise the minimum wage to the level of a living wage. Interfaith Worker Justice is a leader in this coalition.

    www.letjusticeroll.org

National Consumers League is the nation's oldest consumer league and led many of the nation's early fights for minimum wage and child labor protections. Currently, the organization convenes the Child Labor Coalition and produces resources to protect young workers.

    www.nclnet.org

National Day Labor Organizing Network (NDLON) improves the lives of day laborers in the United States by unifying and strengthening its thirty-eight member organizations to be more strategic and effective in their efforts to develop leadership, mobilize, and organize day laborers in order to protect and promote civil, labor, and political rights. NDLON provides excellent resources for those wishing to organize and support day laborers.

    www.ndlon.org

National Domestic Worker Alliance (NDWA) is a vehicle to build power nationally as a workforce. NDWA is organizing to improve the living and working conditions of domestic workers; win respect and justice from employers and government for exploited domestic workers; change the racism and sexism that has led to the persistent devaluing of this labor so that dignity of domestic work is honored; end the exclusion of domestic workers from recognition and protection; build a movement of migrant workers to fight the labor displacement and exploitation created by globalization; and continue a brave legacy of resistance by supporting movement-building among domestic workers and other communities and workers in struggle.

www.nationaldomesticworkeralliance.org

National Farm Worker Ministry (NFWM) is an interfaith organization that supports farm workers as they organize for empowerment, justice, and equality. The organization began in 1920 providing direct charitable support for farm workers in the field, but in responding to Cesar Chavez's call for religious activism for justice in the 1960s, NFWM began mobilizing the religious community to support farm workers organizing for fundamental change in their working conditions. NFWM provides excellent resources for congregations.

www.nfwm.org

Restaurant Opportunities Center United (ROC-United) is a national restaurant workers' association, comprised of restaurant worker organizations around the country.

www.rocunited.org

Student Action with Farmworkers (SAF) brings students and farm workers together to learn about each other's lives, share resources and skills, improve conditions for farm workers, and build diverse coalitions working for social change. SAF works with farm workers to address their concerns through documentation of human rights violations, grassroots education and mobilization, leadership development of young people, policy advocacy, and support of labor organizing. Its website has good resources for student groups.

http://cds.aas.duke.edu/saf

Student Labor Action Project (SLAP) is a joint initiative of Jobs with Justice and the United States Student Association that engages student organizations in economic justice campaigns. JwJ coalitions around the country house local SLAPs that connect students from multiple campuses.

www.jwj.org

Worker Rights Information on the Internet

The following websites offer information to help workers and employers understand their rights and responsibilities in the workplace:

www.aflcio.org is the website of the AFL-CIO. It has some basic workers' rights information and good information for contacting unions in your community.

www.canmybossdothat.org is the worker-friendly website created by Interfaith Worker Justice. It has the only state-by-state information available on the Web written so that a worker or an employer can understand which federal *and* state laws apply and how to protect their rights.

www.dol.gov is the official website of the Department of Labor. There are many excellent fact sheets on hundreds of topics. Unfortunately, the website is a bit hard to navigate and find things.

www.iwj.org has a list of state-specific workers' rights resources as well as workers' rights information that are appropriate for distribution in congregations, such as bulletin inserts.

www.just-pay.org is NELP's new National Wage and Hour Clearinghouse, described above. It is an excellent resource for workers' centers, attorneys, and community advocates.

www.workplacefairness.org is an excellent workers' rights website with issues covered in a simple question-and-answer format. On wage issues, there is an excellent review of federal laws, and for enforcement of state laws, the site refers you to state labor department websites.

Union Federations

Most of the nation's trade unions are members of one of the two following federations:

AFL-CIO is the largest union federation in the nation representing fifty-six national and international unions. The AFL-CIO union movement represents 10.5 million members, including 2 million members in Working America, its new community affiliate. The website can connect you with unions that represent teachers, taxi drivers, musicians, miners, firefighters, bakers, bottlers, engineers, editors, pilots, public employees, doctors, nurses, painters, plumbers, service workers, and many more professions.

www.aflcio.org

Change to Win was formed in 2005 to build a new movement of working people equipped to meet the challenges of the global economy and restore the American Dream in the twenty-first century: a paycheck that can support a family, affordable health care, a secure retirement, and dignity on the job. It represents seven unions and six million workers. Its website provides links to its union members and action information on campaigns.

www.changetowin.org

Appendix G

Congregational Study Guide
for *Wage Theft in America*

Congregations and interfaith groups are encouraged to use *Wage Theft in America* as an adult study program. Below is an outline designed for four 50-minute discussion periods, a common time frame for adult education programs. If you have fewer sessions, or more time during each session, adjust the schedule accordingly. A longer time period, such as 1½ hours per session, is preferable for discussions, guest presentations, and reflection.

Leader Preparation

- Publicize the study program in congregational or interfaith communication vehicles *and* recruit people personally to participate.
- Order books for participants. Books are available from Interfaith Worker Justice and The New Press. Books are also available from major booksellers, including Amazon and Powells Books (a union bookstore).
- Research your denomination/faith body's positions on work and wages. See Appendix E for selected resources. Make copies of appropriate statements, if available. (Statements on living wages and economic justice are appropriate for Session I. Statements on unions and the rights of workers to organize are appropriate for Session II.)
- Recruit people to lead opening and closing prayers or reflections. Urge those who would like prepared responsive readings or prayers to look on the Interfaith Worker Justice website at www.iwj.org.
- Inquire among the congregation's members to see if there are workers who have had their wages stolen. If the congregation has workers in low- and moderate-wage jobs, it should not be hard to locate someone who has had wages stolen. If the congregation is more affluent, talk with young people who have had jobs at restaurants to find someone

who knows about wage theft. Having someone from the congregation who has had wages stolen will reinforce the book's point that wage theft is all around us.

- Contact a local worker center or union leader for participation in Session II. (Many workers' centers and legal clinics are listed in Appendix D.)
- Visit the book's website at www.wagetheft.org to view speaker suggestions, additional resources, and comments from other congregations for improving the study.
- Write each session's outline on a board or newsprint sheet before each session.
- Only Session I suggests introducing each person, but be sure to welcome new participants who join in later sessions.

Session I: The Crisis of Wage Theft

Participant Preparation: Read Chapters 1 through 5.
Opening Prayer/Reflection: (5 minutes)
Introductions: (5 minutes)
Questions and Discussion: (25 minutes if there is a guest or 35 minutes if there is no guest)

Do you believe the nation faces a wage theft crisis? Did you know workers' wages were being stolen?

What surprised you most about *how* unethical employers steal wages?

Did you agree with the arguments about *why* unethical employers steal wages? Are there other reasons?

What can be done to make the laws simpler for employers and workers alike?

What religious principles (and faith body statements if available) address these issues?

Worker from the Congregation—optional: (10 minutes)

Ask the worker to share experiences about getting paid.

Next session's assignments: (2 minutes)

Read Chapters 6, 7, and 8.

Talk with three friends about wage theft and see if they know of people who have experienced problems.

Closing prayer/reflection: (3 minutes)

Session II: Unions, Workers' Centers, and Ethical Employers

Participant Preparation: Read Chapters 6, 7, and 8
Opening Prayer/Reflection: (5 minutes)
Questions and Discussion: (20 minutes if you have a guest or 40 minutes if there is no guest)

> What happened when you talked with friends about wage theft? Had anyone you know had a problem or heard of problems with wages getting paid?
>
> Have you ever had any experiences with unions? Do you think they are a vehicle for stopping wage theft? Why or why not?
>
> Are there any workers' centers in your community? If not, should there be?
>
> What religious principles (and faith body statements if available) support workers' rights to organize? How are congregations in your community supporting workers' centers or unions that are trying to improve working conditions for workers in low-wage jobs?
>
> Guest from a workers' center or a union—optional: (20 minutes)
>
> If either a leader from a workers' center or a union can join the session, ask the person to share his or her experiences with wage theft and how either the workers' center or union fights wage theft.
>
> Which of the ethical business leaders were you most impressed with? Do you know other business leaders who are stepping forth to challenge unethical practice in paying workers?
>
> Next session's assignments: (2 minutes)
>
> Read Chapters 9 through 12.
>
> Read the labor law posters at your office. Are they clear about what the law is and what you should do if you have a problem?
>
> Do you know anyone who tried to organize a union? If so, ask the person what happened.
>
> Closing prayer/reflection: (3 minutes)

Session III: The Department of Labor

Participant Preparation: Read Chapters 9 through 12.
Opening Prayer/Reflection: (5 minutes)
Questions and Discussion: (40 minutes)

Did you find the labor law posters at your office? Were they clear?
Did you talk with anyone who had tried to organize a union? What
was the experience? (Be careful not to let this question take up too
much time, because the real focus of this session should be on public
enforcement efforts in fighting wage theft.)

Had you ever heard of the Wage and Hour Division of the Department of Labor before reading the manual? Do you know anyone
who has ever filed a claim with the U.S. Department of Labor or
the State Department of Labor? What was the experience?

What do you think should be the government-imposed punishments
and disincentives for employers who steal wages from workers?
Next session's assignments: (2 minutes)
Read Chapters 13 and 14.

Talk with a few workers in your community who work in industries
known for wage theft, such as restaurants, residential construction,
or car washes. Ask the workers about their working conditions and
if they ever have problems getting paid all their wages. If you talk
with home health aides, ask if they think they should be covered by
overtime laws. (Make sure not to ask the questions in a public setting or in front of their employers.) Even though it may seem awk-
ward to ask workers you don't know about their working conditions,
you'll be surprised how readily most workers will talk about their
situations if they are comfortable and have time.

Closing prayer/reflection: (3 minutes)

Session IV: What You Can Do

Participant Preparation: Read Chapters 13 and 14.
Opening Prayer/Reflection: (5 minutes)
Questions and Discussion: (35 minutes)

> Did you hear anything interesting in talking with workers in your
> community?
> Why is fighting wage theft good for America?
> What can your congregation do to fight wage theft? Who do you need
> to talk with to make this happen? *Clarify who will follow-up.*
> What will you commit to do to help stop wage theft?
> Evaluation: (5 minutes)
> What did you like about the study?
> What changes in the study would you recommend?
> Closing prayer/reflection: (3 minutes)
> Follow-up: Please type up the evaluation notes and post on the book's
> website at www.wagetheft.org. Thanks.

Notes

1. The Crisis of Wage Theft

1. U.S. Department of Labor, Employment Standards Administration, Wage and Hour Division, *1999–2000 Report on Initiatives*, February 2001, p. 19.

2. Ibid., p. 15. The rate of compliance was significantly better for garment shops that were "effectively monitored." Rates of compliance went up from 11 to 44 percent for shops in Los Angeles and up from 33 to 46 percent in New York City, thus demonstrating the importance of ongoing monitoring.

3. Ibid., p. 24.

4. Ibid., p. 35. In 1999, local Wage and Hour offices undertook eleven targeted restaurant initiatives. Compliance rates ranges from 22 percent in New Orleans to 70 percent in northern New Jersey.

5. Abel Valenzeula Jr., Nik Theodore, Edwin Meléndez, and Ana Luz Gonzalez, *On the Corner: Day Labor in the United States* (Los Angeles: UCLA Center for the Study of Urban Poverty, 2006). The report can be viewed or downloaded at http://www .sscnet.ucla.edu/issr/csup/index.php or http://www.uic.edu/cuppa/uicued.

6. U.S. Department of Labor, *Report on Initiatives*, February 2001, p. 25.

7. Annette Bernhardt, Ruth Milkman, Nik Theodore, Douglas Heckathorn, Mirabai Auer, James DeFilippis, Ana Luz Gonzalez, Victor Narro, Jason Perelshteyn, Diana Polson, and Michael Spiller, *Broken Laws, Unprotected Workers: Violations of Employment and Labor Laws in America's Cities* (New York: National Employment Law Project, 2009).

8. Craig Becker, "A Good Job for Everyone: Fair Labor Standards Act Must Protect Employees in Nation's Growing Service Economy," *Legal Times*, 27, No. 36, September 6, 2004.

9. U.S. Department of Labor Bureau of Labor Statistics, "Construction," available at http://www.bls.gov/oco/cg/cgs003.htm (accessed May 1, 2008).

10. Fiscal Policy Institute, *Building Up New York, Tearing Down Job Quality* (New York: Fiscal Policy Institute, 2007), p. 1.

11. Interview with Cristina Tzintzun on May 7, 2007.

12. Wage and Hour Division, Department of Labor, "US Department of Labor Obtains Default Judgment in Southern California Garment Manufacturer Case: Workers Awarded More Than $887,000 in Unpaid and Liquidated Damages," Wage and Hour Division news release, December 14, 2010.

13. Centers for Disease Control and Prevention, *An Introduction to the National Nursing Assistant Survey*, March 2007, p. 2.

14. Hospital and Healthcare Compensation Service, *The 2006–2007 Nursing Department Report*, 2007.

15. Salary Wizard at www.salary.com. This figure is as of January 2008.

16. Department of Labor, *FY 2004 Department of Labor Annual Performance and Accountability Report*, November 15, 2004.

17. U.S. Department of Labor, Employment and Training Administration, *The National Agricultural Workers Survey*, 2001–2002.

18. U.S. Department of Labor, *2000 Report on Initiatives*, p. 24.

19. Wage and Hour Division, Department of Labor, "Tyson Foods Agrees to Nationwide Injunction Requiring Poultry Workers Be Paid for Time Spent Putting on and Taking Off Protective Items, Sanitization and between Basks," news release, June 3, 2010.

20. Rae Glass, who led many of the compliance surveys, clarified that the restaurant investigations were really directed enforcement activities, not statistically valid surveys like those in garment, health care, and poultry, in e-mail notes of June 2008.

21. Chinese Progressive Association, *Check Please! Health and Working Conditions in San Francisco Chinatown Restaurants* (San Francisco: Chinese Progressive Association, 2010).

22. Find all the Restaurant Opportunities Centers United reports at www.rocunited .org.

23. National Restaurant Association, *2011 Restaurant Industry Pocket Factbook*, available at www.restaurant.org.

24. WKRC Cincinnati, *Did the Work, But No Pay*. This was a television troubleshooter story on Channel 12, WKRC in Cincinnati, February 13, 2011.

25. Business Wire, *Labor Ready Signs Groundbreaking "VIP" Agreement with U.S. Department of Labor to Promote Employee Fairness and Safety*, June 12, 2003.

26. Valenzeula Jr., Theodore, Meléndez, and Luz Gonzalez, *On the Corner*.

27. Ibid., p. 14.

28. Ibid., p. 9.

29. Department of Systems Management for Human Services, *An Account of Day Laborers in Fairfax County* (Fairfax County, VA: Department of Human Systems Management, 2004).

30. Nicholas Norcia, Rafael Perez Jr., Anjana Malhotra, and Bryan Lonegan, *Ironbound Underground: Wage Theft & Workplace Violations among Day Laborers in Newark's East Ward* (Newark, NJ: Immigrant Workers Rights Clinic, Center for Social Justice, Seton Hall University School of Law, July 2010).

31. U.S. Government Accounting Office, *Worker Protection: Labor's Efforts to Enforce Protections for Day Laborers Could Benefit from Better Data and Guidance* (Washington, DC: U.S. Government Printing Office, 2002), p. 14.

32. Philly Online, LLC, "Pay for Phila.-area Landscape Workers to Be Monitored," August 26, 2009.

33. Elizabeth Dwoskin, "Begging for Your Pay," http://opinionator.blogs.nytimes.com/2010/12/15/begging-for-your-pay.

34. Cathy Junia, my IWJ assistant, prepared this table by reviewing Department of Labor press releases from the national and regional offices.

35. Michael Orey, "Wage Wars: Workers—From Truck Drivers to Stockbrokers—Are Winning Huge Overtime Lawsuits," *Businessweek*, cover story, October 1, 2007.

36. Joseph M. Sokolowski and Lindsay J. Zamzow, "Wage and Hour Violations: An Employer's Single Greatest Uninsured Risk," May 2007 article on the website of the law firm of Fredrikson & Byron P.A., www.fredlaw.com.

37. Marta Fernandez, *Time Bomb Waiting to Explode: Wage and Hour Claims over Exempt Employees,* a Hotel Online Special Report, October 2002, www.hotel-online.com.

38. Mountain States Employers Council, Inc., www.msec.org/msecservices/wage_hour_audit.asp.

39. Associated Employers, *Wage and Hour Issues,* www.associatedemployers.org/site/wage-issues/.

40. Mina Kimes, "Overtime Pay: A Ticking Time Bomb," *Fortune Small Business,* January 22, 2008, www.cnnmoney.com.

41. James C. Duff, *Judicial Business of the United States Courts: 2009 Annual Report of the Director* (Washington, DC: Administrative Office of the U.S. Courts), Table C-2A.

42. Leonidas Ralph Mecham, *Judicial Business of the United States Courts: 2005 Annual Report of the Director* (Washington, DC: Administrative Office of the U.S. Courts), Table C-2A.

43. James C. Duff, *Judicial Business of the United States Courts: 2010 Annual Report of the Director* (Washington, DC: Administrative Office of the U.S. Courts), Table C-2A.

44. In many Fair Labor Standards Act suits, workers must "opt-in" on the suits. On most other kinds of class-action cases, members of the class are automatically included unless they "opt-out." Because many workers are fearful of having their names on a suit against their employers, the number of workers seeking stolen wages would be much higher if they weren't required to "opt-in."

45. Orey, "Wage Wars," *Businessweek*, cover story, October 1, 2007.

46. Testimony of Jeffrey Steele before the Domestic Policy Subcommittee, Oversight and Government Reform Committee, U.S. House of Representatives, Tuesday, June 26, 2007. The testimony can be read in full at http://domesticpolicy.oversight.house.gov/documents/20070703121251.pdf.

2. How Employers Steal Wages

1. In this prayer for relief from being mistreated, we know that God gives us confidence to hear the stories of those who have been unfairly compensated and call to account those employers who deprive workers of wages. Checks that bounce, not paying overtime, and illegal deductions are examples of "cunningly conceived" wage theft.

2. Wal-Mart Press Release, *Walmart and Plaintiffs' Counsel Announce Settlement of Most Wage and Hour Class Action Lawsuits Against Company,* Bentonville, Arkansas, December 23, 2008.

3. Dave Copeland, "Wal-Mart Will Pay $40 Million to Workers: Settlement Is Biggest in Bay State History," *The Boston Globe*, December 3, 2009.

4. Jonathan Stempel and Brad Dorfman, *Wal-Mart in $86 Million Settlement of Wage Lawsuit*, Reuters, May 12, 2010.

5. State minimum wages are often higher than the federal minimum wage.

6. The Urban Institute, Immigration Studies Program, *A Profile of the Low-Wage Immigrant Workforce*, November 2003. This figure of two million is based on this report profiling low-wage immigrant workers, which found that 13 percent of foreign-born female workers and 9 percent of foreign-born male workers are paid less than minimum wage. By this estimate, more than two million immigrant workers are earning below minimum wage. Although immigrant workers are probably the most vulnerable in terms of minimum wage, there are many other native-born workers, especially young people and those in the informal economy, who are denied overtime. The three million number is an estimate the noted Princeton economist Alan Krueger, who served as chief economist at the Department of Labor in 1994–1995, gave to the *Wall Street Journal*.

7. Annette Bernhardt, Ruth Milkman, Nik Theodore, Douglas Heckathorn, Mirabai Auer, James DeFilippis, Ana Luz Gonzalez, Victor Narro, Jason Perelshteyn, Diana Polson, and Michael Spiller, *Broken Laws, Unprotected Workers: Violations of Employment and Labor Laws in America's Cities* (New York: National Employment Law Project, 2009), p. 2.

8. Interview with Garrett Stark, organizer, Homeless Power, June 16, 2008.

9. Interview with Laura Boston, worker advocate, Houston Interfaith Workers' Center, March 21, 2008, and follow-up e-mail of May 15, 2008.

10. Interview with Patrick Hickey, director, Madison Worker Rights Center, April 4, 2008, and follow-up e-mail of May 22, 2008.

11. E-mails from Rael Silva of Young Workers United on May 12, 2008, and May 15, 2008.

12. Interview with Boston, March 21, 2008, and follow-up e-mail of May 15, 2008.

13. Wage and Hour Division Statistics Fact Sheets for the last five years, available at www.dol.gov.

14. Wage and Hour Division, Department of Labor, "Levi Strauss Agrees to Pay More Than $1 Million in Overtime Back Wages to Nearly 600 Employees Following US Labor Department Investigation," Wage and Hour Division news release on March 29, 2011.

15. Bernhardt et al., *Broken Laws, Unprotected Workers*, p. 2.

16. Interview with Kader, April 2, 2008.

17. Interview with Hickey, April 4, 2008.

18. Interview with Paul Strauss on May 1, 2008.

19. Interview with Kader, April 2, 2008.

20. Notes from Brian Payne, Centro de Trabajadores Unidos en la Lucha, on March 21, 2011.

21. CS Decisions, "Raceway to Pay $4 Million in Back Wages," April 23, 2010.

22. This lower minimum wage plus tips must still add up to at least the regular minimum wage.

23. E-mails from Silva, May 12, 2008, and May 15, 2008.

24. Interview with Stark, June 16, 2008.

25. Office of the Attorney General, State of California, "Brown Wins Back Pay for Over 200 Construction Workers Denied Fair Wages by Drywall Company," press release, April 5, 2010.

26. Dennis Hoey, "Group Sues Great Wall Restaurant for Wages: Nine Former Employees, All Chinese Immigrants, Say They're Owed at Least $500,000 in Back Pay," *Portland Press Herald*, September 1, 2009.

27. E-mails from Hickey, May 29, 2008.

28. E-mail from Kader, June 10, 2008.

29. Notes of call with Fernando Garcis, March 15, 2011.

30. E-mail from Annica Gorham, executive director, Houston Interfaith Workers' Center on July 2, 2008.

31. U.S. Government Accountability Office, *The Worker Adjustment and Retraining Notification Act: Revising the Act and Educational Materials Could Clarify Employer Responsibilities and Rights* (Washington, DC: U.S. Government Printing Office, 2003).

32. Mark Curnutte, "Did Veterinarians Extort Pay from Undocumented Workers?" *Cincinnati Enquirer*, November 1, 2010.

33. Michael Moore, "Hollister Company Accused of Scamming Employees," *Morgan Hill Times*, January 21, 2010.

3. Payroll Fraud

1. American Rights at Work, *Fed Up with FedEx: How FedEx Ground Tramples Workers' Rights and Civil Rights* (Washington, DC: American Rights at Work, 2007), p. 10.

2. Ibid., p. 28.

3. Judith Graham, Becky Schlikerman, and Abel Uribe, "Undocumented Worker Who Became Quadriplegic Is Moved to Mexico against His Will," *Chicago Tribune*, February 6, 2011.

4. Frankly, the "system" is not much of a system because it is operated by the states, which means that each state has different rules and guidelines.

5. Statement of Senator Patty Murray on Misclassifying Employees as Independent Contractors. Available at www.faircontracting.org.

6. Notes from call with Martin Chartrand, Food AND Medicine, on March 18, 2011.

7. The U.S. Attorney's Office, Southern District of Florida, "Owner of La Bamba Check Cashing and Corporation Sentenced in Connection with $132,000,000 in False CTRS," press release, June 23, 2009.

8. U.S. Attorney, District of Alaska, "Colorado Man Sentenced to Federal Prison for Currency Structuring: Drywaller Who Operated in the Anchorage Bowl and Matanuska-Susitna Valley Attempted to Avoid Government Oversight and Payroll Taxes by Paying Undocumented Workers 'Under the Table,'" press release, September 23, 2010.

9. Oregon Department of Justice, Portland, Oregon, "Attorney General John Kroger Announces Major Racketeering Conviction," press release, January 13, 2009.

10. U.S. Government Accountability Office, *Employee Misclassification: Improved Coordination, Outreach and Targeting Could Better Ensure Detection and Prevention*, (Washington, DC: Government Accountability Office, GAO-09-717, August 2009), p. 10.

11. Ibid., p. 11.

12. Dale L. Belman and Richard Block, *Informing the Debate: The Social and Economic Costs of Employee Misclassification in Michigan* (East Lansing, MI: Institute for Public Policy and Social Research, 2009).

13. James I. Sturgeon and Michael P. Kelsay, *The Economic Costs of Employee Misclassification in the State of Indiana* (Department of Economics, University of Missouri-Kansas City, September 16, 2010) pp. 4–5 of the summary findings.

14. Washington State Department of Labor & Industries, "L&I's Fraud-Fighting Program Collects $137 Million," press release, January 18, 2011.

15. Patricia Smith and Jennifer Brand, *Annual Report of the Joint Enforcement Task Force on Employee Misclassification* (Albany, NY: Joint Enforcement Taskforce, 2009), p. 3.

16. Ibid., p. 4.

17. Joint Enforcement Taskforce on the Underground Economy and Employee Misclassification, *2010 Annual Report* (Boston: Joint Enforcement Taskforce, 2010), p. 4.

18. Rebecca Smith, David Bensman, and Paul Alexander Marvy, *The Big Rig: Poverty, Pollution and the Misclassification of Truck Drivers at America's Ports* (New York: National Employment Law Project, 2010).

19. E-mails from Silva on May 12, 2008, and May 15, 2008.

20. U.S. Government Accountability Office, *Employee Misclassification: Improved Outreach Could Help Ensure Proper Worker Classification*, testimony before the Subcommittee on Income Security and Family Support and Subcommittee on Select Revenue Measures, Committee on Ways and Means, House of Representatives, May 8, 2007.

21. The Internal Revenue Service and National Labor Relations Board use different standards, as do the courts, in enforcing other workplace laws, which is why, in part, this issue is so complicated.

22. U.S. Department of Labor, Employment Standards Administration, Fact Sheet #13: Employment Relationship under the Fair Labor Standards Act (FLSA). Although this list seems fairly clear, the guidelines aren't the same for laws other than those under the FLSA.

4. Why Employers Steal Wages

1. The counterpoint to this strong message in Timothy is the message in II Corinthians 8:8 affirming that God is able to provide you with every blessing in abundance so that by always having enough of everything, you may share abundantly in every good work. The message is that love of money and its consequences cause human misery and estrangement from what God wants for God's people.

2. Wage theft is actually a global problem, not just a national problem. For an interesting analysis of the structures that must be in place to stop wage theft, see section 3 on Workers in Contract Factories in Nike's 2005–2006 *Social Responsibility Report* available at http://www.nikeresponsibility.com/#crreport/main.

3. Bureau of Labor Statistics, *Contingent and Alternative Employment Arrangements*, February 2005.

4. Ibid.

5. Bureau of Labor Statistics, "The Employment Situation—February, 2011," Economic News Release, March 4, 2011.

6. The Economic Policy Institute provides extensive discussion and data about underemployment. For more information, visit http://www.economytrack.org/under employment.php.

7. Office of the District Attorney, "Roofing Contractor Sentenced to 10 Years in Prison in California's Largest Premium Insurance Fraud Scam," press release, November 9, 2009.

8. See SEIU website at www.seiu.org.

9. See Grace Chang, *Disposable Domestics: Immigrant Women Workers in the Global Economy* (Cambridge, MA: South End Press, 2000) for a fuller conversation on disposable workers.

10. Borgna Brunner, *The Wage Gap: A History of Pay Inequity and the Equal Pay Act*, at http://www.infoplease.com/spot/equalpayact1.html.

11. Statistics available at www.bls.gov.

12. Mike Mielke, *Short-Term Profit versus Long-Term Sustainability: CSR & Successfully Competing for the Future* (CSR is corporate social responsibility), The DC Sustainable Business Network, January 27, 2006.

13. Thomas A. Kochan, *Evaluation of Wal-Mart's Performance Management, Incentive, and Control Systems and Their Relation to Unpaid Work of Hourly Associates*, expert report in the case of Nancy Hall, on behalf of herself and all others similarly situated versus Wal-Mart Stores, Inc., and Sam's West, Inc., September 29, 2006.

5. How U.S. Labor Laws Fail Workers

1. This list is from the Department of Labor website, www.dol.gov.

2. National Labor Relations Board, *Seventy Fourth Annual Report of the National Labor Relations Board for the Fiscal Year Ended September 30, 2009* (Washington, DC: U.S. Government Printing Office, 2009), p. 3.

3. U.S. Government Accountability Office, *The Worker Adjustment and Retraining Notification Act: Revising the Act and Educational Materials Could Clarify Employer Responsibilities and Employee Rights* (Washington, DC: U.S. Government Printing Office, 2003).

4. Interfaith Worker Justice has launched a new website, www.canmybossdothat .com, that has workers' rights information organized by topic and by state.

5. Interview with Anne Janks on May 9, 2008.

6. Organizing to Stop Wage Theft: Why Unions Matter

1. Moses went to Pharaoh with a petition and was rebuffed. The king then ordered the Israelite workers to make as many bricks as before, but he insisted that they had to gather their own straw. As the story goes, Moses persists in what becomes the first act of organized labor.

2. Tiffany Hogue at SEIU Local 1 provided the updated information, April 28, 2011.

3. Philip S. Foner, *From Colonial Times to the Founding of the American Federation of Labor*, Vol. 1 (New York: International Publishers, 1982), p. 26.

4. Ibid., p. 71.

5. "School for Organizers," *Time*, November 19, 1951.

6. Much of this section is adapted from a piece I wrote called "Why Unions Matter," which was published by Interfaith Worker Justice (IWJ). The figures were updated by Ted Smukler, director of the IWJ policy department.

7. AFL-CIO, *Union Workers Have Better Health Care and Pensions*, AFL-CIO website.

8. Ibid.

9. A. Suruda, B. Whitaker, D. Bloswick, P. Philips, and R. Sesek, "Impact of the OSHA Trench and Evacuation Standard on Fatal Injury in the Construction Industry," *Journal of Occupational and Environmental Medicine* 44 (2002): 902–905.

10. Much of this section is also adapted from "Why Unions Matter."

11. Peter D. Hart Research Associations, Study 7518, 2005.

12. Kate Bronfenbrenner, "Uneasy Terrain: The Impact of Capital Mobility on Workers, Wages and Union Organizing," September 6, 2000.

13. Bureau of Labor Statistics, U.S. Department of Labor, "Union Members 2010," news release, January 21, 2011.

14. Ibid.

15. Notes from Kim Keller, International Brotherhood of Teamsters, from April 12, 2011.

16. Call with Bob Brock, IBEW organizer, March 16, 2011.

17. Conversations and e-mails with Justin Nickels, March 17-29, 2011.

7. Workers' Centers: Front Lines against Wage Theft

1. This is a Polish name, and my colleague Anka advises me to spell it this way.

2. Kathryn Kish Sklar, Introduction to *The Autobiography of Florence Kelley* (Chicago: Charles H. Kerr Publishing Co., 1986), pp. 12–13.

3. Judag H. Shapiro, *The Friendly Society: A History of the Workmen's Circle* (New York: Media Judaica, 1970), p. 30.

4. Ibid., p. 101.

5. Ibid., p. 127.

6. For more information, visit http://www.circle.org/about-wc.html.

7. Higgins letter in the American Catholic History Research Center and University Archives, Catholic University of America, Collection 10, Box 40, File 15.

8. American Catholic History Research Center and University Archives, Catholic University of America, Collection 10, Box 40, Files 13, 14, 15, 16, 26, 30.

9. See the Labor Guild's website at www.laborguild.org.

10. See the Comey Institute of Industrial Relations' website at www.sju.edu/academics/centers/comey/index.html.

11. Janice Fine, *Workers' Centers: Organizing Communities at the Edge of the Dream* (Ithaca, NY: ILR Press, 2006).

12. For more information, visit www.ndlon.org.

13. For more information, visit www.iwj.org.

14. For more information, visit www.enlaceintl.org.

15. E-mail from Jose Oliva, IWJ Workers' Center network coordinator and former director of the Chicago Interfaith Workers' Center on June 17, 2008.

16. Interview and follow-up e-mails with Veronica Mendez, an organizer with Workers Interfaith Network, May 15, 2008.

17. E-mail from Jose Oliva, IWJ Workers' Center network coordinator and former director of the Chicago Interfaith Workers' Center on June 17, 2008.

18. The agreements give workers' centers the opportunities to participate as nonvoting members at central labor councils.

19. Notes from Brian Payne, Centro de Trabajadores Unidos en la Lucha on March 21, 2011.

20. For more information, visit www.youngworkersunited.org.

21. Just Faith is a terrific educational program for congregations. For more information, visit www.justfaith.org.

22. Interview with Don Sherman, director of the Cincinnati Interfaith Worker Center, on April 3, 2008.

8. Business Leaders Challenge Wage Theft

1. Vision for 2011 taken from the company's website at http://www.marekbros.com/Corporate/GoalsValues.aspx.

2. Statement of values taken from the company's website at http://www.marekbros.com/Corporate/GoalsValues.aspx.

3. View the entire video at http://vimeo.com/19708336.

4. Notes from call with and e-mails from Stan Marek on March 14–16, 2011.

5. Notes from call with Jennifer Piallet on March 17, 2011.

6. Notes from call with Lindsey Lee on March 16, 2011.

7. Taken from the website of the Florida International Association of Arboriculture under the section on how to hire an arborist at www.floridaisa.org.

8. Notes from call with Ron von Paulus on March 18, 2011.

9. See the website for the Maintenance Cooperation Trust Fund at www.janitorialwatch.org.

10. E-mail communication with Yardeena Aaron, Maintenance Cooperation Trust Fund, on March 28, 2011.

11. Notes from conversation with Fabian Loera on March 23, 2011.

12. E-mail notes from Pete Meyers, director of the Tompkins County Workers' Center on March 21, 2011.

9. Leadership Matters: Lessons from Frances Perkins

1. The description of Frances Perkins's life draws heavily from the excellent biographies written by Bill Severn (*Frances Perkins: A Member of the Cabinet*, New York: Hawthorn Books, 1976) and George Martin (*Madam Secretary Frances Perkins: A Biography of America's First Woman Cabinet Member*, Boston: Houghton Mifflin Co., 1976), as well as from her own writings (*The Roosevelt I Knew* and *People at Work*).

2. Martin, *Madam Secretary Frances Perkins*.

3. Ibid., p. 52.

4. Severn, *Frances Perkins*, p. 24.

5. Lillian Holmen Mohr, *Frances Perkins: "That Woman in FDR's Council"* (Great Barrington, MA: North River Press, 1979), p. 56.

6. Severn, *Frances Perkins*, pp. 110–111.

7. Donn Mitchell, "The Gracious Society: Frances Perkins and the Religious Dimension of the New Deal," paper presented at the Mid-Atlantic Regional Meeting of the American Academy of Religion/Society of Biblical Literature, New Brunswick, New Jersey, March 13–14, 2003.

8. To Mr. DeCamp's credit, he spent time initially visiting sweatshops and labor camps to get a better understanding of working conditions.

9. Jonathan Grossman, "Fair Labor Standards Act of 1938: Maximum Struggle for a Minimum Wage," *Monthly Labor Review,* June 1978.

10. Martin, *Madam Secretary Frances Perkins,* p. 49.

10. The U.S. Department of Labor: More Important Than Ever

1. There were some manuals on workers' compensation that attorneys had prepared.

2. Bureau of Labor Statistics, Department of Labor, "Union Members—2010," news release, January 21, 2011.

3. Davi Weil, *Improving Workplace Conditions through Strategic Enforcement: A Report to the Wage and Hour Division* (Boston: Boston University, May 2010).

4. Just Pay Working Group, *Just Pay: Improving Wage and Hour Enforcement at the United States Department of Labor* (New York: National Employment Law Project, 2009).

5. Jonathan Grossman, *The Department of Labor* (New York: Praeger Publishers, 1973), p. 182.

6. The other major federal agencies tasked with enforcing workers' rights are the National Labor Relations Board (NLRB), which protects the rights of workers to unionize, and the Equal Employment Opportunity Commission (EEOC), which enforces our nation's employment discrimination and harassment laws.

7. Grossman, *The Department of Labor,* p. 27.

8. Ibid., p. 50.

9. Ibid., p. 60.

10. Wage and Hour Division History, U.S. Department of Labor website.

11. This figure comes from the 1941 Annual Report of the Wage and Hour Division. Staff "in the field" is roughly equivalent to the current figure of investigators, although it is possible that the figure included some administrative field staff.

12. Wage and Hour Division, *Annual Report, Wage and Hour Division,* 1941.

13. U.S. Department of Labor, 1968 Budget Estimate, Volume II, 90th Congress, First Session, WH-14.

14. Child Labor Coalition, *The Government's Striking Decline in Child Labor Enforcement Activities* (Washington, DC: Child Labor Coalition, 2006), p. 2.

15. National Consumers League, *American Working Teens Fact Sheet* (Washington, DC: National Consumers League, 2003).

16. Child Labor Coalition, *The Government's Striking Decline in Child Labor Enforcement Activities* (Washington, DC: Child Labor Coalition, 2006), p. 3.

17. James Dao, "34th Precinct Is Expanding Police Force," *New York Times,* August 5, 1992.

18. Norman Mineta, secretary of transportation, remarks at the TSA anniversary event, Washington, D.C., November 18, 2002.

19. Interview with Don Sherman, director of the Cincinnati Workers' Center, on April 3, 2008, and follow-up e-mails on May 29, 2008.

20. Conversation with Reverend Bob Coats, April 30, 2008.

21. Program History of the Program in Criminal Justice Policy and Management at www.hks.harvard.edu/criminaljustice/history.htm.

22. Center for Problem-Oriented Policing, "Community Policing," Module 2, Model Academic Curriculum.

23. U.S. Department of Labor, OSHA, Office of Communications, National News Release USDL: 03-306, June 10, 2003.

24. The positions were only advertised within the agency, which raises concerns about whether those in the positions have adequate backgrounds or training in community organizing to create meaningful partnerships.

25. Interview with Patrick Hickey, director, Madison Workers' Center, April 4, 2008.

26. Interview with Don Sherman, director of the Cincinnati Workers' Center, on April 3, 2008, and follow-up e-mails on May 29, 2008.

27. U.S. Department of Labor, 1968 Budget Estimates, Volume II, 90th Congress, 1st Session, WH-16.

28. U.S. Department of Agriculture, Cooperative State Research, Education and Extension Service, *About Us* section of the website at www.csrees.usda.gov.

29. 4-H Youth Department, "The History of the Cooperative Extension Service," Purdue University, West Lafayette, Indiana, 2001.

30. Ibid.

31. National Institute for Literacy, "Fact Sheet: Adult and Family Literacy," April, 2000.

32. Most cases are settled for only two years' worth of back wages, but the law allows for three if the employer is found to have "willfully" stolen the wages. The Just Pay Working Group, a collection of the nation's experts in wage and hour issues convened by the National Employment Law Project, recommends that the Department of Labor recover three years of back wages in willful cases because it is not routinely doing so. See the full report at http://www.nelp.org/page/-/Justice/2010/JustPayReport2010.pdf.

33. The Department of Labor (DOL) defines repeat violations as follows: The current investigation discloses violations, and the employer had prior violations under any statute enforced by WHD. Recurring violations means that the current investigation finds a violation(s) that is identical in nature to the cause of the prior violation(s); and that the employer has not modified its violative behavior to ensure compliance. The statistic in the table plus the DOL definition are from a Department of Labor FOIA response letter to Ms. Kim Bobo dated May 1, 2008.

34. According to data provided in the DOL FOIA letter to Kim Bobo dated May 1, 2008, 49 percent in 2007 and 48 percent in 2006. Although child labor violations are subject to CMP assessment in the first instance, this data is only looking at repeat and recurring violations.

35. The average FLSA CMP was $7904 for 2006 and $8196 for 2007. Data provided in the DOL FOIA letter to Ms. Kim Bobo dated May 1, 2008.

36. Wage and Hour Division press release, "U.S. Labor Department to Distribute

$68,000 in Back Wage Checks to New Jersey Textile Employees Following Resolution of 'Hot Goods' Action," January 9, 1997.

37. This definition is from the Department of Consumer Affairs, Contractors State License Board, State of California, website at http://www.cslb.ca.gov/Consumers/LegalIssuesForConsumers/MechanicsLien/What IsAMechanicsLien.asp.

38. Interview with Cristina Tzintzun, coordinator for Workers' Defense Project/Proyecto Defensa Laboral on May 7, 2008, and follow-up e-mail on May 27, 2008.

39. Fiscal Year 2007 IRS Enforcement and Service Statistics.

40. Interfaith Worker Justice, *Working on Faith: A Faithful Response to Worker Abuse in New Orleans*, 2007.

41. U.S. Department of Labor, Wage and Hour Division, *1999–2000 Report on Initiatives*, February 2001, p. 11.

42. U.S. Department of Labor, 1968 Budget Estimate, Volume II, 90th Congress, First Session, WH-14.

43. Weil, *Improving Workplace Conditions*, p. 2.

44. Ibid., p. 30.

45. Interview with Laura Boston, worker advocate, Houston Interfaith Workers' Center, May 15, 2008.

46. The suit filed actually asked for "double damages," which means the amount of the back wages doubled or $50,000. Nonetheless, the actual wages owed were more than $25,000. Interview with Cristina Tzintzun, Coordinator for Workers' Defense Project/Proyecto Defensa Laboral on May 7, 2008, and follow-up e-mail on May 27, 2008.

47. The suit filed asks for double damages, or double the amount of the back wages owed. Interview with Cristina Tzintzun, Coordinator for Workers' Defense Project/Proyecto Defensa Laboral on May 7, 2008, and follow-up e-mail on May 27, 2008.

48. U.S. Government Accountability Office, *One-Stop System Infrastructure Continues to Evolve, but Labor Should Take Action to Require That All Employment Service Offices Are Part of the System* (Washington, DC: U.S. Government Accountability Office, 2007).

49. Workers without proper government identification cannot even get admitted to many government buildings. The official DOL policy is to accept complaints from undocumented immigrants, but many of its office locations won't let them in the buildings.

50. Interview with Bob Anderson, Equal Rights Division, Wisconsin Department of Workforce Development, by phone on May 19, 2008.

51. Interview with Father Sinclair Oubre, April 23, 2008.

52. Douglas B. Stevenson, Testimony before the House Subcommittee on Coast Guard and Maritime Transportation, June 20, 2006.

53. Minnesota Statute: 181.13 Penalty for Failure to Pay Wage Promptly. For a copy of the statute, visit https://www.revisor.leg.state.mn.us/statutes/?id=181.13.

54. Anwers.com, a website for business and finance definitions. Published by Answered Corporation.

55. John Upton Terrell, *The United States Department of Labor: A Story of Workers, Unions and the Economy* (New York: Meredith Press, 1968), p. 13.

56. Jerold Waltman, *The Politics of the Minimum Wage* (Chicago: University of Illinois Press, 2000), p. 32.

57. For more information about paid sick days, visit www.paidsickdays.org.

58. For an excellent overview of the problems of excessive overtime, read *Stopping the Clock: Controlling the Use of Mandatory Overtime in the Health Care Industry* by the Federation of Nurses and Health Professionals. It can be located at www.aft.org/pubs -reports/healthcare/Stop_the_Clock.pdf.

11. Strengthening State Enforcement

1. Jacob Meyer and Robert Greenleaf, *Enforcement of State Wage and Hour Laws: A Survey of State Regulators,* National State Attorneys General Program, Columbia Law School, New York, NY, April 2011.

2. Irene Lurie, *Enforcement of State Minimum Wage and Overtime Laws: Resources, Procedures, and Outcomes,* Nelson A Rockefeller Institute of Government, State University of New York, December 7, 2010.

3. Zach Schiller and Sarah DeCarlo, *Investigating Wage Theft: A Survey of the States,* report from Policy Matters Ohio, November 2010.

4. Notes on conversation with Marcela Diaz, executive director of Somos un Pueblo Unido, on March 28, 2011.

5. Jackson Lewis, *New York Wage Theft Act Increases Employer Obligations and Penalties for Labor Law Violations,* December 21, 2010.

6. Notes on conversation with Sam Latham, president of the Delaware AFL-CIO, on March 10, 2011.

7. Notes on conversations with Lydia Lowe, Chinese Progressive Association, on March 2, 2011, and Marcy Goldstein-Gelb, MassCOSH, on March 3, 2011.

8. Illinois Department of Labor, *Fact Sheet on Employee Classification Act.* Available at www.state.il.us/agency/idol.

9. David Shaffer, "Construction Workers Sidestepping New Law," *Star Tribune,* May 14, 2009.

10. This entire section is adapted from an article by Ai-jen-Poo, "Organizing with Love: Lessons from the New York Domestic Workers Bill of Rights Campaign," December 1, 2010. The article is available at http://www.domesticworkersunited .org/media/files/287/OrganizingWithLoveFinal.pdf.

11. These lessons were taken from an interview with Ai-jen Poo entitled "Organizing with Love" in an online publication, *Organizing Upgrade,* February 1, 2010. Available at www.organizingupgrade.com/2010/02/organizing-with-love/.

12. Strengthening Local Enforcement

1. This prayer of the Psalmist as well as the scripture from the Qur'an call those with power to listen and take action to protect the lowly and weak.

2. National Employment Law Project, *Winning Wage Justice: An Advocate's Guide to State and City Policies to Fight Wage Theft* (New York: National Employment Law Project, January 2011).

3. Call and e-mails with Hilary Stern, executive director of Casa Latina, April 28, 2011.

4. The "importuning widow" is a biblical story found in Luke 18:1–8 of a widow who appeals to a judge. The text says that the judge gave the widow her request because she kept asking and wouldn't go away.

5. Notes from conversation with Shaw San Liu, lead organizer, Worker Organizing Center, Chinese Progressive Association, on April 1, 2011, and follow-up e-mail on April 3, 2011.

13. Stopping Wage Theft Is Good for America

1. Interfaith Worker Justice, *Working on Faith: A Faithful Response to Worker Abuse in New Orleans* (Chicago: Interfaith Worker Justice, 2007).

2. Dr. Martin Luther King Jr. said, "The arc of the moral universe is long, but it bends toward justice" in his speech given to the Southern Christian Leadership Conference in Atlanta on August 16, 1967.

3. U.S. Department of Labor, SDOL FY 1996 Budget Justifications of Appropriations Estimates for the Committee on Appropriations, Volume II, February 1994, ESA-23.

4. Molly Selvin, "US: Speaking Up for Exploited Workers," Communicating LabourRights.wordpress.com, March 2008.

5. 2000 National Compensation Survey.

6. The National Alliance for Fair Contracting, Inc., at www.faircontracting.org.

7. U.S. Government Accountability Office, *Employee Misclassification: Improved Outreach Could Help Ensure Proper Worker Classification* (Washington, DC: U.S. Government Accountability Office), May 2007.

8. U.S. General Accountability Office, *Tax Administration Information: Returns Can Be Used to Identify Employers Who Misclassify Employees*, GAO\GGD-89-107, 1989.

9. Coopers and Lybrand, *Projection of the Loss in Federal Tax Revenues Due to Misclassification of Workers* (New York: Coopers and Lybrand, 1994).

10. Nick Carey, "FedEx Shares Dip 2 percent on IRS Back Tax of $319 Million," Reuters News Service, December 24, 2007.

11. Federal Policy Institute, *Building Up New York, Tearing Down Job Quality: Taxpayer Impact of Worsening Employment Practices in New York City's Construction Industry* (New York: Federal Policy Institute, 2007), p. 1.

12. Congressional Budget Office, *Options for Responding to Short-Term Economic Weakness*, in section on Assessing Different Types of Fiscal Stimulus, January 2008.

13. Paul Demko, "Gabriel Francois Has a Bridge in Bloomington to Sell You," *City Pages*, Issue 1237, August 18, 2004.

14. Paul Demko, "Gabriel Goes Down," *City Pages*, Issue 1254, December 15, 2004.

15. Paul Demko, "Gabriel Francois Stands Accused of Stiffing Day Laborers," *City Pages*, March 12, 2008.

14. You Can Make a Difference

1. Pew Forum on Religion and Public Life, "U.S. Religious Landscape Survey," June 2008.

2. National Consumers League, *American Working Teens Fact Sheet* (Washington, DC: National Consumers League, 2003).

3. Interfaith Worker Justice offers sample curricula for seminary courses on its website at www.iwj.org.